Frank J

ALSO BY JOHN C. SKIPPER
AND FROM McFARLAND

*Billy Southworth: A Biography of the Hall
of Fame Manager and Ballplayer* (2013)

*Showdown at the 1964 Democratic Convention:
Lyndon Johnson, Mississippi and Civil Rights* (2012)

*The Iowa Caucuses: First Tests of Presidential
Aspiration, 1972–2008* (2010)

*A Biographical Dictionary of the Baseball Hall
of Fame*, 2d ed. (2008; paperback 2014)

*Charlie Gehringer: A Biography of the Hall
of Fame Tigers Second Baseman* (2008)

*Dazzy Vance: A Biography of the
Brooklyn Dodger Hall of Famer* (2007)

*Wicked Curve: The Life and Troubled Times
of Grover Cleveland Alexander* (2006)

*The Cubs Win the Pennant! Charlie Grimm,
the Billy Goat Curse, and the 1945 World Series Run* (2004)

*A Biographical Dictionary of Major League
Baseball Managers* (2003; paperback 2011)

*Take Me Out to the Cubs Game: 35 Former
Ballplayers Speak of Losing at Wrigley* (2000)

*Umpires: Classic Baseball Stories from
the Men Who Made the Calls* (1997)

FRANK ROBINSON

A Baseball Biography

John C. Skipper

McFarland & Company, Inc., Publishers

Jefferson, North Carolina

LIBRARY OF CONGRESS CATALOGUING-IN-PUBLICATION DATA

Skipper, John C., 1945–
 Frank Robinson : a baseball biography / John C. Skipper.
  p.   cm.
 Includes bibliographical references and index.

  ISBN 978-0-7864-7561-2 (softcover : acid free paper) ∞
  ISBN 978-1-4766-1696-4 (ebook)

  1. Robinson, Frank, 1935—Juvenile literature.   2. Baseball players—
 United States—Biography—Juvenile literature.   3. African American
 baseball managers—Biography—Juvenile literature.   I. Title.
 GV865.R59S55 2014
 796.357092—dc23
 [B]   2014038279

BRITISH LIBRARY CATALOGUING DATA ARE AVAILABLE

On the cover: Frank Robinson (National Baseball Hall
of Fame Library, Cooperstown, New York)

Printed in the United States of America

McFarland & Company, Inc., Publishers
 Box 611, Jefferson, North Carolina 28640
  www.mcfarlandpub.com

For Craig Farrar

Table of Contents

Preface

This close.

That's a phrase that applies to many aspects of Frank Robinson's career in major league baseball.

He achieved just about everything a ballplayer could possibly do: Rookie of the Year in 1956; Most Valuable Player in both the National and American leagues—the only player to hold that distinction; World Series Most Valuable Player; All-Star Game Most Valuable Player; first black manager in both the American and National leagues; Manager of the Year in both leagues; and a member of baseball's Hall of Fame.

And yet—he was this close to hitting 600 home runs in his career, finishing with 586—fourth best all-time at the time of his retirement. He was this close to having 3,000 hits, one of baseball's magic milestones, finishing with 2,943. He was this close to setting the all-time record for home runs by a rookie, tying the record with 38 in 1956 (a record since broken by Mark McGuire). He was this close to achieving a 50-home run season, another traditional milestone, hitting 49 in 1966. He was this close to becoming the only player in baseball history to win consecutive Triple Crowns, winning one in 1966 and being a serious contender for another in 1967 until a freak injury shortened his season. He was this close to having a lifetime batting average of .300, needing to average a little more than two more hits a season for his career in which he finished with a .294 lifetime mark.

Before all of that, in the minor leagues, as a teenager a long way from home and feeling tired, depressed and lonely, Frank Robinson was this close to quitting professional baseball before his remarkable major league career had ever begun. (He decided not to go with his Columbia, South Carolina, ballclub on a road trip but to go home instead. The next morning, he changed his mind, found a ride to where his team was playing across the state, and rejoined the ballclub.)

The achievements and the near-misses are mostly statistics—numbers that speak the language of baseball and are proof of both stardom and mediocrity. Every time baseball history is made, it is made of yet a another new statistic.

Frank Robinson has left his mark on all of that. But statistics tell the story of baseball after the game is over. They are void of the life and breath of the game, the sound of the crack of the bat or the thud of a ball being caught in a glove. The statistics don't provide the dust flying up from a slide into second or the sight of an outfielder leaping up against a wall or the wail of an umpire calling, "Steee-rike."

Live telecasts and replays show some of that but often it is up to the written word to put flesh on the statistics, to deliver to the reader the personality and attitude and motivation of the men who compile the statistics.

That is the intention of this work: to provide a portrait not just of a ballplayer but of a man who played ball and played it exceeding well. The statistics tell only one part of the Frank Robinson story. They do not tell of a boy growing up in a home with a single mom and nine brothers and sisters. They do not tell of the boy leaving home to play baseball and experiencing racism for the first time in his life, of his lifelong desire not only to earn respect but to demand it, and of how the chip on his shoulder was knocked off from time to time but never knocked him down with it, or at least not for long.

The author is indebted to J. W. Porter, a former major league ballplayer and a standout amateur player in Oakland 60 years ago, for sharing his memories of Frank Robinson as a teenager. Similarly, the late John Flaherty, an American League umpire, provided a vivid description of the work ethic of Robinson as an established major league player.

Bob Rathgeber, an articulate Cincinnati Reds historian, was helpful with insights on Reds ballplayers from the Robinson era and offered some useful guidance on researching the book.

Thanks also to Nathan Kerr, intellectual property coordinator at the Collections and Information Access Center at the Oakland Museum of California, for guiding the author through the online photo archives.

Personnel at the National Baseball Hall of Fame and Museum, Cooperstown, New York, were helpful, as always, giving access to hundreds of newspaper and magazine clippings and photographs. The Society for American Baseball Research also supplied a helping hand.

The author also thanks Craig Farrar and Arian Schuessler for technical assistance along the way, and Tom Drzycimski, a government employee in Cerro Gordo County, Iowa, and a baseball fan who was a great sounding board who can probably say he heard the book before he had a chance to read it.

Lastly, thanks to Pat Hemm, Robinson's assistant in the commissioner's office, for her patience with an eager author.

Introduction

The years had been kind. He was 77 now. His hair was gray, his body not as sleek at it once was, his walk a little slower, his posture maybe not as straight as it once was, and the uniform shirt he wore had gotten a little tighter. But his mind was sharp and alert and his pride swelled as the roar of the crowd greeted him, like it had so many times in the past 60 years.

On the afternoon of October 10, 2012, Frank Robinson ambled out to the pitcher's mound at Nationals Park in Washington D.C., a perfect setting for a moment that was so richly American, within an easy cab ride of the White House, the Capitol building and the Lincoln Memorial. Robinson was about to throw out the ceremonial first pitch in the first post-season game in the nation's capital in 79 years.

Not since October 7, 1933, when Mel Ott of the New York Giants hit a home run in the tenth inning to clinch the World Series championship in a 4–3 win over the Senators, had a Washington ball club played beyond the end of the regular season.

But it was happening on this day, and to commemorate it, the Nationals asked Robby to come out of the dugout one more time. The crowd shouted and erupted in thunderous applause for the man who took over managing the Montreal Expos as a favor to the commissioner, came with them on their move to Washington, D.C., had them in the thick of the pennant race for the first half of their first season there, and started to develop the nucleus of the team that was on the field now.

He had donned his old uniform shirt on this day, with the familiar No. 20 on it, and slipped it on over his pink shirt and tie. He lobbed what would be charitably called a strike to shortstop Ian Desmond behind the plate and then heard the roar of the crowd one more time as he raised his arms in appreciation and sauntered off the field.

What the Nationals had shown him that day, what the crowd had shown him and what he had shown by his acknowledgment of their efforts, defined much of his 50-plus years in baseball, what he at times craved and at other times demanded. Respect.

He played ten years for the Cincinnati Reds, won Rookie of the Year and Most Valuable Player awards and led them to a World Series, yet was traded away in a manner he thought disrespected him.

He played in the era of Willie Mays, Hank Aaron, Mickey Mantle, Stan Musial and Ted Williams and often was overshadowed by them in the headlines of the day.

In his first year with his new team, the Baltimore Orioles, he won the Triple Crown and became the first player ever to win the Most Valuable Player Award in both leagues. And yet, when Carl Yastrzemski of the Boston Red Sox won the Triple Crown the following year, Robinson groused that Yaz got more attention and was hired for more endorsements than he had gotten, and he suspected the reason was that Yastrzemski was white and he was black.[1]

He was the first black manager hired in both the American and National leagues and was outspoken about how more blacks should be considered for managerial and front office jobs.

It was always all about respect. As a manager, he demanded it of his players. They were to do things his way, superstars and rookies alike, doing spring training drills, everyone working on fundamentals like fielding and sliding and hitting the cutoff man rather than just focusing on hitting and pitching and fielding the ball—and his pitchers were to hand him the ball without comment when he came out to take them out of a game.

He managed at Cleveland, San Francisco, Baltimore and Montreal-Washington and ran into problems at each stop when he didn't think he was getting the respect he deserved from the front office or when his players didn't think they were getting the respect they thought they deserved from him.

Ironically, he would say, in looking back over his career, his worst day as a manager was in the game in which, because of what he felt was the necessity to remove a player in the middle of an inning, he "disrespected" him—and Robinson wept about it when the game was over.[2]

A part of his baseball personality from the time he was a youngster was crowding the plate—literally and figuratively—doing whatever he could within the rules to get the advantage. In the literal sense, he was hit by pitches 198 times in his career because he refused to back off. But he also refused to back off on the bases, in the outfield, battling with umpires, confronting general managers and speaking out on civil rights.

The craving and demanding respect and his propensity to crowd the plate in most everything he did on and off the field translated into an intensity that he wore as if it was part of his uniform.

That was—and is—Frank Robinson, the man who helped usher in a new era of Washington baseball and who was honored for it on that October day in 2012.

He had a playing career in which he was traded three times—by the Cincinnati Reds, the Baltimore Orioles and the Los Angeles Dodgers, and as a manager was fired four times—by the Cleveland Indians, San Francisco Giants, Baltimore Orioles and Washington Nationals. As Bill Corum, a sports writer of a bygone era, once wrote, a life in baseball means both "taking bows and hearing bow-wows."[3]

In Cincinnati and Baltimore, there are statues of Robinson outside the baseball stadiums, just as there is a plaque in his honor in the National Baseball Hall of Fame in Cooperstown, New York.

So, in the end, what he played for, what he lived for, he got. Respect.

As he strolled off the field after symbolically reviving post-season baseball in Washington, with a military honor guard nearby and jets flying overhead, the Nationals took the field and lost 8–0 to the St. Louis Cardinals.

That's baseball.

CHAPTER 1

Something to Prove

Frank Robinson hung up the phone, having just been punched in the gut by one of baseball's cruel realities.

It is a dismaying experience for a ballplayer to be traded, to experience the feeling of not being wanted anymore in what had been your home. It is coming to grips with the reality that baseball is not a game, but a business, and that the players are commodities that have value on the open market.

The business of baseball was such that on December 9, 1965, the Cincinnati Reds traded Robinson to the Baltimore Orioles. He had spent a decade with the Reds—a third of his entire life and all of his adult life—and now he had to accept the fact he was no longer wanted or needed in Cincinnati.

But Baltimore did want him and need him, and so the moment of disbelief for a ballplayer soon shifts to what lies ahead. Robinson was going to the Orioles with the same confidence in his abilities that he had displayed ever since his high school days in Oakland. Instead of questioning his worth, his attitude was one of marching on. Reflecting on it years later, he said, "I had nothing to prove."[1]

During a ten-year career with the Reds, Robinson tied the major league record for most home runs by a rookie (38), won the Rookie of the Year Award in 1956, led the Reds to their first World Series in 21 years in 1961 and was voted Most Valuable Player in the National League that year. He had hit 30 or more home runs in seven of his ten seasons, had driven in 100 runs or more four times, and had led the league in runs scored twice, in doubles once, in intentional walks four times and in getting hit by pitches six times. His career statistics showed he was prolific at getting on base (sometimes painfully), scoring and driving in runs.

Perhaps his most impressive statistic is that he led the National League in slugging percentage three times in an era in which the league featured such stars as Willie Mays of the Giants, Henry Aaron of the Braves and

Duke Snider of the Dodgers. In 1965, Robinson's tenth year with the Reds, he hit .296 with 33 homers and 113 runs batted in. Yet that winter, general manager Bill DeWitt traded 30-year-old Robinson to Baltimore, claiming, as it turned out infamously, that his star was "an old 30."

So when Robinson said he had nothing to prove, he had an arsenal of statistics to back him up. But when he took the field for the Orioles in the spring of 1966, he felt like he had something to prove to Bill DeWitt. He won the Triple Crown that year, leading the league in home runs, runs batted in and batting average. He became the only player in baseball history to win the Most Valuable Player Award in both leagues and led the Orioles to a four-game sweep over the Los Angeles Dodgers in the World Series. He led the Orioles to three more pennants in the next five years, and in 1970 helped them beat the Reds in the World Series.

The "nothing to prove" comment is testimony to the confidence Robinson had in his abilities but is ironic because from the time he was a 20-year-old kid and for the next 50 years, he displayed an attitude of someone who always had something to prove. Indeed, it motivated him, from his minor league days in the Sally League in the segregated South and throughout his career as a player, coach, manager and executive in the major leagues. Frank Robinson had something to prove every day.

John Flaherty, an American League umpire for 21 years, said, "He was the hardest-working ballplayer I ever saw. He never loafed on the ballfield. An umpire can tell when a guy's loafing and he never did."[2]

Veteran American League umpire John Flaherty said Frank Robinson "never loafed on the ballfield. An umpire can tell" (author's collection).

It didn't end when his playing career ended. In 1975, he became the first black manager in major league history when he was named playing manager of the Cleveland Indians. Although he had nothing to prove, he hit a home run in his first at-bat that season. When he was named manager of the San Francisco Giants in 1981, he became the first black manager in the National League and was named Manager of the Year by the United Press International wire service one year later. Still later, he earned Manager of the Year honors in 1989 with the Baltimore Orioles from the Baseball Writers' Association of America. He ended his managerial career by taking over a Montreal Expos team as a favor to major league baseball because the franchise was dying, moved with them when the team became the Washington Nationals, and helped develop them into a playoff competitor.

Robinson described himself this way: "I am not a fancy guy, not a glamor boy. I don't believe I intrigue the fans and I obviously don't interest the sports writers. All that I am is an uncomplicated, single- minded guy. And my single-mindedness is baseball."[3]

On August 1, 1982, this single-minded ballplayer was inducted into the Baseball Hall of Fame in Cooperstown, New York, voted in by the sports writers who apparently did have an interest in him. The induction was the ultimate verdict for a man who had "nothing to prove," but it was a humbling experience as well.

Bob Maisel, a columnist for the *Baltimore Sun,* described the scene on the platform on that sunny Sunday afternoon, with Robinson and the other inductees surrounded by the greats of the game: "When you see such a concentration of legends, past and present ... Luke Appling, Charlie Gehringer, Joe DiMaggio, Stan Musial, Sandy Koufax, Warren Spahn, Bob Feller, and on and on.... Well, if you don't get a few goose bumps and shed a tear or two, you just aren't a baseball fan."[4]

Robinson and the other inductees each represented significant chapters in baseball history. There was Travis Jackson, shortstop for John McGraw's Giants and later Bill Terry's, who played in an era when organized baseball was a white man's game. There was A. B. "Happy" Chandler, a governor of Kentucky who, as baseball commissioner, opened the doors for black players to become major league ballplayers; and there was Henry Aaron and Robinson, two men who benefitted from Chandler's courageous decision and from the grit of Jackie Robinson, who broke the baseball color line with the Brooklyn Dodgers in 1947. As the four men sat on the stage, with more than 20 Hall of Famers sitting behind them, they saw, sitting in the first row of spectators, Rachel Robinson, Jackie's widow.

Travis Jackson was the first to speak. He said his biggest thrills in baseball were playing for the Giants for 15 years, playing in four World Series and having 13 teammates in the Hall of Fame.

Chandler was next. Speaking with a distinct Kentucky twang, he pulled no punches. "My predecessor [Judge Kenesaw Mountain Landis] would not let black men play, and that's a recorded fact. He wouldn't even let them barnstorm after the season. But he was only doing what the owners wanted—and what they wanted was baseball white and segregated," he said.

He recalled that among the 16 club owners, the vote was 15–1 against integrating the game. The "one" was Branch Rickey of the Brooklyn Dodgers. Chandler told the audience Rickey came to his cabin in Kentucky and told him about Jackie Robinson and how he wanted to sign him. Chandler said Rickey told him Robinson had the skills to play major league ball and the temperament to shrug off the bigotry he was sure to face. But Rickey said he couldn't do it without the full support of Chandler.

> "I gave him that support. I didn't think it fair that black men fight in wars but not be allowed to play the great American game although they were talented. I'm eventually going to have to meet my maker and if I explain to him that I didn't let a person play baseball because he was black, that would not be a good answer," said Chandler.[5]

Aaron, baseball's all-time home run leader at the time of his induction with 755 (subsequently surpassed by Barry Bonds) gave the shortest speech of the day. He said in part, "I feel a great sense of humility, gratitude and appreciation for this day." He thanked Rachel Robinson for her husband's trailblazing for black ball players and also Hall of Famer Roy Campanella for helping lead the way. "The sheer majesty of this occasion and its significance is overwhelming," he said.[6]

Robinson actually spoke before Aaron did and kidded that he was finally ahead of him in something. He said,

> "To Hank, I just like to say I've been chasing him for a long time. Always seemed like I was a step behind or a year behind. I broke in, in Columbia, SC, in 1954. Down there after a half a season in Ogden, Utah. And the talk of the league was all about Hank Aaron, the way he tore up the league, the way he did this, the way he did that.
>
> "Two years later I was fortunate enough to make it to the Major Leagues and Hank was an established major leaguer at that time and the talk was about Hank Aaron. And the comparison continued. And I must say we had a long and friendly rivalry on the field and I said this to Hank in New York where he was introduced as being elected to the Hall of Fame.
>
> "But I think he made me a better baseball player because of that, because when Hank would get up with the Milwaukee Braves and hit a home run,

I'd be standing in the outfield watching it go over. I said, 'Well, this is up to you. When you get up there you gotta try to do something as well if not as good, 'cause your teammates are going to be expecting the same.' And my neck got sore watching Hank Aaron's fly balls go over the fence.

"But he was a tremendous athlete, tremendous ballplayer and it's been sad that he didn't get his just dues as a player and I agree, because Hank Aaron was not a flashy individual. He just went about his job and did it very well. But what I also admired about Hank Aaron, not only his athletic abilities, I admired him as a human being and an outstanding person. But I must say that I thought I had drawn even with Hank when we were elected to the Hall of Fame…. I'm going into the Hall of Fame before he does [because he was inducted moments before Aaron]. So, I finally got ya, buddy."[7]

Robinson's remarks were a fine tribute to Aaron but in their own way, they were also another example of that same motivating force in Robinson's career—another example of having something to prove.

Robinson's old teammates as well as players from other teams shared memories of their playing days with him with the press. Paul Blair, Orioles

Frank Robinson was elected to the Hall of Fame in 1982, his first year of eligibility (National Baseball Hall of Fame and Library, Cooperstown, New York).

center fielder, said Baltimore was a good ball club but was missing something until Robinson joined the club in 1966. "He went out and showed us how to win," said Blair.[8]

"I never played with a guy I wanted more on my team," said Jim Maloney, a pitcher for Cincinnati when Robinson was with the Reds. Whatever you needed, he'd do it—a home run, a stolen base, a great catch—and he'd do it when it was needed most."[9]

Jim Russo, a longtime scout with the Orioles who attended the Hall of Fame ceremonies, offered an example of exactly what Maloney was talking about. He recalled the 1966 World Series where the upstart Orioles faced the veteran Los Angeles Dodgers ballclub whose pitching staff was anchored by Sandy Koufax and Don Drysdale. "We were a very young, very nervous team, and he came up in his first at-bat and hit one out," said Russo. "You could feel the whole bench relax. We knew it was going to be all right."[10]

Not all of the early reviews on Robinson were good. Jim Brosnan, a relief pitcher with Cincinnati and a teammate, panned Robinson in his book, *The Long Season,* implying that he was lazy and didn't play up to his ability. Brosnon wrote, "Frank could be the best in the game if he was able to put out in every game."[11]

In those early days, he had the reputation of being kind of a complainer and always seemed to have an injury that was bothering him. Jim O'Toole, another Cincinnati pitcher, said, "He was the only guy I knew who didn't need batting practice and could come out swinging from his ass. But Frank always whined and complained. Hutch [Reds manager Fred Hutchinson] didn't like that. There was a battle of wills…. Hutch always won."

O'Toole said Robinson always seemed to have his arm wrapped because of some kind of injury and Hutchinson, tired of his complaining, benched him for three games.[12]

As Robinson matured, he got tougher, being hit by pitches 198 times in his career and suffering one of his most serious injuries not at the plate or crashing into a wall, but sliding hard to break up a double play in 1967.

Teammate Brooks Robinson summed up Frank Robinson this way: "Frank was not out to make friends but to knock someone on his tail."[13]

In his acceptance speech, which lasted about a half-hour, Robinson touched on many themes. Looking at Rachel Robinson, he said, "Without Jackie around to lead the way, the door might not have been opened for a long time. He made it easier for all black ballplayers. I don't know whether I could have put up with what Jackie put up with."[14]

He talked about his achievements in baseball but said he was never hung up on his statistics. If he had been, he said, he had a sure-fire way of padding them. "A lot of people ask me if I get upset because I fell just short of 600 homers (586) and 3,000 hits (2,943)," he said. "If I wanted to go after personal goals, I could have inserted myself into the lineup a lot more when I was managing Cleveland. I just want to be remembered as a winner."[15]

Robinson's career statistics point out how amazingly consistent he was. His lifetime batting average was .294. His lifetime batting average against right-handed pitching was .294 (.295 against left-handers.) His lifetime batting average against right-handed starting pitchers was .294. His lifetime batting average against left-handed starting pitchers was .294. His lifetime batting average in games he started was .294. His lifetime batting average in games in which he was the starting left-fielder was .294. His lifetime batting average in open air stadiums was .294. He hit .295 on natural grass, .296 in day games, .293 when leading off an inning and perhaps most significantly, .291 with runners in scoring position.

In his Hall of Fame speech, he did not shy away from talking about the insensitive comments made in Cincinnati when he was traded to Baltimore. He acknowledged that baseball management has the right to trade any player but he resented Reds general manager Bill DeWitt justifying the trade by calling him "an old 30."

"That really hurt me because it was the first time in my life I felt I had failed," said Robinson. "But it also served to turn my career around."[16]

At his request, Robinson's Hall of Fame plaque has him wearing a Baltimore Orioles cap, and at the ceremony, he was moved by the number of people from Baltimore who made the trip up to Cooperstown to see him inducted. Orioles owner Jerry Hoffberger was there. So were Bob Brown, Orioles director of public relations, and John McCall, assistant director of the farm system. Eddie Ridgely, the Orioles' clubhouse man, drove up to honor the ballplayer whose locker room he used to clean.

The most vocal contingent at Cooperstown was a large group of fans representing Section 34 of the seats at the old Memorial Stadium where Wild Bill Hagy, usually dressed in tank top, blue jeans, and wearing a straw hat and sunglasses, would lead raucous cheers for Robinson and the Orioles. Before the ceremony started, Hagy stood up and led the crowd in shouting "O-R-I-O-L-E-S" just like he had done for so many years at Orioles games. During his acceptance speech, as his fans hooted and cheered, Robinson smiled and said, "Section 34, I love you."[17]

He told the crowd his happiest days as a player were in Baltimore. He said when Cincinnati traded him to the Orioles, it was a shock. "But then

I realized I was going to a good club and maybe I could help them win," he said. "The love affair I had with the city, the club and the fans still goes on."[18]

In his autobiography, *Extra Innings,* written with Barry Stainback and published in 1988, Robinson said he was more than a little disappointed that the Cincinnati Reds organization did not have anyone in attendance at his induction ceremony. Gabe Paul, general manager of the Cleveland Indians who was Reds general manager during many of Robinson's years there, had called and congratulated him. But he hadn't heard from anyone else in the Cincinnati organization.

"I considered that a slap in the face and I later wrote to Dick Wagner, then the Reds president, and asked him to remove my name from everything pertaining to the ballclub."[19]

(Almost two decades later, Robinson made amends with the Reds as he and his wife Barbara toured the Cincinnati Reds Hall of Fame and Museum, in which he is prominently featured, and attended a ceremony in which his uniform number was retired.)

Robinson paid tribute to the men on the stage with him that day and to other notable baseball personalities—Jackie Robinson, Curt Flood and others. But he had special words for two men who most people on the platform and in the audience had never heard of and yet were most instrumental in developing him as a ballplayer, a manager and a responsible human being.

One was Jerem Quavos, owner of the San Touriste baseball team in the Caribbean Islands who hired him to manage in the winter leagues.

> "He put up with me for eight years down there," said Robinson. "And what he did for me when I became a manager in the big leagues I cannot explain. For we could sit for hours and talk about strategies, what I could do, what I could become …
>
> "But also what Jerem Quavos did for me is he was open and honest with me as a person. And he was able to show me and tell me how other people saw me. And I was able to sit and listen and understand and stand back and say, hey, maybe I'm not as nice, and maybe I'm a little tough on people, maybe I'm a little standoffish And I said, I'm going to try my best to correct it. And I have. I've tried to change for the better."

The other person who impacted his life was someone Robinson met when he was just a youngster. His name was George Powles (pronounced Poles). Robinson said,

> "I was blessed I think to come across a man that set the foundation for my baseball career and made it my life in general, and that man a lot of you will

not recognize, the name is George Powles. He was my sandlot coach, and high school coach, American Legion coach in Oakland, California. And he was a dedicated man.

"He gave to the youth of Oakland his time, his knowledge and his ability that he knew what it would take to play baseball. And what he taught me was how to play the game of baseball the way it should be played and that is to give 100 percent at all times. Do whatever you can do to win a ballgame, short of hurting anyone intentionally. But also I think the biggest thing that he gave to me, and the youth of Oakland was he also taught us how to lose and accept it. Not be happy about it, but how to accept it graciously. Because we all can't win all the time and you have to be able to accept defeat and build from that. George Powles gave me the foundation I'm still building on."[20]

CHAPTER 2

Uncanny Instinct for Baseball

Frank Robinson was a skinny, quiet kid with great athletic ability. He had a bat in his hand from the time he was a toddler, and by the time he was a teenager and met up with George Powles, his American Legion and high school coach, he could swing the bat pretty well.

Robinson was born August 31, 1935, in Beaumont, Texas, the youngest of ten children, most of whom were grown and out of the house when he was growing up. He was raised by his mother, Ruth Shaw, who did her best to hold a tight rein on her youngest son who showed early on that he had a mind of his own. The family moved to Oakland, California, before Frank started school, and that is the place he always considered home. Not much is known about his father except that he introduced his son to the game that would one day make him famous.

Ruth Shaw said Frank's dad died when the boy was about eight years old. When Frank was only three, she said, his dad bought him a mitt, a bat and a ball. "Frank used to carry them around wherever he went, even when he was half the size of that bat," she said. "He lost the ball and the glove or maybe some bigger kids took them away, and then Frank carried the bat around all the time."[1]

Oakland is on the east side of San Francisco Bay. Between 1940 and 1950, the city's population swelled from 302,000 to about 384,000, but was maligned by author Gertrude Stein's comment in her 1937 book, *Everybody's Autobiography*, in which she said, "There's no there there." She was referring to a visit she made to her old hometown and her reaction to seeing that the house where she had grown up was torn down—but the comment was misconstrued to be an indictment of the city as a whole.[2]

During the war years, when Robinson was a boy, the canning industry was the second-biggest in Oakland, with only ship-building being larger. The biggest canneries were the Josiah Lusk Cannery, the Oakland Preserving Company (which developed the Del Monte brand) and the California Packing Company.

The family lived in West Oakland, between downtown and the bay, in a neighborhood in which blacks, Mexicans and Asians all lived in attached, two-story frame tenements. "We were poor and didn't know it," said Frank.

There was never any thought given to the color of someone's skin or their ethnicity. "I knew my skin was different than others in the neighborhood or at school. But I never had any feelings or thoughts about that. We were all just people," he said.[3]

Frank went to Tompkins Grammar School in West Oakland. His mother said he was small and thin but she never worried about it because he was sturdy like his father. When he was an adult, Frank kidded about how small he was as a child. "Well, when you sit down at the table to eat with ten kids, you better be quick," he said. "Less you don't get anything to eat."

But he said there were some definite advantages to being the youngest. "When I was coming along as a kid, I didn't have to do any of the chores around the house because they (my brothers) made the sacrifices for me," said Robinson. "I would say, hey, Johnny or Sylvester, mom wants me to cut the lawn but I got a game to play and they would say go ahead."

So Frank would go off to play ball, and after doing this several times, he realized he had a good thing going. "I got to thinking, say, this is easy. And even if I don't have any baseball games to play and I'm gonna get out of the chores I can just say I do. So a few times I did say that and I didn't have any games to play."[4]

Frank's mother said her son was consumed with baseball. In the summer, he would play in the morning, come home for lunch and then go back to the playground. "I knew I wouldn't see him again until dark. I was always after him to come home early. And later, when he was a teener, I was after him to get a job. He could have had a job at one of the canneries," she said.[5]

Mrs. Shaw said he played American Legion ball in the summer and then joined a winter league and played some more. "He'd leave the house and say he was going to look for work but then when he came home we all knew he had been to the playground," she said. Frank would tell his mother and brothers that he was going to be in the major leagues some day and his brother Sylvester would kid him, saying, "You ain't gonna live long enough to see the big leagues."[6]

Frank went to McClymonds High School at 26th and Myrtle in West Oakland, the third-largest high school in Oakland, named after J.W.

McClymonds, a former superintendent of schools. It was there that he formed what turned out to be a lifelong relationship with George Powles, a teacher and coach. Powles coached at the school from 1947 to 1975, a time in which McClymonds had some tremendous athletes. NBA Hall of Famer Bill Russell was a teammate of Robinson's on the 1952 McClymond Warriors basketball team. The next year, Russell was off to college and Robinson led the team in scoring. In baseball, Robinson and future major leaguers Vada Pinson and Curt Flood all played for McClymonds.[7]

Robinson and Powles first met in the fall of 1949. Frank had just turned 14 and was a student at Westlake Junior High. Powles was a high school coach but he always had an eye open for young talent he could help groom not only for the high school team but for the American Legion team he also coached. He invited Frank to participate in a game with a bunch of 15- and 16-year-olds just to see how he would do. Robinson homered and tripled his first two times up.

George Powles coached Robinson's high school basketball and baseball teams and his American Legion baseball team. He is shown here with Robinson (center) and Brady Hord prior to a McClymonds High School game on January 8, 1953 (unknown photographer, January 8, 1953. Gelatin silver print, 8 × 10 in. The Oakland Tribune Collection, the Oakland Museum of California. Gift of ANG Newspapers).

The following spring, in 1950, Powles invited him to join the Bill Erwin Post 237 American Legion team, which had won the national championship the year before. Frank was stunned to be invited to play for what he considered such a hallowed team and admits to being "just another player" on it. The star was J.W. Porter, who later was a major league catcher. The ballclub won its second straight national championship, helped by a triple Robinson hit in one of the championship playoff games in Omaha.

Powles became a father figure for young Frank. The high school team had mostly black players whereas the Legion team had mostly white players. Powles helped guide his young baseball star through not only baseball situations but life situations as the two of them interacted on an almost daily basis.

One of the baseball lessons Powles taught Robinson might have seemed innocent enough at the time but served him well throughout his major league career. Frank liked to stand close to the plate with his head cocked forward, practically in the strike zone. It is a practice that is commonly called "crowding the plate." Powles taught his teenage hitter that when a pitch was coming high and inside, "tuck your head into your shoulder and spin left. Quickly."[8]

In a 1962 newspaper interview, Powles said, "Frank wasn't much of a student but his instinct for baseball was uncanny. He always had strong wrists. I think today he can stop a swing in the middle better than any man in the majors. And he always had power and a good arm but no speed. I think he gets faster every year."[9]

Powles said many of his former players came to visit him when their teams were playing in the Bay Area but that wasn't Frank's style. "Pinson comes to visit. Robinson hardly ever does That's Frank. Always something of a loner. I never had a shier kid."[10]

A high school team that continually produces talented ballplayers and an American Legion team that wins two consecutive national championships are bound to draw the attention of baseball scouts. One of them was Bobby Mattick, a former major leaguer, who scouted the west coast for the Cincinnati Reds. Mattick's big league career was short and undistinguished—five years, mostly as a reserve Cubs catcher, 206 games, 690 at-bats, no home runs, 64 RBI and a .233 batting average. But as was the case later with managers like Earl Weaver, Walter Alston and Sparky Anderson, he didn't possess great talent but he was an expert in seeing it in others.[11] (To be fair, Alston had a strong minor league career, but he was part of a Cardinals farm system that produced two Hall of Famers; otherwise, he might have had more luck breaking into the big leagues.)

Mattick made several trips to Oakland to take a look at the hitter he had heard the most about, J.W. Porter, who most observers thought had the most big league potential. When he came to watch Porter, whom he eventually signed, he also came across Robinson.

"I was older. Frank was only in the ninth grade," said Porter, recalling those days many years later. "Frankly, I was the star of the team but even though Frank was just in the ninth grade, you just knew if this kid ever put on a few pounds, someone was gonna get hurt."

"He could do everything well except pull the ball," said Porter. "He was way ahead of everyone else. He could hit better, he could run better, he could throw better. He hit the ball to right and right center a lot."

Porter said Mattick, the scout, had never heard of Robinson when he came to Oakland.

"He came to watch me," he said, "and he saw this kid and he came back every year to watch him. He signed Frank and that started it. He later signed Vada Pinson and Curt Flood and lots of other black kids from Oakland for the Reds.

"Bobby sold his house in Los Angeles and moved to Oakland because that's where the action was. Back in those days, it was tough for a black kid to get signed. They didn't get bonuses. If they were lucky, they got a bus ticket.

"Bobby came and watched them play and became friends with them. He bought them burgers and shakes and made them feel good. These kids signed with people they

J.W. Porter was a star ballplayer in Oakland. Cincinnati Reds scout Bobby Mattick came to Oakland to watch Porter when he discovered and eventually signed Frank Robinson (courtesy J.W. Porter).

liked. They signed with Bobby Mattick. He was just an ordinary scout until he discovered all the talent in Oakland. He became a super scout. And it started with Frank Robinson."[12]

In the early summer of 1953, when Frank was 17, Mattick signed him to a $3,500 bonus and salary of $400 a month to play with the Reds' Class C ballclub in Ogden, Utah. It was a long way from the major leagues but it was a start, another opportunity for someone who thrived on having something to prove.

He was a teenager on his way to play with men, and he wouldn't have his mother or George Powles or his brother Sylvester around to encourage him or get him out of jams. He was a kid who wanted to play baseball and he was getting his chance. But for the first time in his life, he was basically on his own.

Ogden was Utah's second largest city, with Salt Lake City, the largest, about 40 miles south. It was situated at the foot of the Wasatch Mountains and was the closest city of any size to the famed Golden Spike, where the Transcontinental Railroad was joined in 1869. The summers were hot and dry with high temperatures typically in the 90s and sometimes reaching 100 degrees or above.

The climate was good for baseball, and Robinson proved he was worthy of being there, even at his young age, just as he had done when George Powles tried him out for a potential spot on his American Legion team in Oakland. The Ogden Reds won the Pioneer League championship with Frank hitting .348 with 17 home runs in 72 games. He was the only player on the team to play one day in the major leagues. Ogden's catcher, Dave Bristol, never made it to the majors as a player but had an 11-year run as a major league manager with Cincinnati, Milwaukee (Brewers), Montreal, Atlanta and San Francisco.

As his statistics showed, young Robinson had no trouble making the adjustment to professional ball on the field. It was the social and cultural climate off the field that was a new, puzzling experience for him. Ogden was in the heart of Mormon country, and that meant "white country," totally different from his old neighborhood in West Oakland where racial and ethnic diversity were a way of life and nobody paid any particular attention to someone's accent or the color of their skin. As Robinson said, "we were just people."

In Ogden, Frank was one of only two black players on the team, and the other, Chico Terry, spoke Spanish and knew only one word of English that anyone could understand, "coffee." Naturally the two black players roomed together. Societal standards in Ogden prevented them from having the same living conditions as their teammates, all of whom lived in private homes of people who had welcomed them into their households. Robinson and Terry lived in a shabby hotel room, victims of the skin color they were born with. Off the playing field, they had only each other, and because of the language barrier, communication between the two of them, while friendly, was limited.

Robinson was depressed and lonely. His only refuge was to call his mother as often as he could and, while it helped to hear her voice, Frank was reluctant to tell her how miserable he was. "I didn't burden her with my problems. I had never done that and never would. I didn't want my mother to be worried about me."[13]

Despite his problems off the field, Robinson had put together good enough numbers on the field that the Reds promoted him to Double A ball, and he reported to Tulsa in the spring of 1954. Cincinnati was well stocked in its minor league system with good, young outfielders, so Robinson was moved to third base. It was an experiment that lasted eight days of what Robinson later described as ineptitude and resulted in his demotion to the Reds' Class A ballclub in Columbia, South Carolina. He was reunited with Chico Terry, who, after hitting .335 at Ogden, was sent to Columbia and was the first Negro to play on a professional baseball team in South Carolina. Terry had a successful minor league career but never made it to the big leagues.

For Robinson, he was back in the outfield again, and was one of three non-whites on the team. He was in the South, where racism was rampant, and he was thousands of miles away from his family.

Columbia was the capital city of South Carolina, with a population of about 120,000. It was the county seat of Richland County but a part of the city was also in Lexington County. The Saluda and Broad Rivers reached confluence in Columbia and merged into the Congaree River.

Columbia had deep roots in southern tradition, culture and mentality. It was the site of the South Carolina Secession Convention prior to the Civil War where delegates voted 159–0 for the state to secede from the union. Eighty years later, the city had shed much of its Jim Crowism. In 1945, a court ruling mandated that the city's black teachers receive equal pay for equal work with white teachers, and there were other indications of the city moving forward in race relations.

Frank Robinson, at age 18, was not caught up in the history of the city and in fact was more comfortable in Columbia than he had been in Ogden.

He and a black teammate, Marv Williams, roomed together and discovered that one of the city's three theaters allowed Negroes in if they sat in the balcony. Going to the movies was one of Frank's favorite pastimes when he wasn't playing ball, so the movie theater in Columbia was an affordable, enjoyable place for him to spend some idle time.[14]

When the ballclub went on the road, particularly in Georgia where they played in places like Macon, Savannah and Augusta, Robinson heard the taunts of "Nigger, go home" and similar outbursts from people in the stands. Still just a teenager, he had to develop a mental toughness that would allow him to concentrate on baseball and not be distracted or react in such a way to jeopardize his goal of playing major league ball. It is likely that Frank Robinson thought often about Jackie Robinson during these days. To calm himself and help him stay focused, he would repeat a little refrain: "Have a good year and get out of here."[15]

The road trips were grueling. Some were all-night jaunts on rickety buses. In Macon, Savannah and other places, the buses would stop at diners where players could get something to eat and use the restrooms, except for Robinson and the other black players. They were not allowed in the restaurant and had to wait for a teammate to bring them a sandwich. They could not stay at the same hotels as other players and certainly not in private homes that were available to the white players. Often they stayed at a YMCA and had to fend for themselves, eating in "Negro restaurants" and taking "Negro cabs" to get to the ballpark. It was a different world for Robinson, far away from the playgrounds of Oakland where no one paid much attention to skin color or someone's accent, and young Frank had to learn to not let the frustration building up inside of him affect how he played on the field.

The Columbia Reds were managed by Ernie White, a former major league pitcher who helped Billy Southworth's St. Louis Cardinals to National League championships in the early 1940s and was also on Southworth's 1948 Boston Braves championship team. The following year, he began a successful minor league managing career. His 1954 Columbia club won 79 and lost 62, good enough only for a fourth-place finish in the South Atlantic ("Sally") League. His leading hitter was his youngest player, Robinson, whose average was .336, fourth best in the league.

The league's best pitcher that year was Humberto Robinson, who won 23 games and later had a five-year major league career with the Milwaukee Braves and Philadelphia Phillies. The best all-around hitter was Jim Lemon, who went on to play 12 years in the big leagues, mostly with Washington and Minnesota, and managed the Senators for one year.

Five other Columbia players, in addition to Robinson, made it to the major leagues, most of them briefly. Pitcher Don Gross had a five-year stint with Pittsburgh and Cincinnati and had a 20–22 lifetime record. Barney Martin pitched two innings for Cincinnati in 1953 before returning to the minors for good. Ken Polivka, another pitcher, pitched three innings for the Reds in 1947. Dick Murphy got one at-bat for the Reds in 1954 and John Oldham got into a Cincinnati game as a pinch-runner in 1956. Hank Ruszkowski logged 84 at-bats over three seasons with the Cleveland Indians.

White was a native of South Carolina and a product of the deep south and its way of doing things. When he held pre-game meetings and said things like "Now how are we going to pitch to this big nigger?" it bothered Frank although White never showed any overt signs of racism. His indelicate language was just the way he talked, and Robinson correctly assessed that nothing more should be made of it.

Frank was invited to spring training with the Reds in 1955 but missed his chance to stick with the big club when he injured his shoulder. It became a chronic injury that affected his throwing and gave him problems for many years, even in the majors. The injury prevented him from sticking with the Reds after spring training. So it was back to Columbia and another season with Ernie White's ballclub. His shoulder bothered him most of the year and his averaged slipped badly to .263. Even the home crowd was starting to get on him. He was relegated to playing first base to save wear and tear on his throwing arm.

One night, some inebriated fans along the first base line started needling him early in the game, and their barbs got louder and more personal as the game went on, including use of the "nigger" term. Robinson was furious and when the game ended, he raced into the dugout, grabbed a bat and headed for the stands. Marv Williams, his roommate, intervened and stopped him from confronting his detractors.

White noticed the commotion and ran over to find out what was going on. Robinson told him and described the three drunks. White ran into the parking lot, saw their car as it was pulling out, and wrote down the license number He learned who the owner of the car was and wrote him a note saying, "If you ever doubt the courage of Frank Robinson, I will arrange a meeting between you and him." The trio never showed up at the ballpark again.[16]

As the season wore on, the pain from the arm injury, the pressure he put on himself to succeed, and the racial slurs he was hearing now at home as well as on the road took their toll on young Robinson, not yet 20 years old. As the team prepared to take another long bus ride, 90 miles to Charlotte, Frank had had enough. He decided to quit the team and go back to Oakland where he could play ball in the summer leagues, hang out with his friends, enjoy the love and support of his mother and family, and sleep in his own bed every night. He might get a job in one of the canneries or maybe he would go back to school. All of that seemed more promising than what he was putting up with in Columbia.

He told Williams his intentions and Williams tried to talk him out of it. Finally, Williams said if Robinson quit the team, he would too. When the team bus left for Charlotte, Robinson and Williams stayed behind, in their room, contemplating their respective futures. Robinson and Williams were at opposite ends of their baseball lives. Robinson's was ahead of him if he chose to continue. Williams was 35 years old, had played in the old Negro Leagues as well as the Mexican League and for about a dozen minor league teams. At his age, he was never going to make the major leagues. So the two players had entirely different perspectives as they sat in their room that night.

The game against Charlotte was rained out. That gave the two men an extra day to decide what they wanted to do. As often happens after a good night's sleep, Robinson changed his mind. He felt like he could be a major league ballplayer some day and he had come this far. He was willing to stick with it at least for a little while longer. Since the game in Charlotte had been rained out, neither he nor Williams had missed any playing time. They found someone who drove them to Charlotte, paying him gas money, and the two ballplayers resumed their minor league careers.

The next spring, Robinson was called up to the Cincinnati Reds, and he never played another inning of minor league baseball. Williams resumed his minor league career and played six more years for various teams before retiring.

Robinson and Williams went their separate ways, one into the beginning of a Hall of Fame career, the other into the twilight of a minor league existence. Yet Frankie, as he was now often called, took something with him from his experience with the older ballplayer that would serve him well for the next two decades.

Just as George Powles, his old high school and American Legion coach, had taught him how to crowd the plate and, when necessary, tuck his chin to his shoulder and spin away from high, inside pitches, Williams taught him how to handle the bat: level bat, parallel to the ground. Lay the bat on your shoulder. As the pitcher comes forward with the delivery, keep your weight on your back foot and raise the bat from your shoulder. As the pitcher strides forward, drop your back elbow to re-level the bat and rip into the pitch.[17]

It created a little bit of a hitch in his swing but it also gave him tremendous thrust from his wrists. For years to come, players, coaches and managers all agreed that Robinson had an amazing ability to stop that thrust almost instantly in the middle of his swing if he didn't like the pitch. Nobody could "check his swing" better than Frank Robinson.[18]

Sometimes life takes unusual twists and turns. Robinson embarked on a major league career in which he was Rookie of the Year, won Most Valuable Player awards in both the National and American leagues, starred in All-Star Games and in the World Series, and hit 586 home runs. All of that may never have occurred if it hadn't rained one night in Charlotte, North Carolina, in 1955.

CHAPTER 3

The Big Leagues

Frank Robinson got the word from general manager Gabe Paul that he had made the Reds ballclub as the team was leaving Chattanooga, on its way north from spring training in March of 1956. At the time, despite the inroads made by Jackie Robinson and others in the past decade, baseball was still pretty much a white man's game, and Cincinnati was still pretty much a white man's city.

After Jackie Robinson broke the color line with the Brooklyn Dodgers in April of 1947, there was a gradual progression of Negro ballplayers into the big leagues. Larry Doby became the first black player in the American League, joining the Cleveland Indians in July of 1947, and Hank Thompson joined the St. Louis Browns 12 days later. Thompson has the distinction of also being one of the first black players on the New York Giants, going with them the same day Monte Irvin joined the club in July of 1949. The Boston Braves integrated their ballclub with Sam Jethroe in 1950. The Chicago White Sox's first non-white player was Minnie Minoso, who debuted in May of 1951. Bob Trice became the first black Philadelphia Athletic in September of 1953, the same month Ernie Banks joined the Chicago Cubs. In April of 1954, Curt Roberts integrated the Pittsburgh Pirates, as did Tom Alston with the St. Louis Cardinals and Nino Escalara and Chuck Harmon with the Cincinnati Reds.

Eight teams had black players on their rosters before the Reds did, and it wasn't until Pumpsie Green played for the Boston Red Sox in 1959, 12 years after Jackie Robinson broke in, that all clubs had at least one black player on their rosters. The Giants and Dodgers were leaders in signing Negro players and it is significant that they were the powerhouse teams in the National League in the 1950s, winning league championships every year from 1951 through 1956. When the Milwaukee Braves won consecutive National League pennants in 1957 and 1958 as well as the World Series championship in 1957, their star player was their young black outfielder, Henry Aaron.

By the time the Reds fielded their first black player, Irvin and Willie Mays were established stars for the Giants, and Jackie Robinson, Roy Campanella and Don Newcombe were dominant players for the Dodgers. On July 17, 1954, the year Cincinnati fielded its first black player and when five major league teams still had none, the Dodgers had a starting lineup with five Negroes—Campanella behind the plate, Jackie Robinson at third; Junior Gilliam at second; Sandy Amoros in left field and Newcombe on the mound.

The city of Cincinnati struggled to achieve racial harmony in the 1950s. It was slow to integrate its schools to comply with the Supreme Court edict of 1954. Its big amusement park, Coney Island, allowed blacks in for the first time in 1955, but, as part of a compromise agreement with white citizens, its swimming pool remained segregated. It was six years later, in 1961, when blacks were finally allowed to use the pool.[1]

Jim Brosnan, who pitched for the Reds, said, "I grew up in Cincinnati. If a black lived in this racist town, particularly in the Avondale area, where blacks and rednecks mixed together, then he had reason to fear for his life."[2]

Greg Rhodes, Cincinnati Reds historian, said, "Cincinnati was a very segregated city in the mid–1950s. Blacks and whites could not stay together in the same hotel. For a young man 19 or 20 coming into the system, he had to make sense of all of that. It could not have been easy.[3]

Robinson recalled, "I came to the major leagues as a 20-year-old kid. There was no one my age, hardly anyone my race [on the team]. I was sure glad to see Chuck Harmon. He took me under his wing and showed me how to do things on and off the field."[4]

Harmon, 31, wasn't exactly a father figure but more of a big brother in helping young Frankie adjust to the rigors of the major leagues. He was a native of Washington, IN, and a tremendous athlete who led his high school basketball team to two consecutive state championships. Harmon tried out with the Boston Celtics but did not make the team. He played semi-pro basketball for several years.

He and Nino Escalara, a Puerto Rican, debuted with the Reds on the same day, April 17, 1954. Escalara actually got into the game before Harmon did. For history's sake, Harmon always said Escalara was the first black to play for the Reds and that he was the first African American.

All the Negro players on the Reds stayed at the Manse Hotel in Cincinnati, a cheap boarding house for Negroes. Among them were pitcher Brooks Lawrence, first baseman George Crowe and outfielder Bob Thurman. They were nice fellows and they stayed out of trouble, but they were older than Frankie and he had trouble fitting in. Lawrence and Thurman liked to go to night clubs after games, which didn't appeal to their young teammate. "I hated to stay in my room by myself. I just hated it. Before I'd go to bed at night, I'd check the papers to see what time the movies started the next day. If there was one in the morning, I'd make it. And the afternoon show too."[5]

Gabe Paul, the general manager who signed Robinson, had been with the Reds since 1951. He was a protégé of Warren Giles, who hired Paul when he was an executive with the Rochester minor league club and brought

Chuck Harmon was the first African American to appear in a game with Cincinnati and was an early mentor for a young Frank Robinson (courtesy Cincinnati Reds).

him along as traveling secretary when he joined the Reds organization. When Giles became president of the National League, Paul succeeded him as general manager of the Reds. Paul began searching the country for good young black and Latin American players and eventually built the Reds into a pennant contender. With young Frankie Robinson, one of his prize finds, he understood the plight of the youngster who pretty much kept to himself. There wasn't much he could do about it. "Frank was like a lost soul. He had no companionship. No guidance," said Paul.[6]

When Robinson did venture out with his black teammates after games, he'd have a Coca Cola while the others had beer or cocktails. He loved to listen to them tell their stories. He wanted to soak up as much information as he could, and he particularly liked hearing Bob Thurman and George Crowe talk about the art of hitting.

Crowe, 35, had played for the New York Negro Giants in the Negro Leagues in the late 1940s and broke in with the Boston Braves in 1952. He was with the club when it made its move to Milwaukee the following year. He was traded to Cincinnati for outfielder Bob Hazle the day before Robinson was offered his contract with the Reds. A first baseman, he didn't see a lot of playing time but served as an able backup to Ted Kluszewski and was a positive influence on young players such as Frankie Robinson.

Thurman, at age 39, was just about old enough to be Frankie's father. He had played for the great Homestead Grays Negro Leagues team from 1946 to 1948 and then played for five minor league teams before joining the Reds as a rookie in 1954. He was full of stories of the old Negro Leagues and its stars such as Cool Papa Bell, Josh Gibson, Ray Dandridge and other black players who never had the chance to play in the big leagues. Both Thurman and Crowe were like a living history book to a young, eager-to-learn ballplayer like Frankie.

Thurman talked one night about the importance of paying attention to a pitcher's sequence of pitches—figuring out how the pitcher thought he was going to get you out, and making him pay for it. "I knew the guy would throw me a slider on the first pitch," he said. "Sure enough, he did. I swung and missed. Okay. I knew he'd come back with it if he got in trouble on the count. I worked him to 3-and-2 and sure enough, here comes the slider. Whack. Base hit."[7]

The one place where Frankie felt comfortable was on the ball field, and now he was going to get a chance to show his stuff in the major leagues. He had had a good spring training, a .271 batting average with four home runs, capped off by Paul offering him a contract. His mother, Johnny, Sylvester and his other brothers would be pretty impressed to hear he was going to earn $6,000 playing ball. He would never have to think about working in the canneries again as long as he kept his eye on the plate and his nose clean.

His manager, George "Birdie" Tebbetts, had high hopes for Frankie but recognized how young he was and knew it would be wrong to expect too much too soon. Tebbetts had been a major league catcher for 14 years with Detroit, Boston and Cleveland. He had exactly 1,000 hits in his career and finished with a lifetime batting average of .270. Tebbetts never hit for power but was known for his defensive prowess, his handling of pitchers and his field leadership. After he managed in the minors for two years, Paul hired him to manage the Reds in 1954.

As opening day approached, Tebbetts talked to the press about his rookie outfielder. "I don't know if Robinson will hit National League pitching sufficiently to be our left fielder," he said. "But the boy certainly packs a powerful wallop, he can field, throw and run well enough to be a regular and he will get a good chance to show if he can make it."[8]

On April 17, 1956, one of those oddities occurred that make baseball such a fascinating game. Three rookies made their major league debut, all of whom eventually were elected to the Hall of Fame—Luis Aparicio, who started at shortstop for the Chicago White Sox; Don Drysdale, who pitched an inning in relief for the Brooklyn Dodgers; and Frankie Robinson, who started in left field for the Cincinnati Reds.

Frankie got up that morning, showered and dressed, and went downstairs to the lobby of the Manse Hotel where he bought a newspaper and had breakfast in the hotel diner. He had his usual, bacon and eggs, toast and juice, and read about today's ballgame—opening day—against the St. Louis Cardinals. The Redbirds' starting pitcher would be Wilmer "Vinegar Bend" Mizell, his nickname coming from his hometown in Tennessee. He was a lefty with a good fastball, which didn't worry Frankie, and a good curve ball that did give him concern. Joe Nuxhall, a veteran pitcher who made his major league debut with the Reds at age 15 in 1944, was to be the Cincinnati starter.

After breakfast, he drove to the ballpark in his green and white 1956 Ford Fairlane and made sure he was there sufficiently before 11 a.m., the time Tebbetts wanted all players to arrive. When he got there he noticed the red Ford Thunderbird convertible in the players' lot and knew that slugging first baseman Ted Kluszewski, "Big Klu," had already arrived. Kluszewski was the team's established star, having hit more than 40 homers three years in a row, and was always among the first to get a pre-game rubdown from trainer "Doc" Anderson. One of Kluszewski's trademarks was that he wore a sleeveless T-shirt under his uniform shirt which he said gave his arms a looseness—but it also showed off his bulging biceps.

The game-time temperature was a crisp 46 degrees as Robinson and his teammates took the field. Joining Frankie in the outfield were Gus Bell in center and Wally Post in right. The infield consisted of Ray Jablonski at third, Roy McMillan at short, Johnny Temple at second and Kluszewski at first. Smoky Burgess was the catcher with Nuxhall on the mound.

More than 32,000 fans crowded into cozy Crosley Field. Robinson had never played in front of a crowd this big, but the ballpark itself, with a 387-foot center field wall and 400 feet at its deepest point in right-center, reminded him a little of Capital City Park in Columbia. One big difference was that Crosley Field had a "terrace" in which the field went uphill for several yards in center field and parts of left-center and right-center.

The Cardinals jumped out to a 1–0 lead in the top of the first inning before the Reds even came to bat. Cincinnati tied it in the second when

Jablonski, who had been traded to the Reds from the Cardinals, hit a home run over the left field wall. The crowd was still buzzing over Jablonski's blast when Frankie Robinson strode to the plate for his first big league at-bat. Tebbetts had him batting seventh, a safe place for a youngster rather than higher up in the lineup where more might be expected of him.

His feet were near the chalk line of the batter's box closest to the plate and his head was cocked forward, practically in the strike zone—"concussion alley," the batters often called it. But Robinson felt confident he could get out of the way of inside pitches, tucking his head into his right shoulder and spinning to the right, as George Powles had taught him years ago. He would easily be able to handle any pitch over the outside corner of the plate. Mizell delivered a fastball on the inner portion of the plate. Frankie reacted, his wrists unleashed, moving the bat through the strike zone from the approach Marv Williams had taught him. The crowd roared again as Robinson smashed a high line drive to deep center field. It hit off the wall as Cardinals center fielder Bill Virdon raced to track it down. By the time he did and threw it in, Robinson was safely on second with a double.

Frank Robinson was one of three future Hall of Famers to debut on April 17, 1956. He doubled in his first at-bat off the Cardinals' Wilmer "Vinegar Bend" Mizell (courtesy Cincinnati Reds).

The game was a dandy, a pitchers' duel between Nuxhall and Mizell in which each pitcher gave up a dozen hits but worked his way out of one jam after another. The ballgame was tied 2–2 in the ninth inning when Stan Musial hit a two-run homer off Nuxhall that turned out to be the game-winner in a 4–2 Cardinals victory. Robinson also collected a single in the game to go 2-for-3 for the afternoon.

Earl Lawson, sports writer for the *Cincinnati Times-Star,* took special note of Robinson's first at-bat, documenting how Frankie was making a habit of great starts. Lawson wrote, "Auspicious debuts have marked the brief but spectacular baseball career of Frankie Robinson, the 20-year-old rookie Redleg left fielder."[9]

He pointed out that Robinson had tripled in his first time up for Ogden, Utah, in the Pioneer League in 1953, homered the next year in his first at-bat for Columbia, South Carolina, in the Sally League, and now had doubled in his first major league at-bat at Cincinnati. "He showed 'em he doesn't scare," said Tebbetts.[10]

His manager said Robinson always had confidence he could hit big league pitching and, while one day was not positive proof, Tebbetts said it was an indication that his confidence was an asset—and there's a difference, he said, between having guts and confidence. "I've seen guys who would fight you until death and fail to make it in the big leagues because they didn't have the personal confidence," said Tebbetts. That would never be Robinson's problem, he said.[11]

St. Louis	AB	R	H
Moon, 1b	4	1	2
Schoendienst, 2b	5	1	2
Musial, rf	5	1	1
Sauer, lf	4	0	0
Boyer, 3b	3	0	2
Virdon, cf	4	0	1
Sarni, c	4	1	3
Grammas, ss	4	0	0
Mizell, p	4	0	0
Kinder, p	0	0	0
Totals	37	4	12
Cincinnati	**AB**	**R**	**H**
Temple, 2b	4	0	1
Burgess, c	5	0	1
Harmon, pr	0	0	0
Kluszewski, 1b	5	0	1
Post, rf	5	0	1
Bell, cf	4	0	1
Jablonski, 3b	4	2	3
Robinson, lf	3	0	2
McMillan, ss	4	0	2
Nuxhall, p	3	0	0
Crowe, ph	0	0	0
Totals	37	2	12

St. Louis	1	0	0	1	0	0	0	0	2–4	12	0
Cincinnati	0	1	0	1	0	0	0	0	0–2	12	0

DP—Grammas-Schoendienst-Moon; Temple-Kluszewski.
Doubles—Moon, Sarni (2), Kluszewski, Robinson, McMillan
HR—Jablonski, Musial.

	IP	H	R	ER	BB	SO
Mizell (1–0)	8.2	12	2	2	2	5
Kinder	.1	0	0	0	0	1
Nuxhall (0–1)	9	12	4	4	3	3

Attendance: 32,095

The Reds beat the Cubs, 10–9, in ten innings in the second game of the season with Brooks Lawrence picking up the win in relief. Frankie went 0-for-5. Jablonski once again had the big bat for Cincinnati, getting three hits for the second day in a row, and had seven RBI in the first two games. On April 20, the Reds got pummeled by the Cubs, 12–1. Robinson got his second double of the year, his only hit in four at-bats.

The Reds then went into their first slump of the year and Robinson hit the skids with them. They lost to Chicago, 3–2, lost again to the Cubs, 5–4, in the first game of a doubleheader and played to a 1–1 tie in the second game. On April 24, Mizell of the Cardinals beat them, 5–3. It was the Reds' fifth straight game without a win (four losses and a tie) and Robinson was hitless in his last ten at-bats. When the Reds returned to Crosley Field to begin a series with the Cubs, Tebbetts decided to give his rookie left fielder the day off.

Robinson said sitting on the bench with Tebbetts provided a good baseball education for him. Tebbetts would tell Frank to watch the opposing pitcher—Warren Spahn, Robin Roberts, Don Newcombe or whoever—and study the way they worked on hitters. He would also point to the way defenses played certain hitters and how positioning the defense for particular hitters—shading them a step to the left or to the right—could mean the difference in a ballgame. He also liked to keep his bench players alert by shouting "What's the count?" or "How many outs are there?"

"Birdie taught me to study the opposition and to think ahead, to anticipate what the opposing manager or players might do in a particular situation," said Robinson. "That very first year, when I was only 20, he made me see how important it was to stay on top of things, to never allow yourself to be surprised by an opponent."[12]

The day off for Frankie paid off. Back in the lineup on April 28, he hit a double and his first major league home run off Paul Minner of the Cubs in a 9–1 Reds victory. By the end of April, the Reds had already had a four-game winning streak, a four-game losing streak and finished the month with a 5–5 record. Robinson's early slump had pushed his batting average down to .167 but he had started to prove to others something he already knew—he could hit major league pitching.

By May, the personality of the 1956 Reds was starting to take shape. Brooks Lawrence, one of Frankie's neighbors at the Manse Hotel, was putting together a great year and won four in a row to up his record to 6–0 going into June. Another starter, Johnny Klippstein, was 4–2. Veterans Joe Nuxhall and Art Fowler were struggling, Nuxhall at 1–5 and Fowler at 3–6. Relief specialist Herschel Freeman was 4–0 and was the beneficiary of some late-inning heroics by the Reds, who were establishing themselves as home run threats up and down the lineup.

Also in May, Robinson was confronted with another fact of life in baseball. Chuck Harmon, who had been one of his mentors from the time he made the team, was traded to the St. Louis Cardinals for Alex Grammas. The two men went their separate ways but maintained a lifelong friendship.

On May 31, the Reds faced Mizell for the third time in the young season and Bell, Kluszewski and Robinson touched him for consecutive home runs—but they came in the ninth inning with the Reds losing 9–0. The final score was 9–3. On June 1, right fielder Wally Post was leading the league in home runs with 11, first baseman Kluszewski and third baseman Jablonski had ten, and center fielder Bell and Frankie each had nine. The Reds were on a pace to set the National League record for home runs.

The Reds swept a doubleheader from the Dodgers at Ebbets Field on June 24, with Robinson hitting the game-winning homer in a 2–1 victory in the nightcap. Three days later, Cincinnati scored nine runs in the eighth inning against the Pirates with Robinson driving in two of the runs. The 10–2 victory gave Brooks Lawrence his tenth win without a loss.

As the season progressed, three stories were developing with the Reds. The first was that they had become legitimate pennant contenders with their thunderous lineup giving them a chance to win almost any game they played. In the seventh, eighth and ninth innings, there was always the possibility that a three-run homer could bail them out of a tough situation. Cincinnati had not won a championship since 1940 but this year, 1956, they had a chance to overtake the Giants and Dodgers, who had won the National League pennant five years in a row and six out of the last seven. Going into August, Kluszewski led the league in home runs with 25; Robinson was second with 24; Bell had 19; and Post had 17, as did catcher Ed Bailey.

The Reds had catapulted into contention by winning 21 of 33 games in July. On July 17, Robinson hit his 20th homer, tying the Reds' rookie record, and Lawrence won his 13th straight game in a 4–3 win over the

Dodgers. Eight days later, Robinson homered again but it was the only run the Reds got in a 2–1 loss to Brooklyn.

On the morning of August 1, the National League standings were:

Team	W-L	GB
Milwaukee	57–35	
Cincinnati	58–40	2
Brooklyn	55–41	4
St. Louis	47–47	11
Philadelphia	45–52	14.5
Pittsburgh	43–52	15.5
Chicago	41–54	17.5
New York	33–58	23.5

The second developing story for the Reds was the emergence of Robinson as a star player. He was not only a good hitter, fielder and base runner, but he was also fearless and tough. In addition to everything else, he was on his way to leading the league in number of times being hit by a pitch as he continued to crowd the plate, refusing to give opposing pitchers the outside corner.

"He was one of the greatest competitors I ever saw," said Johnny Klippstein. "He would stand on top of the plate and always get hit on the arm or leg but he would never rub. If you knocked him down, he'd get up and hit the ball out of the park."[13]

Hersh Freeman noticed the same thing about his rookie teammate. "A pitcher doesn't like a hitter to take the plate away from him but Robby would take it away even if it meant getting hit. He got nailed many times," he said. "He was just a kid but he settled in real quick."[14]

The other pleasant surprise for the Reds was the stellar pitching of Brooks Lawrence, a 31-year-old right-hander acquired from the St. Louis Cardinals. Lawrence won his first 13 decisions, the second-best start in Reds history, topped only by Ewell Blackwell's 18–2 start in 1947. Lawrence was headed for his 14th straight win when Pittsburgh's Roberto Clemente tagged him for a three-run, ninth inning homer on July 21 to secure a victory for the Pirates.

By mid–August, with the Reds in the thick of the pennant race, Robinson was still a shy kid with a big bat but he was becoming somewhat of a celebrity in Cincinnati and especially at the Manse Hotel. Every time he hit a home run, he got a free piece of apple pie from the hotel management. As of August 8, when the *Cincinnati Post* picked up on the story, he had earned 25 pieces of pie.

Theodore Payne, the hotel manager, said Frankie was one of the hotel's most popular guests. He was quiet, went to the movies a lot, and never caused any trouble. "He's a very nice boy. You would never know he was in the place," said Payne. "He never complains or asks for anything special—except apple pie. The staff sort of looks after him."[15]

He continued his torrid hitting in August. On August 15, he drove in the winning run in the 15th inning in a 4–3 win over the Cubs. The next day he homered off Sam Jones but also contributed four of Jones' 13 strikeouts in a 4–2 Chicago victory. Two days later, the Redlegs unleashed eight homers in a game against Milwaukee, with Robinson hitting two of them. That set a National League record, and six of them came in bunches—three sets of back-to-back homers. On August 21, Robinson hit his 31st homer,

Brooks Lawrence won 13 games in a row to start the 1956 season (courtesy Cincinnati Reds).

seven shy of the National League record set by Wally Berger of the Boston Braves in 1930 but equaling the American League mark set by Ted Williams of the Red Sox in 1939. Frankie's 38th home run, tying the National League record, came on September 11. He did not hit any the last two weeks of the season.

(The team was called the Redlegs for a few years in the 1950s—a management reaction in the Cold War era not to have a team name with any connotation to Russians, who were also known as Reds.)

The Redlegs were the surprise team of the National League and remained in a three-way battle for first place with the veteran Dodgers ball club and a Milwaukee team that was coming into its own with its star outfielder Aaron. He, along with third baseman Eddie Mathews and first baseman Joe Adcock, provided the Braves with a 3–4–5 punch that was as good as any in the league. The Braves also boasted a pitching staff led by Warren Spahn, Lew Burdette and Bob Buhl. The race went down to the final weekend with Brooklyn winning ten of its last 14 games to emerge as champions once again. Cincinnati was eliminated on the day before the season ended and finished with a 91–63 record, third behind Brooklyn and Milwaukee.

It had been a year with many remarkable achievements for the Redlegs. Robinson finished with 38 home runs, tying him for most ever by a rookie. He scored 122 runs to lead the league and also led the league in getting hit by pitches, having been plunked 20 times as a reward for his habit of crowding the plate. As a team, Cincinnati averaged five runs a game to lead the league but had a pitching staff that gave up an average of 4.2 runs a game. Their team total of 221 home runs established a new major league record (since broken several times.)

One of many oddities in the season occurred on May 26, when three Redlegs pitchers combined for a no-hitter for 9⅔ innings against the Braves, only to lose the game, 2–1, in 11 innings. Johnny Klippstein pitched the first seven frames and, while holding Milwaukee hitless, he was wild and surrendered seven walks that contributed to the Braves scoring a run. Hersh Freeman pitched a hitless eighth and Joe Black, obtained from the Dodgers, came on to shut Milwaukee down in the ninth. It was a 1–1 tie in the 10th inning when the Braves got their first hit. They got two more hits in the 11th and pushed across the winning run.[16]

There was one blemish at the end of the season involving Lawrence and Tebbetts. On September 17, with the National League championship still in sight, Brooklyn beat the Redlegs, 5–4, with Brooks Lawrence taking the loss in relief, making his record 19–10 for the year. He did not start any games the rest of the way. Tebbetts went with Klippstein, Joe Nuxhall, Hal Jeffcoat and Tom Acker in the remaining 11 games, and Cincinnati won eight of them.

Lawrence thought Tebbetts purposely prevented him from winning 20 games—a milestone for a pitcher—and suspected racism might have been the cause. Sports writers also questioned his selection of pitchers. Tebbetts told the press, "I've got 12 pitchers to choose from. No matter who I pick, someone will say I'm wrong."[17]

Crowe, whose major league career started later than it might have because of the color of his skin, also thought Tebbetts penalized Lawrence because of race. He said he overheard Tebbetts telling someone, "Ain't no black man's going to win 20 games for me."[18]

Lawrence had slumped in the second half of the season after his 13–0 start. In his next 16 decisions he was 6–10, including the September 17 loss, whereas Jeffcoat had won seven of his last nine decisions. But on the last day of the season, when the Redlegs had been eliminated and they were playing a meaningless game against the Cubs, Tebbetts could have started Lawrence and given him his shot at winning 20. Instead, he started Jeffcoat, who won his eighth.

Robinson felt close to Tebbetts, who, like George Powles in Oakland, was a trusted mentor to him. He never saw any hint of racism in Tebbetts.

Robinson's first year in the big leagues was topped off in the fall when he was named the National League's rookie of the year by a unanimous vote. To go along with his 38 homers, he hit .290, scored 122 runs to lead the league, and had 83 runs batted in. He would have had more except, early in the season when Tebbetts had him batting seventh until he settled in, Frankie was hitting behind Kluszewski, Post and Bell and frequently came up after they had already cleared the field of any base runners.

After the 1956 season, he enrolled as a 21-year-old freshman at Xavier University in Cincinnati, the first time he had been in a classroom since his days at McClymonds High School in Oakland. He took 12 credit hours that included courses in psychology, speech, physical education administration, coaching and health/hygiene. It was quite a scene on the day he reported for his first day of classes, with students, reporters, photographers and fans following him on campus.

One of the onlookers was Xavier basketball coach Ned Wulk, who said, "I wish we could get this kind of turnout for the first day of basketball practice."[19]

Frankie had definitely achieved celebrity status in Cincinnati. The Rev. John Reinke, his psychology teacher, said Robinson's first day in class was one of Reinke's most unusual in the classroom. "Late in the hour I noticed the class began to fidget more than they ordinarily did," he said. "Then, as soon as the bell rang, they all jumped up and rushed up to Frank to get his autograph. It was the most hectic ending any of my classes ever had."[20]

CHAPTER 4

High and Inside

The Redlegs got off to a shaky start in 1957, losing their first four games. Then they won four in a row to even their record but lost their next three. By the end of the month they seemed to have found their groove as they embarked on a 12-game winning streak. By May 12, they had a 16–7 record and were tied with Milwaukee for first place in the National League.

Lawrence and Tebbetts had seemingly put any differences they had behind them as Brooks won four of his first five decisions to be the leader on the pitching staff once again. The Redlegs' bats continued to produce a lot of runs, led by Post, Robinson and Bell. Kluszewski, who had been the big boomer in the lineup for several years was experiencing back problems that prevented him from playing much of the season. That was a setback for the team but would have been a bigger one had it not been for the play of George Crowe. Kluszewski's injuries gave Crowe a chance to play on a regular basis, and he began thumping the ball well enough to fit nicely into the starting lineup.

The Redlegs hit their high point on June 2, winning the first game of a doubleheader with the Cubs, bringing their record to 28–14, a .667 winning percentage. On July 4, traditionally the midway point in the season, Cincinnati was in first place with a 44–32 record, a half-game ahead of the Cardinals and Braves, 2½ up on the Dodgers, and three games ahead of the surprising Philadelphia Phillies.

Robinson was having another good year with 96 hits, good for third in the league, and 57 runs scored, second in the league. He also had 13 home runs. The only category in which he was the league leader was in getting hit by pitches, which had occurred eight times already. Frankie refused to relinquish the outside corner of the plate to any pitcher, and hurlers responded by pitching him tight, backing him off the plate. But Tebbetts and others suspected the young outfielder was being targeted for less than honorable reasons.

On the night of July 16, the Redlegs played the Giants at the Polo Grounds in New York. It was an important game because Cincinnati was just coming out of slump in which they had lost seven straight between July 4–11 but had bounced back by sweeping the Pirates in a doubleheader on July 14. The pennant race was up for grabs with the Phillies on top, the Cardinals a half-game behind, the Braves a game and a half out, Brooklyn, two behind and Cincinnati two and a half out.

The pitching matchup was Hal Jeffcoat for the Redlegs and Ruben Gomez for the Giants. The game was scoreless for the first three innings. Robinson doubled in the first inning but was stranded. The Giants put together four singles off Jeffcoat in the fourth inning that produced two runs. The Redlegs got one of the runs back when Robinson tripled, his second extra-base hit off Gomez, and scored on a Kluszewski single. The Giants padded their lead to 4–1 on home runs by Darryl Spencer and Ed Bressoud in the sixth and seventh innings.

In the top of the eighth, Bell led off and grounded out. Robinson came up for his fourth at-bat against Gomez. With the count 0–1, Gomez unleashed a fastball that was head-high and breaking in on Frankie. He could not duck out of the way quickly enough and the ball hit him in the head. He crumbled to the ground semi-conscious and had to be carried off the field on a stretcher.

The Giants held on to win 6–1, but that wasn't what Tebbetts wanted to talk about after the game. In the clubhouse, he told reporters, "I caught long enough to know the difference between a deliberate pitch and a brush-back pitch," but then, as if he wanted to restrain himself, he added, "I am making no accusation."

When he got back to the hotel that night, he became unrestrained. "There is no doubt in my mind that this boy is being picked on because he is colored," Tebbetts told newspapermen gathered around him. "He is at a disadvantage because he can't fight back."

Tebbetts said pitchers didn't throw at hitters like Kluszewski, Musial or Snider because they knew they'd have a fight on their hands. But Frank Robinson, like Jackie Robinson a decade before him, had to gut it out.[1]

Giants manager Bill Rigney defended Gomez. "Robinson is one of those batters who leans over the plate and steps into every pitch. We always pitch him here," he said, pointing toward his body. "Hell, he wasn't trying to hit Robinson. If he was, why would he have yelled 'look out' when the ball was headed toward the plate?"[2]

Robinson was kept overnight at Harkness Pavilion, a midtown hospital, but was released the next morning when x-rays showed no fracture. He got dressed and went to the Polo Grounds, where the Redlegs and Giants were playing a day game. Cincinnati won, 5–4, on the strength of Crowe's 19th and 20th home runs. Frank went 1-for-4, leaning over the plate as usual.

National League president Warren Giles had heard about Tebbetts' outburst and contacted the Cincinnati manager immediately. Prior to the game, Tebbetts talked to the press, and his view had changed from what he had said the night before. "I don't believe Gomez' action was discriminatory in any sense," he said. "I was trying too hard to protect Robinson and I realize now I was being unfair."

After Giles contacted Tebbetts, the manager sent him a telegram in which he said he believed Robinson was being thrown at because he was a good hitter and not because of his race. Giles then released a statement to the press, saying, "I am glad to know directly from Tebbetts that his remarks were unwarranted. They were no doubt made emotionally right after losing a ballgame."[3]

Robinson declined to comment about any racial ramifications but said the Dodgers, Cubs and Pirates threw at him all the time. "I can always count on being in the dirt some time during the series when we play those guys," he said. "If George Crowe has a good day ahead of me or someone has a good day behind me, I'm the one who goes down," he said.[4]

The Redlegs stayed in the pennant race until late August and early September, when they endured a ten-game losing streak, eventually losing 13 out of 14, creating too big a hole and not enough time to climb out of it. They finished at 80–74 in fourth place, behind Milwaukee, St. Louis and Brooklyn. Crowe was among the league leaders in home runs with 31, and Lawrence once again was the top Redlegs pitcher with a 16–13 record. Robinson had another great year, hitting .322 with 197 hits, including 29 doubles and 29 home runs. He was hit with pitches 12 times.

In November, the Associated Press named Frankie as the Sophomore of the Year in the National League to go along with his Rookie of the Year status from his first year. Robinson praised Tebbetts for helping him develop. "He kept after me all the way, and that's what a young player needs because all of us let down too easily, thinking we've got it made," he said.[5]

The Redlegs' fourth-place finish was disappointing and a step backward considering they had won 91 games the year before and were in the pennant race until the last weekend of the season. Gabe Paul decided it was time to shuffle the deck in the off-season. About the only untouchable was Robinson.

On December 9, Don Gross, Frankie's old teammate in Columbia, was traded to Pittsburgh for pitcher Bob Purkey, a deal that would pay big dividends in years to come. On December 16, Wally Post, one of the big bangers, was traded to Philadelphia for left-handed pitcher Harvey Haddix. With those two deals, within a week, Paul had added two starting pitchers to the rotation. Post had served the club well and would be missed, but Cincinnati needed pitching if they were going to make a move in the standings. On December 23, Jim O'Toole, another left-handed hurler, was signed as an amateur free agent. Perhaps the most surprising move of the winter came with the trade of Ted Kluszewski to the Pittsburgh Pirates for Dee Fondy, basically a singles hitter who had played most of his career with the Chicago Cubs. Big Klu had served the Redlegs well for many years but age was catching up to him and he was beginning to have chronic back problems. George Crowe had filled in admirably when Kluszewski was unable to play, which was most of the season in 1957. In picking up Fondy, Paul had acquired a backup for Crowe.

Also in the winter of 1957, the Redlegs invited Vada Pinson, a young, black outfielder, to spring training the following spring. Pinson was from Oakland and was three years behind Robinson at McClymonds High School. But they knew each other from their boyhood days and when Pinson made the opening day roster, Frankie Robinson finally had a friend on the team reasonably close to his own age with a similar background. They became roommates on the road and rented apartments near each other in Cincinnati. For Robinson, Pinson filled a huge void in his life as a ballplayer. He finally had a close friend, a pal.

"We were always together, Vada and I," said Robinson. "We roomed together, lockered and dressed side by side, sat together on team buses and plane rides. Just about everywhere you saw Frank Robinson, you saw Vada Pinson. I had never been very close to anyone before, and it felt good."[6]

As spring training opened in 1958, Robinson decided to try figure out a way of counteracting the high-inside pitches he knew he would be getting all year. "You can't stand by and do nothing about it," he said. "You've got to make adjustments. It calls for careful study of the pitcher." Frank said he didn't believe any pitcher deliberately threw at him with the intent to hurt him. "I crowd the plate and they figure by pitching me close, they've got a better shot at getting me out," he said.[7]

With a bolstered pitching staff, a promising young rookie in Pinson and a happy Frank Robinson, things were looking up for the Redlegs as they approached the 1958 baseball season. But the optimism changed dramatically in a fleeting moment on the afternoon of April 9, 1958, in Portsmouth, Ohio. Cincinnati was headed home from spring training and stopped in Portsmouth to play an exhibition game against the Washington Senators.

It was a meaningless game except to keep the athletes limber and provide them with a few more opportunities to pitch, hit, run, throw and slide against an opponent before the season opened in another week. When Robinson came to the plate for the second time, Washington pitcher Camilo Pascual teased him with a couple of pitches just off the plate, but Frank didn't bite. The third pitch was a fastball that soared in on him head-high, and he could not react fast enough to get out of the way. The ball hit him in the head just beneath the helmet and rendered him unconscious.

Vada Pinson joined the Reds in 1958, became a star and was Robinson's best friend on the team (courtesy Cincinnati Reds).

He was rushed to Mercy Hospital in Portsmouth, where he was examined and treated and had x-rays taken. Outside in the waiting room, Tebbetts and George Crowe sat anxiously in wheelchairs, the only chairs available. Tebbetts wondered whether it was worth it for ballclubs to play exhibition games where an injury could alter a team's prospects for the whole season or, worse, render a ballplayer a career-threatening injury.

"It's the hitting background in these minor league parks," he said. "It's hard to follow the ball. There's always the danger that someone's going to get hurt." Tebbetts smoked one cigarette after another as they awaited the doctor's report on Frankie.[8]

Finally a doctor emerged

and told them Frank would be all right but required a lot of rest. He would be transferred by ambulance to Christ Hospital in Cincinnati for further evaluation. Tebbetts and Crowe were allowed to see him for a moment. He was lying on a table in an x-ray room with an ice pack on the left side of his head. Crowe lifted the ice pack and said, "Gee, Frankie, Easter was a few days ago. Why are you still collecting eggs?" When he arrived at the hospital in Cincinnati a few hours later, Frankie looked at Tebbetts with half-opened eyes and said, "I feel like the devil."[9]

When the season opened on April 15, Frank was in the starting lineup and got a double in four at-bats as Cincinnati beat Philadelphia, 5–4. But Robinson had a headache that day, just as he had every day since the beaning. As the season progressed, he couldn't bring himself to dig in at the plate like he always had. And he had a tendency to bail out on inside pitches.

He knew what the problem was. Fear. For the first time in his baseball career, he was afraid of getting hit. "I was scared to death," he said. "I could no longer bring myself to stride into fastballs. And on curveballs I would flinch and roll back on my heels and then have to reach for the pitch. The fear in my subconscious was just excruciating."[10]

At the All-Star break, Robinson was hitting .240 with just eight home runs—and he knew he was lucky to have that many. The truth was that the fear he felt was robbing him of what had made him one of the most dangerous hitters in the National League; he was afraid to crowd the plate. He knew the fear was all in his mind and the only way to get over it was to get it out of his mind. But how?

He thought about it during the three-day All-Star break and came up with a plan he would try when the Redlegs played an exhibition game in Seattle against their top farm club before the regular season resumed. Robinson, an incessant student of the game, decided that in the exhibition game, he would try to hit everything to right field. If you're not trying to pull the ball, he figured, you're not as likely to bail out and it forces you to hang in there and concentrate on what you're doing. He tried it and got two dinky hits to right field, but he felt better at the plate.

In the first game after the All Star break, the Redlegs played the Giants in San Francisco. His first time up, Frankie hit an Al Worthington curve ball over the left field fence. In his second time up, it was if the fates were playing games with his psyche. Worthington was no longer in the game. The Giants' relief pitcher was Ruben Gomez, the same pitcher who had beaned Robby the year before. Robinson didn't give an inch and lined out to left field. But he felt he was back in the groove, back to crowding the plate like George Powles had taught him, swinging the bat like Marv Williams had taught him and having no fear.

But 1958 continued to be a year of setbacks and disappointments, and the next one came in August when Birdie Tebbetts was fired. The ballclub, which had won 91 games in 1956, was clearly underachieving. General manager Gabe Paul had wheeled and dealed to try to provide a good pitching staff to go along with the club's power-packed lineup. The starting rotation of Lawrence, Purkey, Haddix and Nuxhall was much improved over the staff of two years before. But baseball is a game in which sometimes, inexplicably, a team does not click, even though all the pieces seem to be there. When that happens, often the manager is the scapegoat.

The ballclub went the first half of the season hovering around the .500 mark, at one stretch going nearly three weeks without being more than one game above or below .500. On July 10, the Redlegs were 38–37 but then went on a seven-game losing streak. They climbed their way back to 49–49 by July 31 but August did them in. They lost seven in a row and ten out of 11, and on August 13, after losing a doubleheader to the Braves, Tebbetts was let go. The team was 52–61, in last place, 13½ games behind Milwaukee.

For Robinson, the beanballs had been physical setbacks. The firing of Birdie Tebbetts was an emotional setback. "Birdie was like a father to me," he said. "He was a patient, gentle man. When I made a mistake, he would take me aside and explain what I had done wrong. I was shocked and very upset when Birdie was fired."[11]

He was heartened, however, when he learned the Redlegs had hired Jimmy Dykes to replace Tebbetts. He looked at it as a chance to learn from someone who had been around a long time, someone who had played in the era of Ruth, Gehrig and Walter Johnson, and who had spent 17 years as a big league manager.

Dykes began his managerial career in 1934 with the Chicago White Sox and had managed them for 13 seasons. He had five winning seasons with the White Sox, never finishing higher than third place. In 1951, Connie Mack tabbed him as Mack's successor as manager of the Philadelphia A's, a position he held for three years, guiding the lowly A's to a 79–75 record in one of those years. In 1954, when the St. Louis Browns moved to Baltimore, Dykes became the first manager of the Orioles. In all, he had managed nearly 2,500 big league games.

Cincinnati did all right under Dykes' direction, winning 24 and losing 17 to end the season. But Robinson was not impressed. Dykes was a "rah-

rah" kind of manager who liked to keep things loose and to have a good time. He gave little direction except to clap his hands and say, "Go get 'em, boys," and if the Redlegs lost, he'd say, "Go get 'em tomorrow." His style and approach obviously produced some wins, but for a player as serious as Robinson, where the opponent was the enemy on the field and losing was not a consideration, the new manager was a disappointment. But he did not have to put up with him for long. Dykes was not rehired.

Robinson had another decent year. His batting average slipped to .269 as he tried to conquer his fears in the batter's box. But he led the club in home runs with 31 and in RBI with 83. The Redlegs finished in fourth place with a 76–78 record that would have been worse without the late season turn-around under Dykes. Purkey was their top pitcher with a 17–11 record. No one else won more than 12 and Nuxhall, at 12–11, was the only other hurler who won more than he lost.

The club hired Mayo Smith to be the manager in 1959. Like Dykes, he was an easy-going fellow who had managed the Phillies prior to coming to Cincinnati. In 3½ seasons at Philadelphia, when the Phillies didn't have much in personnel beyond pitchers Robin Roberts and Curt Simmons, he guided them to .500 seasons twice.

In Robinson's estimation, Smith did little more than make out the lineup card every day. The Redlegs did not appear to be inspired by his leadership. On July 5, with the team at a 35–45 record and mired in seventh place, Smith was fired and was replaced with Fred Hutchinson, a gruff, no-nonsense journeyman who had a successful career as a major league pitcher and had managed the Detroit Tigers and St. Louis Cardinals prior to coming to Cincinnati. He was the fourth manager the Redlegs had in less than two years.[12]

Gabe Paul continued to shuffle the deck to try to get the Redlegs back to the contender they had been in 1956. Shortly after the 1956 season, he sent Jablonski to the Cubs for Don Hoak, a younger third baseman who didn't hit with the power of Jablonski but otherwise fit in well. Hoak stayed two years and then was involved in another Paul transaction that had major consequences.

On January 30, 1959, Hoak was traded to the Pittsburgh Pirates along with catcher Smoky Burgess and pitcher Harvey Haddix for veteran Frank Thomas, who could play both in the infield and outfield and had some pop in his bat, and three other lesser players. Paul was trying to rebuild. Kluszewski was long gone but Gordy Coleman was a promising young first baseman. Burgess was expendable because Johnny Edwards was moving up the ladder and would become the Redlegs' regular catcher. Haddix had not produced the kind of season the Redlegs had expected from him.

But in trading Haddix, Hoak and Burgess, Paul had provided the Pirates three key pieces to their 1960 championship team that defeated the Yankees in the World Series. That was an obvious, unintended consequence of the trade for Cincinnati. But the Pirates had been one of the worst teams in baseball in the 1950s and had used their farm system, key trades, and a crafty manager in Danny Murtaugh to climb their way to the top. That is exactly what the Redlegs hoped to do with Fred Hutchinson at the helm.

They had not won a pennant since 1940. In the past 16 years, they had finished in the second division 12 times, had a record of under .500 13 times and, aside from their surprising third-place finish in 1956, hadn't finished that high since 1944. With Hutchinson finishing the 1959 season, the Redlegs went 39–35 to give them an overall record of 74–80, good for fifth place, but another sub-.500 season and another second division finish.

Robinson, playing first base most of the year, had another great season, hitting .311 with 36 home runs and 125 runs batted in. A personal highlight for him came on August 22 when he hit three home runs and drove in six runs in an 11–4 win over the Cardinals. He led the league once again in getting hit by pitches as he was nailed eight times, making it 47 for his four-year career. But after the All-Star break of 1958, he had proven to himself that he could overcome his fears with fierce determination.

Pinson, his teammate and buddy, chipped in with 20 homers, 84 runs batted in and a .316 batting average, best on the club. Bell had a solid year with 19 home runs, 115 RBI and a .293 average. But once again, the pitching was shaky. Don Newcombe, picked up from the Dodgers in the twilight of his career, was 13–8. Purkey also won 13 but lost 18. No one else on the staff won in double figures.

The Reds were still treading water in the National League. It was necessary to continue to shuffle the deck to try to get the right mix of players, the right combination of veterans and youngsters—a period of experimentation and evaluation—and it was likely to be painful until the solution was found. One thing was certain—Robinson and Pinson were untouchables. The ballclub would be built around them.

In December, Johnny Temple, the Reds' second baseman for a decade, was traded to Cleveland for three players, including Gordy Coleman, a young, left-handed-hitting first baseman. Wally Post, who had been traded to Philadelphia the year before, was reacquired. Cincinnati's starting outfield in 1960 would be Robinson, Pinson and Post.

Paul and Hutchinson had determined that changes needed to be made in the pitching staff. Purkey was the untouchable there. Newcombe and Lawrence were let go in favor of a "kiddy corps" of prospects: Jim O'Toole, Jim Maloney and Jay Hook. Jim Brosnan, a bespectacled relief pitcher acquired from the Cardinals, would eventually be the anchor of the bullpen.

Robby had firmly established himself as one of the great hitters of the National League and also one of the toughest players at the plate, in the field and on the bases. He not only conquered his fear of being hit by pitches but became even more tenacious at the plate if he was knocked down. Dodgers pitcher Stan Williams said, "If you knocked him on his ass three times in a row and came anywhere near the plate the fourth time, he'd hit it a country mile. You didn't want to wake him up."[13]

Ryne Duren, a Yankees pitcher and future teammate of Robby's, said, "Robinson was the best competitor I ever saw. I think after he got knocked down, he must have hit .500."[14]

"The fellow is positively fearless," said Stan Musial, the St. Louis Cardinals great. "His determination shows itself more when he steps up to the plate—almost on top of it—practically daring the pitchers to throw at him."[15]

Robinson was also an aggressive runner, believing the base paths belonged to the runner and anyone who doubted it would, in the words of future teammate Brooks Robinson, be "knocked on his tail"[16]

Carl Cannon, writing for the *Washingtonian,* summarized Robinson's approach to the game, calling him, "a legendary hard ass."[17]

On August 15, 1960, the Reds played the Braves in a twi-night double-header at Crosley Field. In the first game, Jim Maloney, a 21-year-old right-hander signed by the Reds the year before, and one of the youngsters the Reds were counting on for future success, won his first major league game, a 5–3 decision over Juan Pizarro.

But that is not what the game is remembered for in Cincinnati's baseball history. In the seventh inning, Robinson blooped a Pizarro offering down the right field line and had what looked to be an easy double. But Robby never stopped as he rounded second and tried to stretch it into a triple, sliding into third with the Braves' third baseman, Eddie Mathews, applying the tag. Suddenly both players were on the ground pummeling one another. Players from both dugouts raced over to try to break up the fight. Pizarro came over from the mound to try to separate them. Hutchinson and Bob Purkey and a swarm of other Reds rushed over.

When order was restored, Robinson was sporting a partially shut right eye as if he had been a losing boxer. He also had a jammed thumb. Mathews had a cut on his lip and bruises on his arm. In the clubhouse afterwards, Robinson explained what happened. "He called me a name," he said, "and I answered him. It was nothing out of the ordinary. I've been called those names before. He was in the baseline and I knew there would be a play and close. But what was I supposed to do—stop and say 'tag me'? Then he made the remark."[18]

Robinson said they exchanged words and then Mathews hit him. "I wouldn't say he sucker-punched me but I was surprised," said Robby. Mathews said the fight started "by mutual agreement" and he knew Robinson got in at least one good punch because of Mathews' bleeding lip.[19]

Mathews was ejected from the game and Robinson was unable to continue because of his swollen eye. But he insisted on playing the second game and had a single, a double and a two-run homer. He also made a great catch in the outfield of a ball hit by Mathews. The Reds won the game, 4–0. Reflecting on the incident more than 20 years later, Robby said he figured, considering what he did in the second game, that he in effect had won the fight.[20]

The Reds finished sixth in 1960, winning 67 and losing 87 in what unfortunately had become a rather typical year for the ballclub. Robinson had another outstanding season, hitting .297 with 31 homers and 83 RBI. Pinson hit .287 with 20 home runs and 61 RBI. Post, reunited with his old teammates, chipped in with 17 home runs and 77 runs batted in.

Purkey did what was expected of him, once again winning 17 while cutting his losses down to 11. Cal McLish, who had come over from Cleveland in the Temple deal, could manage only a 4–14 record, and Nuxhall slumped to 1–8.

But Hutchinson was encouraged by what he saw in the rest of his staff. O'Toole was 12–12 and Jay Hook won 11 though he lost 18. Maloney, the winning pitcher in the game best known for the Mathews-Robinson fight, won two late-season games and was regarded as a future star.

The Reds had only to look at the Pirates, World Series champions in 1960, to see how a team could rise from the ashes of the National League to achieve the ultimate prize.

If the Reds were to do it in 1961, however, it would be without Gabe Paul, their general manager for a decade, who was leaving to help put together the Houston Colt .45s ballclub that would be an expansion team the following year.

Though the Reds did not win a championship in the Gabe Paul era, many of the players he signed were big factors in their next championship.

But his legacy in Cincinnati is that he broke the color line in a segregated city and gave young players like Frank Robinson a chance.

Paul loved to tell the story of how Branch Rickey, the brilliant baseball executive with the St. Louis Cardinals, Brooklyn Dodgers and Pittsburgh Pirates, tried to hoodwink Paul into trading Robinson, then in the minor leagues, to the Pirates in a deal in which Cincinnati was to receive Danny O'Connell, another hot minor league prospect. Robinson was an 18-year-old kid playing in Ogden, Utah, and Rickey acted as if he couldn't even remember the kid's first name. Paul knew that Rickey indeed knew Frankie's first name, and Paul also knew that Frankie wasn't going to be part of any deal.[21]

With Paul's departure, Robinson had much the same feeling he had when Chuck Harman was traded and again when Birdie Tebbetts was fired. In each case, a friend and a mentor had left.

CHAPTER 5

Guns, Hutch and Hoopla

It didn't take Frank Robinson long to realize there was a new sheriff in town—Gabe Paul was gone and things would be quite different with his successor, Bill DeWitt. For one thing, salary negotiations had been fairly easy with Paul. Robinson had joined the ballclub as an unproven rookie making $6,000 a year, had put up good numbers every year and was earning $30,000 in 1960. That was a lot of money for a young man who probably would have been working in a cannery in Oakland for little more than minimum wage if it were not for his baseball career.

The money had provided Robinson with a sense of independence. It gave him a sense of security. He liked automobiles and was able to purchase cars of his choice, rather than clunkers. While he would never be as fancy a dresser as his roommate Pinson, he was now able to have a decent wardrobe. Robby grew up poor, although, as he often said, he didn't realize it as his mother worked hard to meet his needs.

But he was no longer poor and, as if to prove it to himself, he enjoyed having a lot of cash in his wallet, sometimes as much as $2,500. Because of that, during spring training in Florida in 1960, he purchased a handgun, a .25-caliber Beretta that fit in the palm of his hand. He never thought about using the gun. For him, it was just part of the newfound persona of a 24-year-old with some cash in his pocket.[1]

DeWitt had a long history in baseball, dating back to 1916 when, as a 14-year-old kid, he sold soda pop in the stands at Sportsman's Park in St. Louis where he was a protégé of Branch Rickey. As a young adult, he continued to work under Rickey in the St. Louis Cardinals organization and became the club treasurer in 1931.

As he continued to climb the baseball ladder, DeWitt moved over to the St. Louis Browns as vice president in 1936, and he and his brother Charles bought the ballclub in 1949. They sold it to Bill Veeck in 1951 but

Bill stayed on as vice president until 1954, when he accepted a position as assistant general manager of the New York Yankees. He remained there for four years and then spent two years as general manager of the Detroit Tigers before taking his position with the Reds in 1960.

So DeWitt had been around the block many times in major league baseball and had dealt with the likes of Dizzy Dean, Mickey Mantle and Yogi Berra. He had engineered some classic deals, including, as general manager of Detroit, acquiring a young first baseman, Norm Cash, for utility player Steve Demeter. Cash won the batting title the following year for the Tigers and was an integral part of their 1968 World Series championship team long after DeWitt had departed.

Robinson's first salary discussion with DeWitt was far different from any that he had had with Paul. He went to DeWitt's office at the appointed time and had to wait an hour before seeing him. Before they were too far into the talks, DeWitt told Robinson he would have to take a pay cut. Robby was stunned. He had once again led the club in home runs and runs batted in and hit .297.

He told his new boss he deserved at least a little bit of a pay raise. But DeWitt told Robinson he heard he didn't hustle, though he never said who told him that. In the end, DeWitt agreed to pay him the same salary he earned in 1960 and thought that was a reasonable compromise. Robinson left DeWitt's office seething but with a "wait 'til next year" attitude. If he had a great 1961 season, he could crowd the plate a little at next year's salary session.[2]

Not too long after that, Robby and some friends got together one night, went bowling, and then played a pickup basketball game at St. Bonaventure Church in Fairmount. On their way home, they stopped to get something to eat at the Sixty Second Shop, a small diner at Reading Road and Florence Avenue in Cincinnati.

While they were ordering hamburgers, one of his friends, William Webb, got into an argument with three white customers sitting across from them. One thing led to another and, as was often the case, one of the white men uttered a racial slur. Robinson joined in and told the fellows if they wanted trouble, he was ready for them. Instead, the men summoned two policemen who were in the parking lot.

One of the officers used the term "boys" as he was trying bring calm to the situation but Robinson and his friends thought the comment was directed only toward them and was a code word for "nigger." Webb reacted too strongly and was arrested for disturbing the peace. Robinson had the cash to bail him out so he and the other friend went to the police station in Robinson's car to spring their buddy. Then they returned to the hamburger joint to pick up their burgers.

While they sat and ate their meal, Robinson noticed the cook in the kitchen, a. white man, glaring at him. As Robinson stared back, the man raised his finger to his throat and acted like he was slitting it. Robinson stood up and said, "Well, c'mon." The cook came out of the kitchen, walking toward Robby, with a carving knife in his hand. Robinson reached in his coat pocket and pulled out his gun. The cook stood still but by this time, someone had contacted the police and the same two officers who had been there earlier reappeared. They charged Robinson with having no permit for the gun and hauled him off to jail.

What had started out as a night of an innocent basketball game with a couple of friends had catapulted into a major problem. Robinson was a celebrity in Cincinnati and easily recognizable. Not long after he arrived at the police precinct station, sportswriter Earl Lawson showed up. Someone had tipped him off.

Lawson was a legend in the Cincinnati sports community. He had joined the *Cincinnati Times-Star* in 1946, began covering the Reds on a part-time basis in 1949 and became the full-time Reds beat writer in 1951. When the *Times-Star* folded in 1958, Lawson moved over to the *Cincinnati Post* and continued to cover the Reds. It was not surprising that when Frank Robinson got arrested at a hamburger stand, within minutes someone alerted Earl Lawson.

Lawson went to the police station and called DeWitt to tell him what happened, that his star outfielder was in jail. DeWitt said he could spend the night there, that he would tend to it in the morning.

The citizens of Cincinnati read all about it the next day. "ROBINSON IS ARRESTED ON WEAPONS CHARGE" screamed the headline in all capital letters in the *Cincinnati Post*. The story was vivid, containing comments from employees of the diner, whose version of what happened differed from Robinson's account.

One of the workers, Carl Smiddy, said an argument broke out between Robinson's group and some other patrons. When Robinson and his friends got up and headed toward the booth of the others, Smiddy got on the diner's loud speaker and called for help from two police officers, Howard Simpson and Max Luttrell, who had gotten sandwiches at the drive-in and were eating in their patrol car. That's when Robinson and his friends objected to being called "boys" and the police arrested Webb, who apparently had objected too strenuously.

After Robinson bailed Webb out of jail, they returned to the diner to pick up their sandwiches. The same two officers were outside. Webb joked with them about the incident and said he was back to get the meal he had paid for. Meanwhile Robinson went inside and had the encounter with the cook, Arthur Messer.

Robinson contended he never pointed the gun at Messer, and Messer agreed but said he didn't pick up the knife until Robinson pulled the gun. As the officers questioned Robinson further, they discovered he didn't have a permit for the gun. So they placed him under arrest. It all made for juicy reading in the newspaper and made radio and television broadcasts throughout the nation.[3]

Robinson was bound over to a grand jury that indicted him on the weapons charge. On March 20, he pleaded guilty and was fined $250. He told the court he was sorry it happened and that it wouldn't happen again. He apologized to his teammates, who were at spring training in Florida, and to the fans in Cincinnati.

In addition to the fine, he received a scolding from Judge Frank Gusweiler, who told him, "No one of your character should be in this court. You are an outstanding athlete but yours is a greater responsibility to the public than other individuals. It is incumbent upon you that your conduct be above reproach. You should be a good example."[4]

Robinson headed to Florida to join his team for spring training, not knowing how they were going to react or how players and fans throughout the National League would treat him once the season started. Two thoughts that stayed with him: He didn't know he needed a permit for the gun, but he should have known; and if Gabe Paul had still been general manager, he would not have had to spend the night in jail. When Robinson arrived in Florida, manager Fred Hutchinson, as was his way, summed up Robinson's situation in a succinct sentence. "It was a stupid thing to do."[5]

Hutchinson brought a world of baseball knowledge and experience to Cincinnati, and an unequaled brashness. A native of Seattle, he was named "Minor League Player of the Year" in 1938, when he won 25 games at the age of 19 for the Seattle Rainiers. In his pitching career with the Detroit Tigers, he won more than ten games for ten straight seasons, including years in which he won 17 and 18. He became the Tigers manager at the age of 32 and also managed the St. Louis Cardinals before taking over for Mayo Smith in Cincinnati in 1959.

Hutchinson was known in both leagues for his fiery temper. It was not unusual for him to come into a clubhouse after a close game and break water coolers, light bulbs or chairs. He always maintained his anger was over losing ballgames he thought his team should have won. He had no patience for ballplayers who made excuses for their poor play, saying things like "I've never hit well in Pittsburgh" or "The background bothers me in Philadelphia."

"The hell with that," he said. "I want men. I want big leaguers, guys who grind and fight until somebody gives in, guys who can play every day under all kinds of conditions."[6]

He scoffed at fans and sports writers who criticized him and his team. "They've never been there, never crossed those white lines," he said. "What do they know? Do they know what it's like to hit against Newcombe or bunt against him with Hodges coming down your throat? Hell, anybody can play ball in a saloon."[7]

Hutchinson instilled that kind of spirit into his 1961 ballclub, composed of youngsters who were maturing quickly under his forceful guidance and veterans who respected his unwavering will to win. For Robinson, Hutchinson was a catalyst to keep him on his toes and motivated as he tried to overcome the disdain he had for his new general manager and the embarrassment of the gun incident.

Robby witnessed some of the temper tantrums that were part of his manager's character. One night after a loss in Milwaukee, as he walked down the runway to the clubhouse, Hutch reached up, tore up the wire casings around light bulbs above him, and smashed every bulb with his hands as he made his way to the clubhouse.

Another night, after the Reds blew a 6–0 lead with two out in the ninth inning and lost, 7–6, Hutchinson came in the clubhouse, picked up a wooden chair, raised it above his head and slammed it to the ground. It bounced around but did not break. He picked it up again, as his players watched in silence, and once again slammed it to the ground. Again, it bounced but did not break. After a third futile attempt to break the chair, he looked at his players and said, "Well, I think I've met my match." That broke the tension, at least for that night.

One Sunday, after the Reds lost a doubleheader to the lowly New York Mets, Hutch sat in the dugout for a few minutes while his players headed for the locker room. As they showered and dressed, the phone rang. A clubhouse attendant answered it. He got off the phone and said the caller was Hutch. He said he'd be there in 15 minutes and if anyone was still there he would tear them apart.[8]

Beyond all the bellowing, Hutchinson and the Reds front office were piecing together the kind of ball-club that would have the right blend of veterans and young-sters, offense and defense, good starting rotation, good bullpen. Some of the players had come up through the farm system. Others had been acquired in trades.

The rebuilding of the pitch-ing staff actually started in 1957 when Gabe Paul was still the gen-eral manager and before Hutch got there. The Reds signed left-hander Jim O'Toole to a minor league contract and acquired right-hander Bob Purkey from Pittsburgh. In 1958, they signed another right-hander, Ken Hunt, and they signed Jim Maloney in 1959. The young pitchers took tours of duty for a year or two in the minor leagues but were ready for prime time action in 1961. Also in 1959, they acquired relief specialist Jim Brosnan from the Cardinals in exchange for Hal Jeffcoat.

Fred Hutchinson was the no-nonsense manager of the Reds who led them to their first National League championship in 21 years in 1961. He died of cancer three years later (courtesy Cincinnati Reds).

In December of 1960, DeWitt pulled off a trade involving three teams that improved the Reds immensely. Veteran shortstop Roy McMillan was traded to Milwaukee for right-handed pitcher Joey Jay and left-hander Juan Pizarro. He then traded Pizarro and Cal McLish to the Chicago White Sox for hard-hitting third baseman Gene Freese. The Reds were now set with a starting pitching staff of Purkey, Jay, Hunt and O'Toole, with Brosnan the key figure in the bullpen. In July of 1960, they released Brooks Lawrence and sold Don Newcombe to the Cleveland Indians. In that same month, they signed a cocky young Cincinnati native to a minor league contract. His name was Pete Rose.

Also in 1960, Joe Nuxhall was dealt to Kansas City. A final deal as the 1961 season got underway sent catcher Ed Bailey to the Giants for catcher Bob Schmidt, pitcher Sherman Jones and veteran second baseman Don Blasingame.

The new season brought with it some new concepts in major league baseball. The American League expanded from eight to ten teams with the addition of franchises in Los Angeles and Washington. The new teams were heavily stocked with players from the other eight teams who had been put on the auction block. One of the new Los Angeles Angels was the former Reds slugger, Ted Kluszewski.

The other big change occurred in the National League and involved only one team—the Chicago Cubs. Chicago's owner, Phil Wrigley, apparently tired of finishing in the second division, which the Cubs had done for 14 consecutive years, decided to operate the team without a manager. Instead, the Cubs had eight coaches who would rotate from the minors leagues to the major league team. The idea was to bring some continuity between the minor league and major league teams. (After two years of continued futility and much player frustration, the system was altered so that one coach, Bob Kennedy, was considered the head coach. He was, in effect, the manager.)

The Reds lineup now featured rookie catcher Jerry Zimmerman behind the plate, backed up by Johnny Edwards, a future star; Gordy Coleman at first base, acquired from Cleveland in the Johnny Temple deal; Blasingame at second; Eddie Kasko at short, acquired from the Cardinals in 1958 in exchange for George Crowe; Freese at third; and an outfield of Robinson, Pinson, and Wally Post, who was back in familiar territory after a year in Philadelphia.

On April 11, the Reds hosted the Chicago Cubs in the traditional opener of the baseball season and came away with a 7–1 victory behind O'Toole. They won four of their next six to find themselves in first place on April 19 with a 5–2 record. But they lost eight straight before winning again on April 30. Going into May, they were in last place with a 6–10 record and it was beginning to look like business as usual for the Reds.

But they reeled off eight straight wins to start the month, giving them a nine- game winning streak. Led by the pitching of Jay, O'Toole and Purkey and the hitting of Robinson, Pinson, and Freese, which they expected, and from Gordy Coleman, which was a pleasant surprise, Cincinnati continued its hot streak, winning 20 and losing only six in May. They headed into June tied for first place with a 26–16 record. Robinson had 12 home runs, Coleman had eight and Freese had seven. Jay led the pitching staff with six wins, and O'Toole, Purkey and Hunt each had five.

The early season was filled with individual accomplishments throughout the major leagues. On April 28, Warren Spahn of the Milwaukee Braves threw a no-hitter against the San Francisco Giants. Two days later, in the same series, Willie Mays of the Giants hit four home runs in the same game. On May 9, Jim Gentile of the Baltimore Orioles hit grand slam home runs in consecutive innings against the Minnesota Twins—with the same three men on base for each homer.

Baseball has a way of producing intriguing scenarios, and one was developing in Cincinnati, because just as the once-lowly Pirates had done the year before, the Reds were beginning to gel. But the Dodgers were also playing well and, by mid-month, had a half-game lead on Cincinnati.

While the Reds were playing well, one blip on their radar screen occurred on June 8 when the Braves hit four consecutive home runs off them in the same inning. Eddie Mathews and Henry Aaron connected off Jim Maloney. Hutchinson brought in Marshall Bridges, who gave up homers to Joe Adcock and Frank Thomas, the first two batters he faced.

On June 16, the Reds and Phils matched up in a pitching duel between Cincinnati's rookie, Ken Hunt, and Philadelphia veteran Johnny Buzhardt. The Reds broke it open when they opened the eighth inning with four straight hits—singles by Coleman, Freese and Post, and a double by pinch-hitter Jerry Lynch. A sacrifice fly and an error produced two more runs, enough to give Cincinnati a 4–1 victory.

Meanwhile, Milwaukee played the Dodgers with LA's Sandy Koufax gunning for his tenth win of the year. He might have gotten it had he not given up a home run to his pitching opponent, Lew Burdette. The Braves won, 2–1. The Dodgers' loss, coupled with the Reds' win, put Cincinnati in first place, a half-game ahead of the Dodgers. By the end of the month, they sported a 45–28 record and had increased their lead to 2½ games.

They continued their winning ways in July and by July 15 had a six-game lead and seemed to be on their way to their first championship in 21 years. But the tables turned when they lost six in a row, including two to the Dodgers. The Reds then won six out of seven to get just about back to where they were before the losing streak.

Nonetheless, when they split a doubleheader with the Cubs on July 30, they fell to second place, a half-game behind the Dodgers. The Giants were third, eight games back, and everyone else was starting to think about next year. It was clearly a two-team race with two months to go. Coleman, Freese, Robinson and Pinson were leading the Reds attack, with Robby having a shot at the Triple Crown.

By this time, much of the attention of the baseball world was on the American League, where the New York Yankees and Detroit Tigers were battling for top honors. But the big story was with two Yankees sluggers, Roger Maris and Mickey Mantle, who were challenging Babe Ruth's home run record of 60 in one season. Mantle had 39 while Maris had 38. Whitey Ford, the Yankees' brilliant left-hander, was also having a sensational year, compiling a 19–2 record through the end of July.

On August 2, when the Reds beat the Phillies in a doubleheader and Juan Marichal and the Giants downed the Dodgers, Cincinnati recaptured first place by one game over LA. But they lost six out of their next ten games. They went to Los Angeles for a crucial three-game series, a single game on August 15 and a doubleheader on the 16th, trailing the Dodgers by two games in the standings.

In the series opener, Joey Jay was matched up with Sandy Koufax. Wally Post hit his 15th home run and Robby had a single, a double and two runs batted in (plus he was hit by a pitch) as Cincinnati prevailed, 5–2, to climb within a game of the National League lead. The next day, in the first game of a doubleheader, Bob Purkey held the Dodgers to four harmless hits, shutting out LA, 6–0. Robinson hit his 34th home run, a two-run shot, singled, and once again was hit by a pitch. With the win, the Reds were in a virtual tie for first place with the Dodgers going into the second game of the twin bill. In that one, Jim O'Toole tossed a two-hit shutout, Robby had two hits and two RBI and Gene Freese hit his 21st and 22nd home runs.

The Reds left Los Angeles in first place after complete game performances from Jay, Purkey and O'Toole. Things were looking up as they headed home to Crosley Field for an 11-game homestand, including four with the Dodgers, before hitting the road again. They managed to win only three out of the first seven and absorbed a 14–0 pasting by the Giants during that stretch. But the Dodgers limped into St. Louis on a ten-game losing streak that helped Cincinnati to a 3½-game lead. Meanwhile the Giants were inching forward, in third place, just five games out.

The Dodgers cut the lead to 1½ games with Koufax and Johnny Podres besting the Reds in the first two games, but Cincinnati won the final two to keep the Dodgers at arm's length going into September.

The seven games in August marked the last time the two contenders played each other in 1961, so the Dodgers were going to need some help from other teams in September if they were to overtake the Reds. But Cincinnati won 14 and lost only eight in the final month while Los Angeles, playing seven more games than the Reds, could muster only a 16–13 record. On September 26, the Reds played the Cubs at Wrigley Field in Chicago. The Cubs jumped out to a 3–1 lead. Cincinnati got a run on a Johnny

Edwards homer in the sixth, and Robinson tied it with a two-run shot, his 37th of the year, in the seventh. The Reds tacked on three more runs before it was over to get a 6–3 victory. That, coupled with the Dodgers' 8–0 loss to Pittsburgh, gave Cincy a 4½-game lead with LA having only four games left on the schedule. The Reds were the National League champions for the first time since 1940.

They took a jubilant plane ride back to Cincinnati and then, at the direction of Hutchinson, boarded buses and headed for Fountain Square downtown to join a city celebration already well under way.

Many of the players headed for a nightspot called the Rendezvous, a place frequented by some of the Reds' white ballplayers when they were in town. Jim Brosnan was headed there when he saw Robinson and Pinson. "I suggested they come along. It seemed appropriate that they be part of our celebration," he said.

Brosnan had been in the bar many times and had never seen a black person there. "I thought, here's a damn good chance to integrate the bar. Who in the hell is going to turn down Frank Robinson and Vada Pinson?" he said. So Robinson and Pinson joined their teammates and were not turned away. They drank Cokes and stayed for about 45 minutes. Brosnan picked up their tab.[9]

Robinson recalls the celebration at the nightclub a little differently. He said when the team flew back to Cincinnati, he and Pinson heard there was going to be a party for the ballplayers at a downtown club. He and Pinson

Jim Brosnan was a relief pitcher for the Reds and was instrumental in helping them win the pennant in 1961 (author's collection).

hailed a cab and headed for the party. When they arrived at the club, the owner stopped them at the door and told them, "No Negroes allowed." When an onlooker told the guy the men were Frank Robinson and Vada Pinson from the Reds, he let them in. He said he and Pinson went in, walked through the club, walked out the back door and went to a nightspot where they knew they would be welcome.

Robinson said that was one of many examples of how black people have to be careful about how they handle things, even when they are right. They were allowed into the place, not because they were entitled to be there, but because they were Vada Pinson and Frank Robinson. Had they stayed, they would have felt self-conscious because of the circumstances. Had they not gone in at all, prejudice and discrimination would have won. It was a difficult situation and one that blacks faced all the time, he said.[10]

The circumstance at the Rendezvous was significant because there was still some underlying racial tension on the ballclub, most of it off the field. Pinson and Robinson kept mostly to themselves because they felt isolated from the white players. Many of the white players looked upon the two black players as being content to remain in their own world, isolated from the others.

But nobody questioned what they had done on the field because the Reds would not have been the National League champions without their efforts.

	AB	R	H	2B	3B	HR	RBI	AVE.
Robinson	545	117	176	32	7	37	124	.323
Pinson	607	101	208	34	8	16	87	.343

Robinson led the league in slugging percentage (.611), stole 22 bases and, as was his custom, led the league in getting hit by pitches (9). Pinson led the league in hits (208) and stole 23 bases. Of the 710 runs produced by the Reds in 1961, Robinson and Pinson either scored or drove in 376 of them.

Robinson was named the league's Most Valuable Player, though Orlando Cepeda of the Giants put up some big numbers—46 home runs, 142 runs batted in and a .311 batting average. His teammate Willie Mays had 40 homers, 123 runs batted in and a .308 batting average. But the Giants finished third. Robinson led his team to the pennant.

In the American League, Roger Maris of the Yankees hit his 61st home run on September 29, surpassing Babe Ruth's record of 60, which had held for 34 years. Because Maris did it with the American League's expanded schedule of 162 games, the records were listed separately until 1981, when the games played differential was eliminated. Mickey Mantle, plagued with injuries late in the season, finished with 54 home runs.

The Yankees won 109 games and were overwhelming favorites to beat the upstart Reds. New York's pitching staff was led by Whitey Ford, a lefty who compiled a 25–4 record and was sure to start three games in the World Series if it went that far. The Reds' leading hurler was Joey Jay, a castoff from the Braves who had never won more than nine games in his seven-year career. He won 21 for Cincinnati and lost only ten. Jim O'Toole was 19–9, Bob Purkey was 16–12 and Jim Brosnan, coming out of the bullpen, was 10–4 with 16 saves.

One of the big differences in the Reds in 1961 was Robby's emergence as a team leader. The gun incident before the season started haunted him in some ways but helped him in others. He had to put up with the derisive shouts from fans, the ribbing from teammates and other players, and the constant mention of it in the press.

In August, Larry Merchant wrote a column about it in the *Philadelphia Daily News*, and Milton Gross wrote about in October as the Reds were playing in the World Series. Both concluded that Robinson's arrest was a wake-up call for him—a not too subtle pronouncement that it was time for him to grow up. Robinson didn't disagree. "It made me think a lot. I guess it made me more mature," he told Merchant.[11]

"I just had to grow up," he told Gross. "You don't pick a player and say to him 'you're going to be the team's leader and that's it.' If you can't swing the bat and catch the ball and run the bases and maybe give a little more besides, nobody's going to follow you."[12]

Another thing that gnawed at Robinson was the shabby treatment he felt he received from DeWitt, the general manager, both during the gun incident and with contract talks. When contract talks came up next year, Robby wanted to have some ammunition.

His teammates noticed his change in demeanor on the field. Brosnan, the year before, had publicly ridiculed Robinson in his book, *The Long Season,* saying, "He could be the best if he put out every game. A great player is great all the time, not just three months of the season, Robinson has never been able to keep up to that level."[13]

But in August, Brosnan told columnist Merchant, "He's 100 percent better as a player than last year and 1,000 percent better as a leader. If you need a base stolen, he steals it. If you need a great catch, he makes it. If you need a hit, he gets it."[14]

Hutchinson, who in February dismissed Robinson's gun episode as "a stupid thing to do," said in August, "He's the kind of leader Joe DiMaggio was. He leads by example."[15]

The Yankees made short order of the Reds in the World Series, beating them four games to one. Jay got the only win for Cincinnati in Game Two. In his autobiography, *Extra Innings,* written with Barry Stainback, Robinson devotes exactly two sentences to the World Series: "Unfortunately, we lost the World Series to the Yankees in five games. I didn't get too upset, perhaps because we had tried our best and been beaten by a better ballclub."[16]

Robinson managed to set a World Series record the hard way, by getting hit by a pitch twice in the same game. Getting hit was not unusual for Robinson—he had once again led the National League in that department—but twice in the same game, a World Series game at that, was a feat unto itself.

Whitey Ford, usually a master of control, and Jim Coates each plunked him in Game Four. Coates said afterwards it bothered him the way Robinson crowded the plate and that he would never get away with it in the American League. "There'd be plenty of guys pushing him away from the plate in our league," he said. "His arms are over the plate. Even his right foot is over the plate and part of his body when he strides. You never see a real good hitter do that."

Coates said it was therefore hard for him to understand how Robinson hit over .300 with 37 home runs and was obviously a "real good hitter." A reporter asked him what was the best way to pitch to Robby. He said he didn't know. He only threw him one pitch—and he hit him.[17]

During the heat of the pennant race, when Robinson was leading the charge, writers asked him if the gun incident in February or his problems with Bill DeWitt or his penchant for getting hit by pitches angered him and therefore motivated him to play harder. "I do my damnedest," he said, when I get mad at Frank Robinson. In that sense, I've been mad all year. I had such a terrible winter—I had to have a good summer."[18]

Years later, reflecting on the 1961 season, Robinson said he got two clutch hits that were among his proudest moments in baseball. "I get paid to hit in the clutch. It's a burden, a big burden. But I make the most money on the Reds and it's during a pennant race that people feel I've got to show I'm worth it," he said.[19]

In September, with the Reds holding a one-game lead over the Dodgers, Cincinnati played the Cardinals at Crosley Field. Ernie Broglio pitched for the Cardinals and took a two-run lead into the eighth inning. The Reds got a couple of base runners and Robinson came up with two out. The count went to two-and-two when Robinson fouled off five pitches in a row, fighting off Broglio's best stuff. On the fifth foul ball, Robby felt a stinging on his left hand. A blister had broken on his middle finger. He called time out and had the Reds trainer apply a band-aid to it.

Robinson took his time getting back in the batter's box. He said he had a theory that too many batters stay in the batter's box too long—that they should step out from time to time and think about what they're doing. Robby said he always thought about four things—the situation; what the pitcher was trying to do; what he as the batter was trying to do; and to concentrate.

With bandaged finger, Robinson stepped back into the batter's box against Broglio and hit a double off the scoreboard in left-center field. The tying runs scored and Cincinnati went on to win the game. The Dodgers lost, giving Cincy a two-game lead.

The next night, the Reds and Cardinals went to extra innings. In the 12th inning, Leo Cardenas doubled and, after two outs, Pinson walked. St. Louis pitcher Al Cicotte got two quick strikes on Robinson. He tried to sneak another strike by him but Robby smashed a single to left field, scoring Cardenas with the winning run. Los Angeles lost again, putting the Reds up by three games.

"I'll always remember those two big hits," said Robinson, "not that I won the pennant with them. I'll remember them because they meant I was doing my job. Earning my money. It's a satisfying feeling."[20]

Perhaps Robinson's reluctance to dwell on the outcome of the World Series was because he was in love. In August, when the Reds were playing the Dodgers at the Los Angeles Coliseum, Robby came out in the parking lot after a game with a friend and came across a group of people who got lost in the Los Angeles Coliseum parking lot while they were trying to find their car.

As it turned out, Robby's friend knew one of the men, who was accompanied by his niece, Barbara Ann Cole. Robby struck up a conversation with Barbara and, as he describe it later, it was love at first sight. He called her almost every night after that and they were married October 28, two months after they met and two weeks after the World Series.

Robinson had spent so much of his adult life as a loner, a black man in a white man's world in the minor leagues, sitting by himself in movie theaters that would have him watching movie after movie to pass the time away and making his way in the major leagues, with a teammate or two as his companions.

Now he had met Barbara Cole, the love of his life, a woman among thousands in a crowded parking lot whom he encountered under the most unusual of circumstances—and he would never really be alone again.

CHAPTER 6

Transitions

The National League expanded to ten teams in 1962, adding franchises in New York and Houston. The New York Metropolitans (Mets for short) would be managed by Casey Stengel, who was canned by the Yankees after losing to Pittsburgh in the 1960 World Series. The Houston Colt .45s would eventually play their home games in the Astrodome, major league baseball's first venture into indoor stadiums, bringing on such concepts as "Astroturf" and ground rules covering what happens if a batted ball hits the roof or one of the rafters.

In order to stock the two new teams, each existing team had to put some of its players in a pool to make them eligible to be drafted by either New York or Houston. The Reds lost pitchers Jay Hook, Ken Johnson and Sherman Jones; Dick Gernert, a veteran first baseman but a fringe player; Elio Chacon, a young infielder; and Gus Bell, a mainstay of the Reds in the 1950s whose best days were behind him. With the departure of Bell, Wally Post was the only Red who had been there when Robinson came up in 1956.

The Reds actually had a better year in 1962 than in their pennant-winning year, winning 98 games. Robinson had a better year also, hitting .342 with 39 homers and 136 RBI. He scored 134 runs and led the league in doubles with 51. Pinson hit .292 with 23 home runs and 100 runs batted in. Purkey had his career year, winning 23 and losing only five and Jay was a 21-game winner for the second year in a row.

But the expansion teams gave the good teams someone to beat up on—and the Reds' 98 wins were good for only third place. The Giants and Dodgers tied for first, each with 101 wins. San Francisco won a best-of-three playoff to win the pennant.

The season took a toll on Robinson. For the first time in his career, or in his life, for that matter, baseball wasn't much fun. Injuries nagged at him and he had been hit by pitches 77 times in his career. He was not only a married man now but also a father to Frank Kevin. As the Reds dropped out of the pennant race in late September, Robinson mentioned to sports writer Earl Lawson that he was going to retire at the end of the season. As always, when there was a tantalizing story to be told about the Reds, Lawson was there to tell it.

On September 29, 1962, Lawson broke the story in the *Cincinnati Post*. "I know it sounds phony," Robinson told Lawson, citing the physical beating that was wearing him down. "If someone else were giving the same reason, it would sound phony to me."[1]

Robinson said money was not an issue although he told Lawson the ballclub could not afford to pay him what it would take to make him change his mind. When Lawson told him he probably couldn't find work outside of baseball that would pay him what he was making now, Robby said he didn't care. He said he had grown up in poverty and learned there were more important things in life than money.

As was the case in the 1961 gun incident, Lawson informed Bill DeWitt about Robinson's situation, not as a snitch but as a reporter seeking a reaction to Robby's revelation. The general manager responded in the same brusque manner in which he seemingly had always treated his star ballplayer. "Robinson is free, 21, and can do what he wants. It's up to him," said DeWitt.[2]

The next day, prior to the Reds' final game of the year against the Phillies at Crosley Field, Robby's teammates came up to him in the clubhouse to wish him well. Kasko presented him with a gift from the players, something they thought he could use at his next job. He opened it up to find an old, beat-up lunchbox. It was as if they were telling him, in a joking way, what Lawson had told him about the prospects for him finding lucrative work in another profession.

They all laughed, said their good-byes and then went out and beat the Phillies, 4–0, denying Art Mahaffey his 20th win. Robinson hit his 50th and 51st doubles. After the game, as players were clearing out their lockers, Robinson stuck his head in Hutchinson's office and said, "See you in the spring," marking the end of quite possibly the shortest retirement in baseball history. Hutchinson responded with a rare smile.[3]

The 1963 season brought the emergence of Pete Rose into the Cincinnati baseball picture. Rose, a Cincinnati native who was a star athlete at Western Hills High School, signed with the Reds as an amateur free agent in 1960 when he was 19 years old. He played a partial season with Geneva, New York, in Class D ball and hit .277. In 1961, he hit .331 for Tampa, also in Class D, and was moved up to the Reds' Class A ballclub at Macon, Georgia, in 1962, where he hit .330.

Rose was a switch-hitter who sprayed the ball all over the field. He earned an invitation to spring training with the Reds in 1963 and performed well enough to make the ballclub. He also drew resentment from many of his teammates. Robinson described him this way: "He was a cocky little dude who moved chest out like a bantam rooster and ran every place he went on a ball field, even to first when he drew a walk. That ticked off a lot of guys who regarded Pete as sort of a hot dog."[4]

Some of the players started calling him "Charlie Hustle," which in later years writers and broadcasters used as a term of endearment. But in 1963, it was a term of resentment by ballplayers who thought Rose was show-boating—and the resentment grew when he replaced popular second baseman Don Blasingame in the starting lineup.

Rose quickly became an outcast on his own team, mocked in the dugout when he sprinted to first base after drawing a walk, and left out when players socialized after games. Robinson noticed what was happening and it reminded him of the loneliness and isolation he felt when he first came up with the Reds in 1956. Pinson noticed too.

They felt sorry for him. So one day after a game, Robby asked Rose if he would like to go out to dinner with him and Pinson—and Rose jumped at the chance. Soon the three of them became companions—and that did not sit well with many of their teammates.

"Nobody had to show Pete how to hit but they wouldn't show him how to be a major leaguer. So we did," said Robinson.[5]

It was not an easy time. Hutchinson was concerned about how the other guys were reacting as Robinson Pinson and Rose warmed up together before games and went out to eat afterwards. Rose said his father, who was not a bigot, told Pete he probably shouldn't be hanging out so much with the black ballplayers.

Rose appreciated the friendship. "The only guys who treated me with any dignity and decency were Frank Robinson and Vada Pinson," he said. "It was a cliquish team in those days. The black guys were just like me when I was a kid. No car. No money. No suit of clothes. All they had to do was play sports."[6]

Hutchinson and the Reds' front office were convinced Rose was ready for the big leagues, making the jump from Class A to the majors in one year. When he was in the Opening Day lineup at second base, instead of the veteran Blasingame, it did not sit well with Blasingame or his buddy, veteran Gene Freese, ringleaders of what amounted to the hazing of Rose. It did not help his cause when he went hitless in his first 12 at-bats.

Meanwhile, pitcher Jim O'Toole, who was white, tried to give Rose some friendly advice—don't fraternize so much with the black players. Bill DeWitt took the unusual step of calling young Rose into his office to offer the same advice. Rose explained that Robinson and Pinson were the only two friends he had on the team.

Whether his explanation to DeWitt had any bearing on future events is unclear. But by mid–July, Freese was sent down to the minor leagues and Blasingame was shipped off to the Washington Senators. Rose hit .273 for the season, scored 101 runs, and was the National League's Rookie of the Year.

In August, Dick Young, a no-nonsense columnist for the *New York Daily News*, reported dissention on the Reds' ballclub and pointed the finger directly at Robinson and Pinson. "They say the two have formed a clique that is gnawing at the morale of the club," he wrote.

Young said all ballclubs go through it and it isn't something that is talked about openly or written about because it involves race. There's a two-way resentment, he said. The Negro players think they are being picked on and the white players think the Negro players are getting away with things that wouldn't be tolerated with white players.

Young did not mention the relationship of Pinson and Robinson with Pete Rose, which the white players resented, but he said Robby and Pinson were abrasive to white sports writers to the point of shoving them and swearing at them.

It was not an easy time for race relations in the United States. Earlier in the year, Alabama Governor George Wallace stood at the entrance to the University of Alabama, blocking a black student from enrolling. Civil rights leader Medgar Evers had been assassinated by white extremists in the driveway of his Mississippi home. The month before Young was writing about racial troubles in baseball, Dr. Martin Luther King, Jr., delivered his "I Have a Dream" speech in Washington, D.C.

In baseball, wrote Young, it was referred to as "the situation." Alluding to it nationally, he wrote, "If the president of the United States can't handle it overnight, how can Hutch be expected to?"[7]

Hutchinson dismissed all the talk of dissention, saying nobody pays any attention to it when a ballclub is winning. The Reds had slipped to fifth place in the National League, where they eventually finished.

Robinson had an off-year, hitting just .259 with 21 home runs and 91 runs batted in. Jim Maloney had a banner year, winning 23 and losing only seven. O'Toole was 17–14. Nuxhall had one of his best seasons at 15–8, but Purkey and Jay, mainstays of the pennant-winning ballclub, both faltered badly, Purkey at 6–10 and Jay at 7–18.

In the winter, the Reds sold Gene Freese to Pittsburgh and traded Eddie Kasko to Houston. With the departure of Blasingame the previous July, Cincinnati's infield was taking on a whole new look. Deron Johnson was now the starting first baseman, with Gordy Coleman backing him up. Chico Ruiz was the third baseman on Opening Day but gave way to Steve Boros. Ruiz and Leo Cardenas shared shortstop duties, and Rose had established himself at second base. Johnny Edwards was now the regular catcher. Robby and Pinson were joined in the outfield by a speedster named Tommy Harper. The pitching staff was still solid, anchored by O'Toole, Maloney, Purkey and Jay, perhaps the best starting rotation in the National League.

Gene Mauch's Phillies, who three years earlier had set a major league record by losing 23 in a row, had changed their ways and had become a pennant contender. Their pitching staff was led by Art Mahaffey and Jim Bunning, and they had a rookie third baseman, Richie Allen, who seemed destined to be a star in the caliber of Frank Robinson.

The Reds were dealt a huge psychological blow in January when Hutchinson announced that he had terminal cancer. He continued to manage the ballclub, taking time off periodically to undergo radiation treatments, with Dick Sisler, a coach, filling in as manager. As the season wore on, Hutchinson lost weight and became weaker. In August, with his body failing him, he resigned and Sisler was named interim manager.

The Reds devoted the season to their manager, wanting to win the pennant in his honor, but the Phillies seemed to have the championship well in hand. After games of September 20, Philadelphia had a 6½-game lead over both the Cardinals and the Reds with 12 games left.

On September 21, Cincinnati opened a three-game series with the Phillies at Connie Mack Stadium which they had to sweep to have any kind of chance at all of catching Philadelphia.

In the opener, Cincinnati's John Tsitouris and the Phillies' Art Mahaffey got locked in a pitchers' duel in which neither team scored for the first five innings. In the top of the sixth, after Pete Rose grounded out, Chico Ruiz singled and went to third when Vada Pinson singled. Pinson was out trying to stretch it into a double. So Robinson came up with two outs and a runner on third. He worked the count to 2-and-2 when, inexplicably, as

Mahaffey delivered the next pitch, Ruiz broke for home. He was safe, scoring what turned out to be the only run of the game.

Years later, in recalling the play, Mahaffey was still baffled by why Ruiz would even try it. It's a scoreless game, he said, with the potential winning run on third base and one of baseball's greatest hitters at the plate with two strikes on him. If Robinson swings at the pitch and pulls the ball, he's likely to maim the base runner. If he takes the pitch and it's a strike, it's a strikeout and the inning's over. Even if it's a ball, if catcher Clay Dalrymple makes the tag on Ruiz, the inning's over. There's no logical reason why Ruiz should try to steal home in that situation—but he did.[8]

The win moved the Reds to within 5½ games of the Phillies. The Cardinals, who were idle, were now in third place, six games out.

On September 22, the Reds beat the Phillies 9–2 with Robby contributing his 28th home run. The Cardinals beat the Mets 2–1. Philadelphia's lead had shrunk to 4½ games over the Reds and 5 over the Cardinals. But there were only ten games left in the season.

The next day, Cincinnati completed the three-game sweep of the Phillies with a 6–4 win, aided by two home runs from Pinson. The Mets beat the Cardinals, 2–1. So the Reds had crept to within 3½ games of the lead while St. Louis remained 5 games out.

On September 24, Cincinnati had an off-day but the Cardinals played a doubleheader against the Pirates and Milwaukee beat the Phillies. The Reds were now 3 games out, with the Cardinals 3½ back, but both were running out of time. The Phillies had lost five in a row but still controlled their own destiny. The next day, Cincinnati took two from the Mets while the Phillies lost to the Braves again and the Cardinals beat Pittsburgh. On September 26, the Reds and Cardinals each won again while Milwaukee beat the Phillies.

On September 27, with Philadelphia leading Cincinnati now by just ½-game and the Cardinals by 1½ games, the Reds beat New York in a doubleheader by scores of 4–1 and 3–1. St. Louis beat Pittsburgh, 5–0. Milwaukee completed a four-game sweep of the Phillies with a 14–8 victory. At the end of the day, Cincinnati was in first place, having made up a 6½-game deficit in one week. The Phillies were now in second, 1 game out, and the Cardinals were in third, 1½ back. It looked as though the Reds might miraculously fulfill their goal of winning the championship for their ailing manager.

The Reds were idle on September 28 as the Cardinals opened a crucial three-game series against Philadelphia. Bob Gibson tossed a shutout, pulling the Cardinals to within a game of the Reds and dropping Philadelphia to third place 1½ games out.

On the next two days, the Reds, who had ridden a nine-game winning streak to jump into first place, played the Pirates, whose only role now was to be the spoiler. And they succeeded. Bob Friend shut out the Reds, 2–0, on September 29, while the Cardinals were beating the Phillies again. The next day, Pittsburgh beat Cincinnati, 1–0, in 16 innings while the Cardinals beat Philadelphia, 8–5. At the end of the day, the Cardinals had a one-game lead over the Reds with the Phillies 2½ back. On October 1, with both the Cardinals and Phillies idle, the Reds bounced back and beat Pittsburgh, 5–4, with Robinson smashing his 37th double and driving the deciding run.

On October 2, with the Reds ½-game out and the Phillies trailing by 2½, the Phillies' only chance was to win their last three and for the Cardinals to lose all of their remaining games. The Reds had to keep winning and hope for a Cardinals loss somewhere along the way. As it happened, both the Reds and Cardinals lost, with the Phillies beating Cincinnati to move within 1½ games of the lead with two to play. When the lowly Mets beat the Cardinals, 15–5, on October 3, with both the Reds and Phillies idle, St. Louis and Cincinnati went into the last game of the season tied for first with the Phillies one game out. If the Cardinals lost and the Phillies beat the Reds, there would be a three-way tie for first place for the first time in major league history.

But it was not to be. On the final day of the season, the Cardinals beat the Mets, 11–5, but the Phillies, who looked like a sure champion just two weeks before, now played the true spoiler by blanking the Reds, 10–0. The Cardinals were the National League champions. The Reds and Phillies tied for second, just one game out.

The Reds had made a valiant try, at one point winning nine in a row in the September stretch drive, all the time watching their manager waste away. Hutchinson would come to the ballpark when he was able, but each time he came, the players noticed how much he had failed since the last time they saw him.

"It was so trying, so tough on everyone on the ballclub, seeing Hutch wasting away, and everyone was trying so hard to win the pennant for him," said Robinson. He said he thought in some cases, the players tried too hard, as if every misplay or missed opportunity might intensify Hutch's pain.

In the last week of the season, with the pennant on the line, Hutch made his last appearance at Crosley Field. He was helped into the clubhouse and onto a chair where he said, in a voice barely above a whisper, "I don't want you to win it for me; I want you to win it for yourselves."[9]

The pressure of a pennant race can bring out the best—and worst—in individuals, and on Friday, October 2, with the Reds still in the race, they played the Phillies and jumped out to a 3–0 lead. Frank Thomas started the rally in the eighth inning for Philadelphia with a one-out bloop single that fell just out of the reach of Reds shortstop Leo Cardenas. That opened the floodgates. The Phillies scored four runs and won the game, 4–3. In the locker room after the game, O'Toole, the losing pitcher, shouted at Cardenas that he should have caught the ball Thomas hit. Cardenas responded by picking up an ice pick and started moving toward O'Toole. Robby stepped between them. Manager Dick Sisler separated everybody and cooler heads prevailed.[10]

Hutchinson died November 12, 1964. He was 45. Perhaps one of his lasting contributions to the Reds was the confidence he had in Pete Rose. He and the Reds dealt away Blasingame, the veteran, to give the rookie a shot at second base, and when he slumped in his rookie year, Billy Klaus filled in. But the Reds eventually dealt Klaus away as well.

The most bizarre move that Hutchinson made to try to help Rose with the social adjustment to the major leagues came at the time the Reds were concerned about his fraternization with Robinson and Pinson. Hutchinson convinced Johnny Temple, a former popular Reds second baseman, to join the team. Temple, who was white and who had retired after being released by Houston, the previous year, was to be a player-coach for the Reds. His job—to make friends with Rose, to be his companion, his mentor, his confidante. Aside from being a former Reds second baseman, his major qualification was that he was white.

According to Rose biographer Michael Sokolove, Hutchinson told Temple, "Pete Rose is your project. The first thing I want you to do is teach him to use a knife and fork. [The second thing:] Keep him away from the god-damned niggers."

Temple told Sokolove that Rose was head-strong and told him he would do what he wanted to do and hang out with whoever he wanted to hang out with. After ballgames, he began frequenting nightspots that were a little too risqué for Temple's tastes, and before long, they went their separate ways. As Sokolove put it, "The Johnny Temple experiment failed."[11]

The record shows Temple was with the Reds from April to early July and played in exactly six games. He was not there to play.

The Phillies' collapse, losing a 6½-game lead with 12 to play, is one of the greatest folds in baseball history, and Frank Robinson was a part of the play that got it all started. It was Chico Ruiz's steal of home with Robinson at bat—a stupid play by conventional baseball wisdom—that gave the Reds their only run in the 1–0 victory that started the Phillies on their deadly ten-game losing streak.[12]

The individual numbers for the 1964 Reds showed why they were contenders. Robinson hit .306 with 29 homers and 96 RBI. Pinson slipped in batting average to .266 but contributed 23 home runs and 84 runs batted in. Deron Johnson had 21 homers and 79 RBI. Rose hit .269. (He would hit over .300 in 14 of the next 15 years). The starting pitching was once again solid with O'Toole at 17–7, Maloney at 15–10, Purkey at 11–9 and Jay at 11–11.

The Reds slipped to fourth place in 1965 though they won 86 games. Robby had a solid year, hitting .296 with 33 home runs and 113 runs batted in. Pinson hit .305 with 22 homers and 94 RBI. One of the guys scoring many of the runs that Robby and Pinson drove in was Rose, who crossed the plate 111 times. He had 35 doubles and a batting average of .312.

A highlight of 1965 for Robinson occurred far away from the ballpark. In August, he and Barbara became parents of a baby girl they named Nichelle.

The Reds didn't have any trouble scoring but their pitching lacked the depth it had enjoyed in recent years. Sammy Ellis, moved from the bullpen to the starting rotation, responded by winning 22 games and losing ten. Maloney was 20–9. Joe Nuxhall, an up-and-down pitcher most of his career, had 11 wins. No other pitcher was in double figures. O'Toole, the ace of the staff in 1964, won just three games and lost 12.

There were signs of better days ahead. Tony Perez, a young slugger, made his way into the starting lineup. DeWitt and his assistant, Phil Seghi, had an excellent amateur draft, picking up Bernie Carbo in

JOHNNY TEMPLE   2B

Johnny Temple was a former Reds second baseman; he was hired by the Reds to be a "white friend" to Pete Rose (courtesy Cincinnati Reds).

the first round, Johnny Bench in the second round and Hal McRae in the sixth round. It was the embryo of what would become "The Big Red Machine" of the 1970s.

But DeWitt and Seghi realized that while the Reds were strong offensively and had drafted wisely enough to continue to produce big bats, their pitching was becoming suspect if they wanted to compete with the Dodgers, who had Don Drysdale and Sandy Koufax, the Giants with Juan Marichal and the Cardinals with Bob Gibson.

Their solution was to trade one of their hitters in order to get another front-line starting pitcher. Their solution was to trade Frank Robinson.

CHAPTER 7

The Trade

On Thursday, December 9, 1965, President Lyndon Johnson, wrestling with public protests and violence at home and an unpopular war thousands of miles away, was starting a long weekend at his ranch in Texas.

On that day in the little town of Kecksburg, Pennsylvania, residents were unnerved by the sight of what they believed was an unidentified flying object that crashed and burned into a remote, wooded area.

Many Americans were enjoying the Christmas season by watching the premier of *A Charlie Brown Christmas*, a CBS television special whose stars were all animations derived from the popular comic strip *Peanuts*.

It was also the day that Branch Rickey, the baseball icon who had been a player, manager and baseball executive with the St. Louis Cardinals, Brooklyn Dodgers and Pittsburgh Pirates, died at the age of 83.

But in Cincinnati that day, baseball fans were absorbing an entirely different shock though many of them mourned as if it was a sudden death. For it was on this day that the Reds traded Frank Robinson to the Baltimore Orioles.

Baseball transactions are a part of the business. Thousands of them have occurred over the years. But only a select few reach the level of notoriety that this one did.

"Bad trades are a part of baseball. Now who can forget Frank Robinson for Milt Pappas, for God's sake," says Susan Sarandon's character, Annie Savoy, in the 1988 movie, *Bull Durham*, 23 years after the trade.[1]

In 2001, 36 years after the deal, ESPN.com, rated it the seventh-worst trade in the history of all sports.[2]

It had an impact on almost everyone involved, including Reds general manager Bill DeWitt, who made many deals to help establish "The Big Red Machine" of the 1970s but is better remembered for dealing Robinson, whom he described at the time as being "not a young 30."[3]

Robby was traded to the Baltimore Orioles for pitchers Milt Pappas and Jack Baldschun and outfield prospect Dick Simpson. The transaction was actually the last in a series of three deals involving several players. It was not a knee-jerk reaction on anyone's part. On December 2, Baltimore traded first baseman Norm Siebern to the California Angels for Simpson, the young outfielder. On December 6, Philadelphia traded Baldschun, their veteran relief pitcher to Baltimore in exchange for outfielder Jackie Brandt and pitcher Darold Knowles. Three days later, Baltimore traded Pappas, their journeyman pitcher along with the newly-acquired Baldshun and Simpson to the Reds for Robinson.

The trade is often judged on the basis of its results—Robinson won the Triple Crown and the Orioles won their first World Series in 1966 while the Reds slipped to seventh place. But it is instructive to look at the needs of

Milt Pappas was traded from Baltimore to Cincinnati in December of 1965 in what is regarded by many as one of the worst trades in baseball history (author's collection).

the two teams at the time the deal was made and at how the trade looked to benefit both teams.

After being in the pennant race up through the final day of the 1964 season, the Reds slipped to fourth place in 1965. Though their record was a very respectable 89–73, there were indications of troubled days ahead unless some changes were made. Their lineup was full of good hitters. Robby had another good year, hitting .296 with 33 home runs and 113 RBI. Pinson hit .305 with 22 home runs and 94 RBI. Deron Johnson, who could play third base, first base or in the outfield, hit .287, delivered 32 home runs and led the league in RBI with 130. Pete Rose had his first of what would turn out to be many years of 200-plus hits. In addition, the Reds had a farm system that was producing good young hitters—Tommy Harper, Tommy Helms, Tony Perez and Johnny Bench, among others.

Two pitchers had great years for the Reds. Young Sammy Ellis was 22–

10 and Jim Maloney, fast becoming the ace of the staff, was 20–9. But Jim O'Toole and Joey Jay, two prominent members of the 1961 pennant winner, had slipped to 3–10 and 9–8, respectively. Joe Nuxhall contributed 11 wins but no other pitcher was in double figures and most of the staff had earned run averages hovering around 4.00 or above. Reds management liked what they had in Ellis and Maloney but felt they were one starting pitcher shy of being a pennant contender.

The Orioles were well stocked with pitchers. They won 94 games in 1965, finishing in third place. They had a starting rotation that included Milt Pappas, Steve Barber, Dave McNally, Wally Bunker and a 19-year-old up-and-comer named Jim Palmer. Their bullpen was anchored by two of the best relief specialists in the game, Stu Miller and Dick Hall, who between them won 25 games in 1965.

The Orioles were solid defensively, especially with Brooks Robinson at third base. He was also their most potent batter, hitting 18 home runs and driving in 80 runs. First baseman Boog Powell had some power, with his 17 homers and 72 RBI, and Curt Blefary turned in an impressive show-ing, batting .262 with 22 homers and 70 RBI. The Orioles brass thought they had good enough pitching depth to compete with the Yankees and White Sox but needed a thumper in the middle of the lineup to win some games for them.

The deal was made at baseball's winter meetings in Florida. The Reds decided that Deron Johnson, four years younger than Robinson and coming off his 32-homer and 130-RBI season, was the slugger to keep, instead of Robby. The Orioles needed to give up a frontline pitcher and more if they were going to land Frank Robinson. Jim Palmer and Wally Bunker were young with bright futures ahead of them. They truly represented the future of the Orioles. Dave McNally and Steve Barber were good left-handers who provided great balance to the Baltimore starting rotation. Milt Pappas, a 26-year old right-hander with 109 big league wins, was the most expendable pitcher, from the Orioles' standpoint. When Baltimore also offered relief pitcher Jack Baldschun and a young reserve outfielder, Dick Simpson, the deal was approved by all parties.

Robinson chafed at being referred to as "an old 30," and Pappas was miffed because two days earlier he had been assured by Baltimore manage-ment that he wouldn't be traded. He had been in Florida for baseball's winter meetings as the Orioles' player representative.

Baldschun appeared to be a key pick-up for the Reds. In his career, the relief pitcher had weathered the storm with the 1961 Phillies, who lost

23 games in a row, and the 1964 Phillies, who folded in the last two weeks of the season. Without ever starting a game, he had seasons where he won 11 and 12 games, and had 21 saves in 1964. ("Saves" did not become an official statistic until 1969, so the qualifications beforehand are somewhat subjective.) Simpson was 22 and pretty much untested at the major league level.

In February of 1966, Robinson honored a commitment by appearing at a banquet featuring Reds players that was attended by hundreds of baseball fans. Ironically, the event was called the "Ballplayers of Yesterday" dinner. When Robinson walked into the ballroom of the Netherland Hilton Hotel, he was greeted with a standing ovation that moved him to tears.

"When I first put on a Cincinnati uniform, I was so happy," said Robby. "If someone had told me I was going to be here for ten years…." He stopped to hold back tears. "I just hope that someday, I'll be able to come back," he said.[4]

He wasn't so gracious two months later in reacting to comments by DeWitt when the Reds general manager once again defended the trade by mentioning Robinson's age. DeWitt, in an interview with the *Miami Herald,* said, "The Reds dealt Robinson away to Baltimore to strengthen our ballclub. Nothing personal at all. Robinson is not a young 30. If he had been 26, we might not have traded him."[5]

It was no secret in the baseball world that Robinson and DeWitt had a frosty relationship dating back to the 1961 gun incident, when DeWitt let Robby cool his heels in jail overnight, as well as their annual squabbles over salary, the standoffish relationship he had with Pinson, and the befriending of Pete Rose that caused some dissention on the ballclub—so much so that DeWitt, in effect, purchased a white friend for Rose (Johnny Temple). So for DeWitt to say there was nothing personal might have been a bit of diplomacy. When he said if Robby had been 26, he might have kept him—that happened to be the age of Deron Johnson, whom he did keep.

Robinson said, "I can't argue with DeWitt if he said he traded me to strengthen his club but that comment about me being an old 30 is hitting below the belt. It was uncalled for. It seems I suddenly got old last fall between the end of the season and December 9."[6]

In Baltimore, news of the trade was received with excitement but it was clear that Robinson's reputation off the field was baggage he was bringing with him.

General manager Lee MacPhail had resigned at the end of the 1965 season to take a position in the office of baseball's new commissioner, William Eckert. But the Orioles asked him to stay on long enough to attend baseball's winter meetings in Florida, the annual setting in which many transactions were discussed and carried out. MacPhail agreed to stay on that long.

It was there that he ran into his old friend Bill DeWitt. The two had worked together years earlier with the Yankees. They got to talking about the needs of their respective ballclubs. DeWitt was willing to part with one of his sluggers but he wanted a relief pitcher in addition to a front-line starter like Pappas. So MacPhail included Baldschun and the trade was made.

MacPhail said he was excited to get Robinson but had some reservations about this deal, the last one he would make as general manger of the Orioles. "Frank had had a few problems," he said. At one point, the story was he had a gun in the dugout, which bothered me. You know, we were giving away half the team to get this guy."[7]

But MacPhail said another friend from his Yankees days, Jim Turner, was now a coach with the Reds. He called Turner for his honest opinion about Robinson, and Turner assured him Robinson would be no problem.

"No one really knew what to think when they made the trade," said Brooks Robinson, the Orioles' star third baseman. "I mean, Frank was coming over here with a reputation—had been a little hot and cold and had been picked up with a gun…. He had a strong personality."[8]

Second baseman Davey Johnson said, "He kind of had a chip on his shoulder and dared everyone to knock it off…. He just kind of set it up there and said, OK, if you're good enough, knock it off. And nobody really could."[9]

Pappas had heard rumors when the season ended that he was trade bait. He went to the winter meetings in Florida as the Orioles' player rep. His wife was to join him in a few days. One night she called and said the newspaper was reporting rumors that he was going to be traded to San Francisco. Pappas said he ran into Orioles manager Hank Bauer and MacPhail and asked them about the rumors. He said he was assured he wouldn't be traded. A few days later, he was traded to the Reds.

The irony of the situation was that when his wife arrived in Florida, and he told her he wasn't going to be traded, they decided to relax and go to a movie. The movie they saw was *The Cincinnati Kid*.

Interviewed 44 years later, Pappas said the trade, nor the eventual notoriety that came with it, bothered him. "There's nothing I could have done to prevent it. What frosted me was the Orioles told me I wouldn't be traded. Then two days later I was."[10]

Baseball is a results-oriented numbers game, and the 1966 season showed how unforgiving those numbers can sometimes be. Robinson, with something to prove to DeWitt and to the American League, won the Triple Crown and led the Orioles to their first World Series championship. Cincinnati fell to seventh in the National League. Pappas was one notch better than a .500 pitcher at 12–11. After a 16–13 season in 1967, he was traded to the Atlanta Braves and later to the Chicago Cubs. He won 209 games in his major league career, most of them with sub-par teams, and threw a no-hitter with the Cubs.

As Cincinnati fan and blogger Dean Hanley points out, if the Orioles had kept Pappas and traded another pitcher instead, Pappas might have pitched in four World Series and been elected to the Hall of Fame.[11]

Even without the benefit of pitching for the Orioles, baseball historian Bill James points out Pappas's career statistics match up pretty well with Hall of Famer Don Drysdale.[12]

	W-L	Pct.	ERA	ShO
Pappas	209–164	.560	3.40	43
Drysdale	209–166	.557	2.95	49

Then there is the question of whether Robinson would have continued to put up big numbers with Cincinnati and whether the Reds would have been a championship team with him.

Baseball is full of moot points because "what ifs" have no home runs, runs batted in or batting averages. What is for certain is that on December 9, 1965, Robinson was traded to the Baltimore Orioles, and the fortunes of the ballplayer and his new team changed dramatically because of it.

CHAPTER 8

New Beginnings

In 1966, Americans were laughing at the antics of Dick Van Dyke on the *Dick Van Dyke Show* and at the ineptitude of the lovable sheriff's deputy, Barney Fife, played by Don Knotts on *The Andy Griffith Show*. Many young people were caught up in "Beatlemania," enamored by four British singers who called themselves the Beatles and who had taken America by storm. Simon and Garfunkel hit the top of the music charts with "The Sounds of Silence," and Nancy Sinatra, daughter of music legend Frank Sinatra, had a hit of her own, "These Boots Were Made for Walkin." The average price of a home in America was $14,200, and a new car cost $2,650. Working Americans brought home incomes on the average of $6,200 a year.

The nation found itself in turmoil on at least two fronts. There was growing opposition to America's involvement in the war in Vietnam. Protesters burned their draft cards and took part in mass demonstrations on college campuses, on public streets and in front of public buildings all over the country. The other lightning rod was the quest for racial equality and an end to discrimination of minorities. President Johnson had signed the Civil Rights Bill in 1964 and the Voting Rights Act of 1965, guaranteeing the rights of all citizens, including the right to vote. But some communities, particularly in the South, were slow to comply with the law of the land, leading to violent protests in many cities.

Baseball was a diversion that helped millions of Americans have a little enjoyment, watching athletes of many races and creeds compete together on ball fields.

In 1966, Baltimore, Maryland, was a racially mixed city of nearly one million in population, and had a rich baseball history, though it didn't have a major league team from 1915 until 1954. Its first professional team was in 1882 and was part of the American Association. In 1892, it joined the old National League and experienced great success for several years.

Managed by Ned Hanlon, the Orioles were known for their toughness, hustle and ingenuity, and won championships three years in a row, 1894–1896. Its players included John McGraw, Wilbert Robinson, Hughie Jennings, Wee Willie Keeler and slugger Dan Brouthers, all of whom went on to have Hall of Fame major league careers. The franchise broke up as major league baseball expanded and players went in several different directions.

In 1903, the St. Louis Browns joined the American League and remained there through 1953. The Browns experienced some difficult times both on the field and at the box office, winning only one pennant (1944) and playing in the same city—and in the same ballpark—as the popular National League team, the St. Louis Cardinals.

In 1953, ownership made the decision that a change of scenery might improve the ballclub and increase attendance. So the Browns moved to Baltimore and the Baltimore Orioles were reincarnated.

The new ballclub in town, managed by Jimmy Dykes, who would manage Frank Robinson a few years later, was not an overnight success. In 1954, the Orioles won 54 games and lost 100. Their leading hitter, Vern Stephens, hit .285 and also led the team in home runs with just eight and RBI with just 46. The offense did not give the pitchers much to work with. The hurler who suffered the most was right-hander Don Larsen, who won three games and lost 21.[1]

The Orioles needed some good, young players if they were going to be able to compete with New York, Chicago, Detroit, Cleveland, Boston and even less talented teams like Kansas City and Washington. These were the days before the major league draft system came into being. Young ballplayers were signed by scouts who scoured the countryside looking for kids who could hit a curve ball or throw one accurately. The goal was to find them, praise them, pamper them, woo their parents and, finally, sign them and assign them to teams in the Orioles' minor league system.

In the early 1960s, the Orioles set the stage for the success they would experience in the latter half of the decade and for many years to come. In 1960, they signed pitchers Dave McNally and Tom Phoebus. In 1961, they signed catcher Andy Etchebarren and pitchers Eddie Watt and Darold Knowles. In 1962, infielders Davey Johnson and Mark Belanger signed. Pitchers Jim Palmer and Wally Bunker signed in 1963 as well as outfielder Paul Blair. The Orioles already had three veterans in third baseman Brooks Robinson, whom they signed in 1955, pitcher Milt Pappas, who signed in 1957, and first baseman John "Boog" Powell, who signed in 1959. The pieces were starting to come together.

From 1954 through 1959, they were under .500 all but one year. They finished seventh twice, sixth three times and fifth once, in 1957, the year they finished at exactly .500 with a 76–76 record. The breakout year was 1960 when they climbed to second place behind the Yankees with an 89–65 record. The "Kiddy Corps" pitching staff produced Chuck Estrada, age 22, 18–11; Milt Pappas, age 21, 15–11; Steve Barber, age 22, 10–7; and Jack Fisher, age 21, 12–11. They also had veteran Hal "Skinny" Brown, age 35, who was 12–5, and the Hoyt Wilhelm, age 37, who was used in both as a starter and in relief, at 11–8.

In the next few years, the pitching staff was bolstered by the emergence of Wally Bunker, Dave McNally and Jim Palmer. Third baseman Brooks Robinson was an established star and the Orioles picked up shortstop Luis Aparicio from the White Sox, giving them the best defensive combination in baseball history on the left side of the infield. Gradually, Baltimore began knocking on the door of the American League championship but couldn't quite get in.

Paul Richards was the manager who was one of the architects of the reformation, but he left in 1962 to be part of the management team of the new Houston Colt .45s in the National League. Billy Hitchcock, an Orioles coach, took the reins for a couple of years. Hank Bauer, an outfielder with the great Yankees teams in the 1950s, became the Orioles manager in 1964.

The Orioles won 95 games in 1961 but that was the year of Mantle and Maris with the Yankees, and Baltimore finished third behind New York and Detroit. They slipped to seventh place in 1962 and finished fourth in 1963, both years with Hitchcock at the helm.

When Bauer took over in 1964, all the pieces seemed to come together—great pitching, great defense, timely hitting. Brooks Robinson hit 28 home runs and drove in 118 runs, taking home the MVP award for the season. Boog Powell hit 39 homers and had 99 RBI. Wally Bunker, at age 19, won 19 games and lost only 5. Pappas won 16, McNally and Barber each won 9 and 37-year-old Robin Roberts, a past star with the Philadelphia Phillies, won 13 games. The bullpen was outstanding with Dick Hall going 9–1 and Stu Miller winning seven games. The Orioles won 95 and lost 67, finishing in third place, but just two games behind the pennant-winning Yankees.

The 1965 Orioles had another good year, finishing at 94–68, the second straight 90-plus-win season under Hank Bauer. Pappas was 13–9, Barber was 15–10, McNally was 11–6 and Bunker was 10–8. The bullpen once again had big numbers. Stu Miller was 14–7 and Dick Hall was 11–8. Brooks Robinson was once again the leading hitter with a .297 average 18 homers and 80 runs batted in. Powell dropped to 17 home runs but had 72 RBI. Outfielder Curt Blefery led the team in homers with 22 and drove in 70 runs.

The Orioles' farm system had done about all it could expected to do. It had produced a great assembly of talent that was nurtured in the minor leagues and was paying big dividends in the big leagues. The ballclub was now a consistent pennant contender but didn't seem to have quite enough to win a championship. While the Yankees were starting to fall on hard times with the retirements or waning careers of Mantle and Ford and Yogi Berra, other teams were making big improvements.

The Minnesota Twins won their first American League pennant in 1965 with 102 wins. The Twins had solid pitching led by Jim "Mudcat" Grant, they had a batting champion in Tony Oliva and an MVP shortstop in Zoilo Versalles. But they also had power hitters, guys like Bob Allison and Harmon Killebrew who could bail the ballclub out with a three-run homer late in a game.

The Baltimore brass determined they needed someone with a big bat to help protect Brooks Robinson and Powell in the lineup and to be the three-run homer guy. At the winter meetings in Florida, they learned Frank Robinson might be available. The Cincinnati Reds needed pitching and were willing to part with a hitter. The trade seemed like a perfect fit for both teams if they could pull it off. On December 9, they did.

Robinson had many mixed feelings about going to Baltimore. Being a former Rookie of the Year, an All-Star, a Most Valuable Player, and always among the league leaders in home runs and runs batted in, he felt like he had nothing to prove. And yet, there was that Bill DeWitt comment about his age and rumblings about his reputation.

"I definitely had something to prove after Bill DeWitt told the press he traded me because I was 'an old thirty,'" said Robby. "And I took a new approach, having been labeled a troublemaker and called hostile. I was tired of hearing those things." He said he wasn't going to stop knocking shortstops on their butts but would try to be less intense all the time.[2]

Sports columnist Jimmy Cannon ran into Robinson in spring training with the Orioles and was impressed with his composure. "He gives me the impression he performs for no one but himself," wrote Cannon. "He doesn't demean his ability with the actor's tricks so many ballplayers use to excite the buffs. He demands appreciation for only what he accomplishes."[3]

Robby told Cannon what he had been telling everyone else—that he was hurt by the trade but he was not surprised. He was the highest-paid

Red and the oldest of the regulars, and, after the Reds fell flat in 1965, someone had to go.

Cannon said it was hard to think of Robinson playing anywhere but with Cincinnati, like thinking of Mantle playing with someone other than the Yankees or Willie Mays playing for someone other than the Giants. "But if Baltimore wins the pennant this year, that will be Robinson's town," he wrote. "There will be no doubt about his identity then. They got him for only one reason. The people who own the Orioles are positive he will bat them into the World Series. They could be right."[4]

Phil Pepe, another New York sports writer, talked with Orioles manager Hank Bauer at spring training, before Robby arrived. Bauer mentioned how Boog Powell had slipped from 39 homers in 1964 to just 17 in 1965 because pitchers could pitch around him. With Robinson in the lineup, Powell would be a better hitter. He expected 100 home runs from Robby, Powell and Brooks Robinson.

Bauer talked about how Robinson had averaged 32 home runs and 100 runs batted in for ten years in Cincinnati and how excited Bauer was when he heard the deal was in the works. He got a call at 8 a.m., on the morning of December 10 from Orioles general manager Harry Dalton, telling him the deal was done; he could celebrate.

"Did you get drunk?" Pepe asked him. "Not that early," said Bauer. "I had to wait until the kids got on the school bus."[5]

There was another factor that played into Frank Robinson coming to Baltimore as the top gun in the lineup and, for that matter, in the franchise. How would Brooks Robinson react? It would be hard to find two players from more culturally different backgrounds.

Here was Frank Robinson, a black man from Oakland, the youngest of ten children from a broken home, who was moody and outspoken and had been arrested for carrying a gun. Brooks Robinson was a white man from Little Rock, Arkansas, where, just a decade earlier, President Eisenhower sent in federal troops to allow black students to enroll at Central High School. He came up to the Orioles as an 18-year-old kid in 1955, which meant he had been with Baltimore longer than Frank Robinson had been with Cincinnati. Orioles fans watched him grow up, become the top fielding third baseman in baseball and hammer out more than 1,000 hits. In 1964, he even led the league in RBI with 118—a Frank Robinson- like number.

Mark Kram, writing about the two Mr. Robinsons, put it this way: "For the Orioles, he [Frank] alone could mean a pennant. The only question was, on or off the field, would tip the balance that was Frank Robinson, and would his vast presence change Brooks Robinson?"[6]

Kram answered his own question: "The wingspread of Frank never showed on the face of Brooks when he suddenly became the other Robinson. The town still belongs to him but the club, at least visually, is the property of Frank."[7]

Orioles players sensed something special when Frank Robinson arrived at spring training. He had permission to arrive late because of some personal business. When he got there, he made his presence felt immediately. It was as if his reputation of being the bad guy, the guy with the gun, the trouble maker, the guy who gives the front office fits—all of those thoughts seemed to dissipate.

"All of a sudden, you could see it. Everyone was thinking, now we've got it. We got the hitter we needed to win it," said relief pitcher Dick Hall.[8]

Jim Palmer, the up-and-coming pitching star, said, "One day in spring training, a bonus kid from the Braves threw an off-the-table curve, and Frank hit a rocket, right down the line, bringing up chalk. I turned to Davey Johnson and said, 'We just won the pennant.' He made everyone believe they could win."[9]

While Frank was enjoying the experience of adjusting to his new ball-club in Florida, Barbara Robinson was frustrated trying to find a home for the family in Baltimore. She told Frank she called different places, identified herself as Barbara Robinson, and said that her husband played for the Orioles. They were anxious to find a place for her until they met in person and they realized she was Mrs. Frank Robinson, not Mrs. Brooks Robinson. Suddenly, for the black woman, no housing was available. When Frank heard about it, he contacted Orioles owner Jerry Hoffberger. He put up the family in a nice Baltimore hotel and personally helped them find decent housing.

When the season opened, the Orioles were hot out of the gate. He began his American League career characteristically. On April 12, in his first at-bat in the league, he was hit by a pitch thrown by Earl Wilson of the Red Sox. Brooks Robinson then homered and the Orioles were off and running.

Robinson homered in each of his first three games, and Baltimore won 12 of their first 14 games, which ordinarily would have given them an early first-place cushion. But the Cleveland Indians, managed by Birdie Tebbetts, Frank's first manager in Cincinnati, were even hotter, sporting a 12–1 record. Cleveland had a solid starting pitching corps of Gary Bell, Sonny Siebert,

Sam McDowell and Luis Tiant. Two aging veterans, Rocky Colavito and Leon Wagner, put some pop in their lineup. Robinson had a tremendous April, hitting .463 in a dozen games with five home runs, 16 runs scored and ten driven in.

Turning points in seasons can come at any time and can even affect teams that are already playing exceptionally well. Many Orioles players look to Sunday, May 8, as a turning point in their young season. The Orioles and Indians played a doubleheader, the last two games of a four-game series at Baltimore. They had split the first two games, leaving the Orioles two games behind Cleveland in the standings.

In the first game of the twin bill, Robby hit his sixth home run and Baltimore moved to within a game of the top with an 8–2 victory. In the first inning of the second game, following an Aparicio single, Robinson tied into a Luis Tiant offering and hit a towering drive that cleared the roof at Memorial Stadium, the first ball ever hit clear out of that stadium. The Orioles went on to an 8–3 win, hanging the first loss of the year on Tiant. The Orioles moved into a first place tie with Cleveland, each having 15–4 records.[10]

"Sometimes you can point to one incident in a season as a big one," said relief pitcher Moe Drabowsky. "To me, when Frank hit that ball out of the stadium off Tiant, it galvanized the whole team. It was like 'we're going to be tough to beat this year.'"[11]

Both the Orioles and Indians settled into more normal patterns of wins and losses in May, and Robinson encountering his first slump of the season. He hit his tenth home run on May 20 and did not hit another one until June 3. His batting average, which was bound to go down after his blistering start, dropped more than 100 points in the month. Going into June, the Orioles had a record of 25–17, three games behind the Indians.

In June, the Orioles doubled their win total for the year, winning 25 games while losing only 8. The Indians won 18 games, losing 12—not a bad month but they dropped to third place as Detroit sneaked into second. Robby hit eight home runs in June to give him 18 for the year, but experienced another drought in which he went homerless from June 18 to July 1. Nonetheless, he was on pace to win the Triple Crown by leading the league in batting average, home runs and runs batted in.

The Orioles' starting pitching was outstanding. Entering July, Barber was 8–2, Palmer and Bunker were each 8–4, and McNally was 6–2—a combined record of 30–12.

On June 21, in the first game of a doubleheader against the Yankees, the Orioles held a 7–5 lead when Roy White came up with two on and two out in the bottom of the ninth. He hit a line shot headed for the right field stands. Robby gave chase and, diving over the short right field wall, caught the ball while falling into the seats. Yankees manager Ralph Houk protested that he did not have control of the ball, but to no avail. Robby had preserved the win in this game with his glove, not his bat.

Remarkably, on August 11, he did the same thing against the same team. With the Orioles winning 7–5 in the 11th inning, Robinson dived into the left field stands and snatched what would have been a home run by Clete Boyer.

In the space of one year, Baltimore had been transformed from a team that tried to win every game to one that expected to win every game. Robinson was clearly the team leader, not only with his bat and glove, but with the attitude he displayed. Many ballplayers will try to pump up their team by saying something like "Let's go" as they return to the dugout after an at-bat. Robinson shouted it on his way to the batter's box, exhorting himself as well as his teammates.

Brimming with confidence, the Orioles put together two seven-game winning streaks in late June and July while other contenders faltered and opened up a 13-game lead over the Tigers and 14 over Cleveland by the end of the month. Robby led the league in runs with 82, home runs with 31, RBI with 82, and was first in on-base and slugging percentage.

Brooks Robinson and Robby were second and third in batting average, behind Tony Oliva, and second and third in hits. Aparicio led the league in stolen bases and in triples. The starting pitching staff was stellar with Palmer at 12–4, McNally at 10–3, Barber at 10–5 and Bunker at 8–4. Eddie Watt was the leader in the bullpen with an 8–2 mark.

As invincible as the Orioles seemed to be, an incident away from the ballpark in August could have changed everything. On the night of August 22, many of the players attended a private party at the home of Leonard F. Ruck, a wealthy funeral director and ardent Orioles fan. As Paul Blair, Boog Powell, Moe Drabowsky, Davey Johnson, Andy Etchebarren and others sat around the Rucks' swimming pool, having drinks and cavorting, one thing led to another and players started to try to throw their teammates into the pool. At one point, as Powell pulled at Drabowsky, trying to throw him in, he slipped and hit his head, cutting it open. The cut was so deep that he had to go to the hospital and have stitches. As it turned out, that was minor compared to what happened a few minutes later.

Robby was sitting with the others at poolside but did not want to get tossed in the pool. The biggest reason, unknown to most of his teammates, was that he didn't know how to swim. He ducked away for a moment, put on his swimming trunks and got in the shallow end of the pool, away from the horseplay. As he meandered about in the water, he inadvertently moved into the deep end and was immediately in trouble.

"I went down a couple of times and kept yelling for help every time I surfaced," he said. "My wife thought I was kidding and I guess everyone else did, too."[12]

Etchebarren saw him and thought he was just fooling around at first, but when he saw Frank go under and not come up, he jumped in the pool to try to help him. Robby was dead weight at the bottom of the pool. Etchebarren shoved him a couple of times but then had to resurface to catch his breath. He went under again, pushed Frank to the surface and pulled him to the side of the pool.

Other players helped get him out, and he lay by the side of the pool for about five minutes, then got up, shaken, embarrassed, but okay. "No one seemed too excited right away," said Paul Blair. "But it hit us when we realized what could have happened."[13]

Davey Johnson, in recalling the incident years later, said he and Etchebarren were standing by the side of the pool and caught sight of Robby in the deep end. "We both looked down and said, 'Hey, look, there's Frank, he's swimming—no, he ain't.' So we went after him. That was a scare."[14]

Everyone recovered from the party and the Orioles continued to roll. When they beat Kansas City, 6–1, behind Palmer on September 22, they clinched their first American League pennant. By season's end, they had won 97 games and lost just 63 finishing nine games ahead of second-place Minnesota, the defending league champion.

Robinson won the Triple Crown with his .316 batting average, 49 home runs and 122 runs batted in. Those numbers also earned him the Most Valuable Player Award, making him the only player in baseball history to win it in both leagues.[15]

The Orioles finished 1–2–3 in the MVP voting, a rare accomplishment for one team, with Brooks Robinson and Boog Powell finishing second and third respectively. Their numbers told the story:

	AB	R	H	D	T	HR	RBI	AVE.
F. Robinson	576	122	182	34	2	49	122	.316
B. Robinson	620	91	167	35	2	23	100	.269
Powell	441	78	141	18	0	34	109	.287

The young pitching staff came through. Palmer was 15–10, McNally 13–6, Barber 10–5 and Bunker 10–6. The bullpen was also effective, keeping the Orioles close enough to pull off late-inning victories—and their records showed it. Miller went 9–4, Watt 9–7, Drabowsky 6–0, Hall 6–2 and Eddie Fisher 5–3.

"The bullpen was the key to the season," said Robby. "Those guys were experienced and knew what to do. They didn't ever walk anyone. You had to earn your way on."[16]

But the season wasn't over yet. The young, upstart Orioles had to face a veteran Los Angeles Dodgers team in the World Series, a team with a pitching staff, led by Don Drysdale and Sandy Koufax, that promised to give the Orioles hitters all they could handle.

The Dodgers carried with them a proud tradition, winning National League championships most recently in 1953, 1955 and 1956 while they were still in Brooklyn, and in 1959, 1963, 1965 and 1966 in Los Angeles. They wore "Dodger Blue" and they expected to win.

Their ballclub was built around speed, pitching and defense. Infielder Jim Lefebvre led the team with 24 homers and 74 runs batted in. Outfielder Lou Johnson had 17 homers and 73 runs batted in. No one else on the team drove in more than 61 runs. Shortstop Maury Wills, who four years earlier set the major league record with 102 stolen bases, had 38 steals this year for the Dodgers and center fielder Willie Davis had 21. Wills, Lefebvre and first baseman Wes Parker were all switch-hitters as was veteran utility man Junior Gilliam. This gave manager Walt Alston the ability to stock his lineup with left-handed or right-handed batters. The Dodgers were adept at what became known as "small ball"—getting on base and methodically moving runners around.

They were aided by a pitching staff that held the opposition down much of the time so that the offense didn't need to produce a lot of runs. Sandy Koufax, pitching in his last year, won 27 and lost nine with five shutouts and 27 complete games—more than the entire Baltimore staff. Claude Osteen, like Koufax a left-hander, was 17–14. Don Drysdale and Don Sutton, two right-handers, were 13–16 and 12–12 respectively. So Los Angeles had two right-handers and two left-handers in their starting rotation—and three of the four were eventually elected to the Hall of Fame.

Whereas the Orioles had a bullpen corps of Watt, Miller, Drabowsky and Hall, the Dodgers had Phil Regan, who appeared in 65 games, had a 14–1 record with 21 saves. In other words, of the 95 Los Angeles wins during the season, Regan won or saved 35 of them.

The World Series opened in Los Angeles on October 5. As expected, the Dodgers were heavy favorites. The Orioles were subjected to acts of disrespect, some from the press, some from the Dodgers brass. Sports writer Jimmy Cannon wrote that the American League had to be kidding to call itself a big league. Dodgers vice president Fresco Thompson said the Orioles didn't have near the pitching staff that Minnesota had in 1965, when the Dodgers beat the likes of Jim "Mudcat" Grant and Jim Kaat to win the World Series. The Dodgers front office also provided Orioles owner Jerry Hoffberger and his entourage with seats down the right field line near the foul pole, an unnecessary indignity. Among Hoffberger's guests were pitcher Steve Barber and his wife. Barber had suffered a sore arm late in the season and could not pitch in the Series.

One break the Orioles caught was that the National League pennant race had come down to the final day, with Koufax winning his 27th game to clinch it. But because of that, he was unable to pitch the World Series opener. That duty fell to Drysdale. Baltimore manager Hank Bauer sent out McNally as his starter.

In the first inning, with one out, Drysdale walked Russ Snyder, bringing Robby to the plate. He took the first pitch and hit the next one into the left field stands to give the Orioles a 2–0 lead barely five minutes into the ballgame. As he had done all year, it was another example of Robinson's "Let's go" spirit and leading by example. Brooks Robinson was up next and he too parked a Drysdale pitch in the left field bleachers.

Staked to a 3–0 lead, McNally was plagued with control problems. The Orioles added a run in the second inning but gave it back in the bottom of the second when McNally gave up a long home run to Lefebvre, a double and a walk, and was bailed out when Snyder made a diving catch in the outfield to end the inning.

In the third inning, McNally simply could not find the plate and walked the bases loaded. Bauer brought in Drabowsky to try to put out the fire. He walked a batter to force in a run but otherwise got out of the inning unscathed. He proceeded to put forth the best relief pitching performance in World Series history. He pitched 6⅔ innings, allowing no runs on one hit, and striking out 11—a World Series record for a relief pitcher, including six in a row at one point, another record. Final score: Baltimore 5, Los Angeles 2.

The second game pitted 27-game winner Koufax and Palmer, the 20-year-old right-hander for the Orioles. Both pitchers breezed through the first four innings. In the fifth, After Powell singled, Blair hit a lazy fly ball to center field that Willie Davis circled under and dropped. Etchebarren hit another fly ball to center and Davis dropped this one too. Powell scored and Blair followed him home after Davis rushed a throw to third base, committing his third error of the inning. The Orioles scored a third run on an Aparicio double and went on to win the game, 6–0.

The action moved to Memorial Stadium in Baltimore with Bunker on the mound for the Orioles versus Osteen for the Dodgers. A great pitching dual ensued with the only run of the game coming on a home run by Blair in the fifth inning. It was one of only three hits given up by Osteen but it was enough for a 1–0 win and a three games to none lead in the series.

Game Four matched Drysdale and McNally, the starters from the Series opener. McNally had his control on this day and so did Drysdale. In the fourth inning, Frank Robinson lit up Drysdale for a home run, just as he had done in the first game, and it turned out to be the only run of the game.

Moe Drabowsky was a fun-loving relief pitcher who set a World Series record by striking out 11 men in a relief appearance in 1966 against the Los Angeles Dodgers (author's collection).

The Orioles were the world champions in spectacular fashion. They outscored the Dodgers, 13–2, and reeled off three consecutive shutouts, holding Los Angeles scoreless for 33 consecutive innings.[17]

Robby was named the Series' Most Valuable Player. Later he would be named the league's Most Valuable Player. The Orioles had traded for him, hoping to put some thump in their lineup to put them over the top. Robinson responded by winning the Triple Crown, two MVP awards and hitting the game-winning homer to cap a World Series sweep.

Sports writer Peter Gammons described Robinson as "a man whose style is the seeming rejection of everything superfluous. It is as if he is forever conserving his energy for one powerful, violent stroke as in hitting a baseball or hurling his body into a second baseman."[18]

Orioles broadcaster Chuck Thompson, reflecting on 1966, said, "We couldn't believe it. We had to slap ourselves to prove we were awake. It was like we were in a dream—that our reality was fiction."[19]

Frank Robinson had an interesting view on the Orioles' World Series success. "Do I think the Dodgers expected to win? Sure," he said. "I don't think they were overconfident. The key for us was Koufax didn't start the first game. They went with Drysdale and we only had to face Koufax once. And then there was the thing with Willie Davis. He didn't have another day like that in his entire career."[20]

Bunker put it in this perspective. "It was just a fluke. Everybody says we weren't that good and they weren't that bad. And, well, you know, that's about right. You know what I'm saying?"[21]

Meanwhile, Cincinnati and Bill DeWitt were licking their wounds. Milt Pappas won 12 games and the Reds finished seventh in the National League.

CHAPTER 9

Falling from Grace

Baseball is a strange game. With individual players and teams alike, there can be seasons or stretches of seasons in which everything clicks—the bloop hits fall in for singles and doubles; the opponents' line drives are hit right at somebody; the pitchers are all hitting the corners and getting the calls when they're close; the aging veteran has one more good year left in him; the rookie who was thought to be a year or two away from full development surprises everyone by hitting 30 home runs.

Just as common are the situations in which, with basically the same personnel, everything seems to go wrong. Batters have off years; pitchers can't find the plate; managers' decisions, which seemed brilliant last week or last year, all suddenly backfire; and injuries pile up.

In 1967, the Orioles were the defending world champions and were heavily favored to win the American League championship once again. They had the best starting pitching staff and the best relief corps in the league. They had a dynamic defense led by Brooks Robinson and Aparicio on the left side of the infield and Paul Blair in center field. Boog Powell was part of a powerful one-two punch in the middle of the lineup. And they had Frank Robinson.

All the pieces were in place—and yet most of them fell apart, and the best team in baseball in 1966 struggled to stay above .500 in 1967. In fact, they didn't do it. A harbinger of what the season was to be like occurred on April 30 when Barber threw a no-hitter against the Detroit Tigers—and lost the game. He walked 10 batters in $8\frac{2}{3}$ innings but took a 1–0 lead into the ninth inning. A couple of walks, a wild pitch and an error doomed him and the Orioles lost, 2–1.

Palmer was sailing along with a 3–1 record in May when tendonitis in his elbow shelved him for the rest of the season. Bunker, who struggled with arm problems at the end of the 1966 season, won only three games in

1967, losing seven. Powell dropped from 34 home runs in the championship year to 13 in 1967. One bright spot for Baltimore was the emergence of Tom Phoebus, a right-handed pitcher. Phoebus came up from the minors in September of 1966 and threw consecutive shutouts. In 1967, he became the surprise mainstay on the pitching staff with a 14–9 record.

Robinson, coming off his Triple Crown, MVP year, had surgery on his right knee in December. He hurt the knee during a ballgame in June when he was running the bases and felt something pop. It caused some pain but did not disable him, and he managed to play through the pain and rack up the great numbers that he did. But Orioles doctors recommended surgery in the off-season for removal of cartilage and a small piece of bone. He was reluctant at first but decided to go through with it.

"Sure I was leery," he said. "It was my first operation, and when you make your living with your arms and legs, you don't exactly welcome the idea of being cut." He had the surgery on December 6 and it was deemed a success.[1]

He picked up in 1967 where he left off in 1966 and appeared headed for a second consecutive Triple Crown year, something that had never been done before. In late June, Robinson was leading the American League in hitting with a .337 average, with Carl Yastrzemski second at .336; was second in home runs with 21 to Harmon Killebrew's 22; and was first in RBI with 59, just ahead of Killebrew, who had 57.

Robby also continued to be a daring defensive player. On May 24, in a game against the Yankees, he made a leap for a long drive hit by Mickey Mantle. He caught it, but as he hit the wall, the ball popped out of his glove and over the wall for a home run. The Yankees won, 2–0. Had he held on the ball, it would have been the third time in two years that he robbed the Yankees of a homer with a game-saving catch.

A strange play that occurred on Tuesday night, June 27, sealed the Orioles' fate for the season. It not only wiped out Robinson's chance for a second straight Triple Crown, it threatened his career.

The night before, Chicago had won a 5–4 thriller, scoring two runs in the ninth inning. The Orioles held a 4–3 lead going into the ninth. Tommy McCraw led off for Chicago with a single. Pete Ward followed with another single. Jerry McNertney laid down a sacrifice bunt, advancing the runners to second and third. Wayne Causey was intentionally walked to set up the double play. Pinch-hitter Jim King made the strategy look good by hitting a tapper that Powell moved in on and threw to the plate for the force out. But McCraw's slide upended catcher Etchebarren, and he was unable to throw to first for the easy double play to end the inning. Ken Berry singled to center, driving in two runs that decided the game.

The Orioles thought McCraw was out of the baseline and should have been called out. It was a tough loss in a tough season, dropping the Orioles to 32–35 for the year. Their hope had been to sweep the series with the White Sox and get to .500 for the year. That was no longer possible. Robinson's feeling was that Chicago had won because of an illegal slide, and the Orioles needed to send a message on how they felt about plays like that. The opportunity came the next night.

In the fourth inning, Robby singled and was on first when Brooks Robinson hit a ground ball to the third baseman. He threw to second baseman Al Weis to start the double play. Robby barreled into second, intent on breaking up the double play but also wanting to crash into Weis in a decisive way. But somehow, his slide missed Weis who, in leaping to avoid the collision, hit Robinson across the left eye with his knee. The force of the blow rendered Robinson unconscious.

"Knocked me cold," said Robby, recalling the play years later. "When I finally got up, they asked me where I was and I said, 'It's a great day for UCLA basketball.'"[2]

He had a concussion, some swelling of the brain and nerve damage. He also incurred double vision. He was able to recover from most of it quickly but the double vision lingered on for quite a while.

Robby had been injured many times in his career. There were the nagging arm injuries that impeded his throwing early on in his career. There were the beanings by Ruben Gomez in July of 1957 and by Camilo Pascual in April of 1958. There was the fight with Eddie Mathews in August of 1960 and the day he felt something give in his knee that eventually required surgery in 1966. This one was different and he knew it. He went home to rest and recover and was out for four weeks, the longest departure in his career.

When he came back, the double vision still bothered him. He managed to hit nine more home runs and drive in 33 runs. At the time of his injury, he was on a pace to hit 42 homers with 122 RBI. Instead he finished with 30 home runs and 93 runs batted in to go along with a .311 batting average.

Sports columnist Jim Murray wrote, "It's interesting to speculate what might have been if Frank Robinson had jogged into second base standing up that day. Ballclubs don't keep Triple Crown winners around to take out pivot men. They want a Frank Robinson to trot around the bases, not slide around them."[3]

Robinson worried about what effect the injury would have on his career. Would he be able to play again? If he did, would he have the same drive and ability that has sustained him? And if not, would it be worth it to return? It was during this time, assessing his future, that he thought about the possibility of someday managing. Actually, he had been thinking about it off and on for at least a year. It was a tough field for blacks to break into. Gene Baker, who played second base in the big leagues, was managing in the Cubs' farm system, but there weren't many others.

Robby knew it wasn't because they weren't qualified; it was because they were black. Even after he broke the barrier a decade later and became the first black manager in the big leagues, he became outspoken about the lack of opportunities for blacks to advance in the sport in which they had excelled.

In December of 1966, after winning the Most Valuable Player Award, Robby mentioned the possibility of someday managing in an interview with *The Sporting News.* He said he might have to put in some years as a coach or manage in the minor leagues or, if he played a few more years, he might be ready without having the other experience.

He said he thought Maury Wills, Ernie Banks, Junior Gilliam and Willie Mays were qualified to break the color barrier and manage in the major leagues. "I would say Gilliam and Banks have the quickest opportunity because they are at the right point in their careers," he said. "They are highly respected by their clubs, the ownership of which is not expected to change, which means a lot."[4]

Robinson returned to the ballclub two weeks after the collision, played catch on the sidelines prior to games, and took "soft" batting practice—with Orioles coach Sherm Lollar pitching to him. The headaches were gone but he still had double vision unless he held his head a certain way.

The double vision was always the same—one image above the other, rather than side by side. He discovered that if he cocked his head in a particular way, the double vision would disappear. He began trying to hit with his head down, his chin almost against his chest. Doctors had assured him the double vision would go away.

He was back in the Orioles lineup on July 29 and gutted out the rest of the season. When he was at the plate he sometimes saw two balls coming in. He'd swing at one and hope for the best. The eye condition created some potentially dangerous situations in the outfield as well as he tracked down fly balls hit his way.

"I wasn't the same player, really," said Robinson, "and really, I wasn't the same player for the rest of my career. My motor skills and reflexes weren't the same."[5]

Weis, the White Sox shortstop who collided with Robinson on that fateful play, incurred a knee injury and was out for the rest of the season.

The disappointing year was not without its share of highlights. On May 17, the Orioles hit seven home runs in a 12–8 win over the Red Sox at Fenway Park—by Andy Etchebarren, Sam Bowens, Boog Powell, Davey Johnson, Robby, Brooks Robinson and Paul Blair. A week later, they lost a 2–0 game to the Yankees on a two-run homer by Mickey Mantle—a ball that Robby caught as he dived into the right field stands but could not hold onto when he landed.

The Orioles' dismal play in 1967 prompted some changes that began in August when Barber, the left-hander whose wildness cost him a potentially brilliant career, was traded to the Yankees. With young Mark Belanger ready to take over at shortstop, Aparicio was traded back to the White Sox, where he had starred earlier in his career, along with outfielder Russ Snyder, for pitchers Bruce Howard and Roger Nelson and infielder Don Buford, who turned out to be the key acquisition in the deal.

But what turned out to be the most significant personnel changes occurred on the Orioles' coaching staff. Harry Brecheen, the only pitching coach in club history and the man who had groomed the "Kiddy Corps" of Orioles hurlers, was let go and replaced by George Bamberger. And a 12-year manager in the minor leagues, a feisty little guy named Earl Weaver, was moved up from being manager at Triple A Rochester to coach first base for the Orioles.

Bamberger was a minor league pitcher for most of his professional baseball career, once throwing 68⅔ innings straight without issuing a walk. He had stints in the major leagues with the New York Giants and the Orioles that amounted to 14⅓ innings of work. He hooked on with the Orioles as a minor league pitching instructor in 1960 and had worked with many of the young Baltimore hurlers before they made it to the big leagues.

Brecheen had been with the Orioles since their first days in Baltimore, but Bauer justified the change in pitching coaches, saying he was tired of the sore arms. Bamberger believed pitchers needed to pitch more innings, not fewer innings, to keep their arms in shape—but the key was to throw strikes. He believed a ball thrown out of the strike zone was a mistake, and that a walk was the result of four mistakes. He wanted his pitchers to throw the ball over the plate but to change speeds and keep hitters off-balance. In the next decade, he had eighteen 20-game winners.

Weaver grew up in St. Louis and started his professional career as an infielder in the St. Louis Cardinals organization in 1948. He had a minor league career in which he had to keep his suitcase packed—Winston-Salem, Denver, Houston, Omaha, New Orleans, Knoxville—making it to Triple A one year but never playing an inning in the big leagues.

While he was toiling for the Knoxville Smokies in the South Atlantic League, their manager was let go and Weaver was asked to fill in for the rest of the season. As it happened, Dalton, the Orioles' personnel director, was in town, and while attending some Smokies games to look at some ballplayers, he took particular interest in their young interim manager.

Knoxville was an unaffiliated team, which made rising through the ranks more difficult. So when Dalton offered Weaver the opportunity to manage an Orioles Class-D ballclub, he jumped at the chance. He managed four years at Elmira and two at Rochester before being named the Orioles' first base coach.

Weaver was a fiery, take-charge guy who didn't take guff from anybody, including umpires, and many baseball people, including Bauer, believed it was only a matter of time before he would be a big league manager somewhere.

Bauer, who had been a star outfielder for the great New York Yankees teams of the 1950s and who had guided the Orioles to their first World Series two years earlier, was suspicious of the Orioles bestowing upon him their choice for a first base coach, someone who had never even played in the big leagues. He had been around baseball long enough to know his days might be numbered if the Orioles didn't produce, and his relationship with Weaver was professional but not cordial.

As the O's left spring training in 1968 and headed north, they were filled with high hopes, as all teams are at that time of year. Robby was intent on rebounding from his eye injury but he was sidelined for nearly three weeks in April when he came down with a case of mumps. When he came back from that, he soon realized his double vision was still there.

Robinson struggled most of the year as did several other veterans. At the All-Star break, with their record at 43–37, the Orioles brass decided to make a change. Bauer was fired and replaced by Weaver.

The new manager immediately started playing his kind of ball, platooning his players to get the best possible match-ups, not only at the plate but in the field; shunning the sacrifice bunt because he didn't believe in giving outs away; and relying on pitching, defense and the three-run homer to win ball games.

The Orioles won 48 and lost 34 under Weaver, giving them a 91–71 record for the year, finishing in second place behind the Detroit Tigers. Dave McNally was the leader of the pitching staff with a 22–10 record.

Detroit had an outstanding ballclub and its pitching staff was led by right-hander Denny McLain, who won 31 games, and lefty Mickey Lolich, who won 17. The most amazing part of Detroit's success to Robinson was that this team, which won 103 games, was managed by Mayo Smith, who had been Cincinnati's manager for a brief time in 1959 and who Robinson thought did little more than make out the lineup card every day.

But Robby had more serious concerns than figuring out Mayo Smith's success in Detroit. He had his worst year in the big leagues, hitting .268 with just 15 homers and 52 runs batted in. For the first time in his career, he was getting booed in his own ballpark. His vision got better as the season went along but had not cleared up altogether.

The booing had as much to do with Robinson's attitudes and actions off the field as it did with his batting average. Prior to the season, he had held out for a raise and was earning a well-publicized $115,000, so fans were now questioning whether he was worth it. He had chided the performances of some of his teammates, without naming anybody, saying they might be jealous of him. And he had made disparaging remarks about Boston's Carl Yazszstemski, who won the Triple Crown the year after Robinson won it. He was a little perturbed that Yaz was making a fortune in commercial endorsements after his Triple Crown year whereas Robby hardly got any attention. The reason, Robinson believed, was that he was black and Yaz was white.

With his numbers down, his popularity waning and his future uncertain, he began thinking about managing once again.

One night late in the season, the Orioles were in New York for a series with the Yankees. Some of the players got in a conversation with Weaver, and he mentioned he had been managing the Santurce ballclub in the Puerto Rican League in the winter months but was going to give it up now that he was managing the Orioles.

Robinson told Weaver he might be interested. Weaver seemed incredulous at first, and who could blame him. A 33-year-old black ballplayer with no managerial experience going to a foreign country to take the helm of a team? It was indeed an unlikely scenario. But Weaver made some phone calls and arranged for Robinson to meet with Hiram Cuevas, owner of the Santurce Crabbers.

When the Orioles got home from their road trip, Robby and Cuevas had lunch at the Baltimore Hilton Hotel. "We cut a napkin in half," said Cuevas. "Each of us was to put down a 'fair' dollar figure. I put down $1,800 but Frank left his blank—he was willing to take whatever I offered. I gave him $2,000 (per month) and we became good friends."[6]

The Orioles front office supported Robinson. "Frank has said he wants to manage someday and this is the way to go about it," said Harry Dalton of the Oriole front office. "He gets a chance now, some experience, before his playing days are over. This is pretty indicative of how much he does want to manage, being willing to spend the off season away from home.[7]

Robinson became the first American black person to manage a professional team in Organized Baseball. More importantly to him, it was a training ground, a possible stepping stone to managing some day in the big leagues.

Several Orioles players joined the Santurce team that winter—Jim Palmer, Paul Blair, Elrod Hendricks, Dave Leonhard, and Dave May as well as ex–Oriole Wally Bunker, who had been selected by the Kansas City Royals in the expansion draft. Santurce already had veteran major league pitcher Juan Pizarro. Cuevas signed big leaguers George Scott, Joe Foy, Leo Cardenas and Julio Gotay. Going into his first experience as a manager, Robby had a team loaded with talent.

Robinson's 1968–1969 Santurce club won 49 games, which included a 15-game winning streak, and won the league championship with a 49–20 record. Highlight of the season was a no-hitter by Palmer. Gotay, a veteran of winter league ball, said Robinson was the best manager he ever had.

Robby learned a lot about managing that winter. "I learned you can't handle men as a group," he said. "You handle them as individuals. Some guys don't play well if they're not praised. Some you got to kick on the tail. Some you don't have to say a word to. But if they make the same mistake twice, you must be tough as nails."[8]

He also learned that managers must have a thick skin. "If you don't make the right move at the right time and you're wrong, you must accept the criticism of the press and the fans," said Robby. "It's easy to take bows when things are going well. But the thing is to keep your head up when they're not."[9]

CHAPTER 10

Movin' on Up

The Orioles made one strategic trade after the 1968 season that might have seemed questionable at the time. They sent outfielders Curt Blefary and John Mason to Houston for pitcher Mike Cuellar and utility man Elijah Johnson.

Clearly, Blefary and Cuellar were the key players in the deal. In four years with the Orioles, Blefary hit 82 home runs and contributed many clutch hits. But after the 1967 season, the Orioles traded Luis Aparicio to the White Sox as part of a multi-player deal that sent Don Buford to the Orioles. Buford was a speedy runner who drew a lot of walks and could play third base, shortstop, second base or the outfield. He was an infielder for most of his time in Chicago but Weaver wanted to use him primarily as an outfielder. With Paul Blair and Frank Robinson established in their positions, Blefary became the odd man out.

Cuellar was a left-handed pitcher with a good screwball, but had an up-and-down career in the major leagues. He signed with the St. Louis Cardinals at age 21 and appeared in two games for them in 1959, giving up seven runs on eight hits in just four innings. He did not emerge again until 1964, when he was 5–5 with the Cardinals. Peddled to Houston, he was 12–10 in 1966 and 16–11 in 1967 before slipping to 8–11 in 1968.

Orioles fans had to wonder which Cuellar they were going to get—the 16-game winner of 1967 or the eight game winner of 1968? The Baltimore brass saw him as a left-hander who could fill the void for a second lefty in the starting rotation missing since Steve Barber was traded to the Yankees the year before. Also, the Orioles needed a pitcher to fill the slot left when Bunker was picked up by the new Kansas City Royals in the expansion draft.

Cuellar's problems in 1968 had more to do with the fact he was playing for a bad team that had trouble scoring as well as some off the field problems

Don Buford, shown here with Angels infielder Jim Fregosi and umpire Bill Valentine, was traded from the Chicago White Sox to Baltimore after the 1967 season and helped the Orioles to several championship seasons (author's collection).

stemming from a marriage breaking up and bills piling up. Harry Dalton helped his new pitcher pay off some debts with some no-interest loans from the Orioles, with payments deducted from his paychecks. Just as the Orioles had helped Robby's family find suitable housing in 1966, they came to the aid of Cuellar and made him feel part of the family. Cuellar responded with several outstanding years with the Orioles, beginning in 1969.

Robinson and the Orioles got off to a great start in 1969. By the end of April, Baltimore was 16–7 and had a 3½-game lead over second place Boston. Robby was seeing the ball better—and seeing only one of them— and had ten home runs, setting a major league record for most home runs in April. McNally was 4–0, Phoebus was 3–0 as was Palmer, who was over his arm problems from the previous year.

Robby, fresh from a winter of managing in Puerto Rico, where he had become a student of how to run a ballclub, was impressed with how Earl Weaver ran his. "He knew how to use all 25 men on the roster and he wasn't afraid of being criticized for using the 25th man," said Frank. "He kept everybody relatively happy because you didn't just sit on the bench with Earl—you played."[1]

Weaver had his regulars—Robby, Brooks, Blair and Powell, he had platoon players that included even his catchers, Etchebarren and Elrod Hendricks, and he had role players that entered the game in certain situations. Long before the age of computers, he kept statistics on 3x5 cards—so he might use a .200 hitter as a pinch-hitter because he knew the guy hit .400 against whoever was on the mound at the time.

On April 27, the Orioles swept a doubleheader from the Yankees, 6–0 and 10–5, as Robby had two homers, four singles and eight RBI. On July 27, Baltimore registered its most lopsided shutout in team history, a 17–0 whitewashing of the Chicago White Sox with Robinson banging two home runs and driving in five.

It was in July, shortly after the All-Star break, that the Orioles instituted a new gimmick in their clubhouse—a kangaroo court in which players were held accountable, in a comical setting, for bonehead plays they had made during that day's game. They only did it after they won—because there was no fun in losing—and the whole team bought into it. Robinson, who served as judge, often wore a mop on his head as if he were a British barrister.

A player could get fined a dollar or two if he missed a sign, missed hitting the cutoff man or failed to execute a sacrifice bunt. Players would nominate one of their teammates for a fine and the other players would give it a thumbs-up or a thumbs-down. If the vote was thumbs-down, the player who made the nomination got the fine.

It was a ploy that could have caused a lot of hard feelings on some teams, but it worked for the Orioles. "It made you pay attention and you learned from your mistakes," said center fielder Paul Blair. "Guys didn't make those same mistakes again. That helped tremendously. And it brought the club closer together, made us more of a family to the point where we could laugh at our mistakes—but we didn't make 'em twice."

Baltimore won 18 games in May, losing only eight, but Boston and Detroit, the two most recent pennant winners, stayed close, trailing by three games and six games respectively. Robby continued to hit well though he managed only two home runs in the month. The starting pitching continued to be outstanding—McNally was 7–0, Phoebus was 5–1, Palmer was 5–2 and Cuellar, after a slow start in April, won five games in May and was 6–4. The quartet of starters accounted for 23 of the club's 34 wins.

In May, Doug Brown, the Orioles beat writer for the *Baltimore Sun*,

In 1969, the Orioles instituted a good-natured kangaroo court after games the Orioles won, in which players were fined for, in the opinion of their teammates, making bonehead plays. Robinson, shown here wearing a mop to look like a barrister, was the judge (National Baseball Hall of Fame and Library, Cooperstown, New York).

asked Robby what the difference was between the Robinson of 1968 and the Robinson of 1969. "The first guy you mentioned hit .200 something. The second guy you mentioned is hitting .400," Robby said with a laugh. He explained that he was healthy this year for the first time in a long time.

Robinson said injuries alone don't affect a player's performance. It's the layoff they cause and the time it takes to get back into shape and into the rhythm of the game. "Once you fall behind and have to stay out of the lineup for a few weeks at a time, it's tough," he said. Robby said it's especially tough at the start of the year when no games have been played, whereas in June or July, a player tries to pick up where he left off before he got hurt.[2]

Robinson had made no secret of the fact he wanted to manage someday, and his stint in the winter in Puerto Rico, coming off such a poor year at the plate in 1968, gave rise to speculation that he might retire as a player sooner rather than later. His hot bat in 1969 changed nearly everyone's thinking. "Players who win Triple Crowns don't have to give their futures a thought," wrote Doug Brown. "But players who drop to .268 two years later...."[3]

When he opened the season with an 11-game hitting streak in which he hit .419 and belted six home runs, and hit safely in 14 of 15 games between May 4 and May 22, he was back in Triple Crown form, and thoughts of his immediate ventures into managing disappeared as the Orioles continued to roll.

Heading into July, the Orioles had opened up an 11-game lead on second-place Boston and showed no signs of weakening. Not only had Robby come back from a bad year the year before, but Boog Powell was also on a tear and Paul Blair was having his best offensive year. All three had 17 home runs. On the mound, McNally was still undefeated at 11–0, Palmer was 9–2, Phoebus was 7–2 and Cueller was 8–6. A pleasant surprise was Dave Leonhard, who was 6–0 out of the bullpen.[4]

In the National League, the Chicago Cubs seemed headed for their first title since 1945, holding an eight-game lead over the second-place New York Mets. The Cubs had a lineup with four future Hall of Famers: Ernie Banks, Billy Williams, Ron Santo and Ferguson Jenkins, and were the talk of baseball, despite the fact the Orioles were on a pace to win well over 100 games and had the potential for four 20-game winners. This was the first year of divisional play, however, so winners of their respective divisions would have to win playoffs to get to the World Series.

The Orioles continued to cruise in August. On August 13, Palmer threw a no-hitter against the Oakland A's, and by August 19, Baltimore was 51 games over .500 and 17 games ahead in the American League East. They finished the season—Weaver's first full season—with 109 wins. Robby had a .308 batting average with 32 home runs. Powell hit .304 with 37 homers. McNally won 14 straight before finally losing and ended up with a 20–7 record. Palmer was 16–4. Phoebus was 14–7. But the big winner was Cuellar, woman problems and money problems behind him, who won 23 and lost just 11.

An oddity occurred with the Orioles' fan base. As they continued to win and their lead in the American League East continued to widen, their attendance actually gradually dropped. In September, as they moved toward the division championship, they were drawing fewer than 20,000 fans a game.

The O's, who had won as many games as the 1927 New York Yankees, and who were considered to be one of the greatest teams ever, now had to play the Minnesota Twins, who were no slouches, in the inaugural League Championship Series. They still had many of the same players from their 1965 championship team, including Harmon Killebrew, who led the league in home runs in 1969 with 49, Tony Oliva, who had won consecutive batting titles in his first two years in the big leagues, and Rod Carew, this year's batting champion. The Twins' manager was Billy Martin, like Weaver a firebrand, who was in his first year with the Minnesota.

The first-ever American League Championship Series game took place on October 4, 1969 at Memorial Stadium—and 43,000 fans showed up to see a pitching matchup of Cuellar and Jim Perry. Robby hit a home run, which was no surprise, and Belanger also hit one, which was a surprise but the Twins rallied for a 3–2 lead until Powell hit the Orioles' third home run of the game off veteran reliever Ron Perranoski. The Birds won the game in the 12th inning on a suicide squeeze bunt by Blair.[5]

The second game was a classic pitching matchup with McNally going for the Orioles and Dave Boswell for the Twins. The game was scoreless after ten innings. In the bottom of the 11th, Baltimore's Curt Motton singled home Boog Powell from second to give the Orioles a 1–0 victory and a 2–0 lead in the series.

The scene shifted to Minnesota for the third game, with the Twins hoping their home field would help turn things around for them. It didn't. The Orioles won 11–2 to advance to the World Series. Their victory was not unexpected. But in the National League, the New York Mets, once the laughingstock of the league, overcame an 8½-game Chicago lead in late August and roared past the Cubs to win their division. Then they polished off the Atlanta Braves in the League Championship Series. It would be the mighty Orioles versus the pesky Mets in the World Series.

The Mets were heavy underdogs going into the Series, and the odds makers appeared to be right on the money when leadoff hitter Don Buford hit Tom Seaver's second pitch in the first game over the fence. The Orioles, behind Cuellar, won 4–1, and it seemed like business as usual for the American League champions.

Robby was not impressed with the Mets and, shunning all baseball protocol and diplomacy, made derogatory remarks about them to the press. "They didn't show any life on the bench until the ninth inning," he said. "I looked over there several times and there was nothing."

He said even when the Mets got a couple of base runners on in the seventh inning, their dugout was quiet. "Nobody was jumping up and down, standing on the dugout steps, the way winners do. It surprised me," he said. "They looked like losers."[6]

The Mets showed some life in the rest of the Series. In Game Two, Jerry Koosman took a no-hitter into the seventh inning and outdueled McNally in a 2–1 Mets victory. In Game Three, Tommy Agee led off the Mets' first inning with a homer off Palmer and made two great catches in the outfield while Gary Gentry was silencing the Orioles bats in a 5–0 shutout. The fourth game of the Series went ten innings with the Mets prevailing once again and Seaver picking up the victory in a 2–1 decision. In Game Five, which turned out to be the decisive one, Robby connected for a home run, just his third hit of the Series, and McNally also homered but Koosman and the Mets won, 5–3, to become the World Series champions.

Prior to 1969, the Mets had never finished higher than ninth place and had never finished with a record above .500. Now they were the world champions. Manager Gil Hodges had beaten Weaver using many tactics that had spelled success for the Orioles manager—great pitching, great defense, timely hitting and effective platooning to create good matchups for his hitters.

Orioles hitters didn't hit. Robby was just 3-for-16. Buford and Blair were both 2-for-20. Brooks Robinson was 1-for-19. Davey Johnson was 1-for-15. Powell was 5-for-19, better than the rest, but had no RBI.

"They had the pitching and they made all the plays. Plain and simple," said Frank Robinson. "We were better but what did that matter? They got the big hits. They did what they had to do."[7]

Robby went back to Santurce for a second season of managing in winter ball. The Crabbers went 35–33, well off their pace of the previous winter, but they set an attendance record for the second straight year and made the playoffs with their third-place finish. Robinson got a pinch-hit single in the All-Star Game played on January 6, 1970, and one of his pitchers, Freddie Beane, threw the club's second no-hitter (including Palmer's the year before).

On November 28, 1969, Santurce went to San Juan, where they faced Robinson's teammate in the big leagues, Mike Cuellar. He didn't have his good stuff that day and the Crabbers shelled him. The San Juan fans were not happy with his performance. Merv Rettenmund, a Baltimore teammate who was playing for Santurce, said, "We beat him bad. The fans were all over him. He was a superstar in the big leagues. Some fan came down and threw beer all over him."[8]

George Scott of the Boston Red Sox, Santurce's first baseman, still had thoughts about the World Series. "Those Mets proved that Baltimore isn't invincible," he said. "It should open up the eyes of other teams in the American League who have the idea the Orioles were unbeatable."[9]

The Orioles went into the 1970 season with one goal in mind—to win the World Series. After what happened to them against the Mets in 1969, winning the division championship and league championship would not be enough to satisfy them. They needed to make a statement to prove to themselves and the rest of the world that losing the World Series was a fluke.

"If we had beaten the Mets in 1969, I don't know that we would have come back as strong," said Robby. "That was a lesson for us. The best team doesn't always win. You also have to be the best prepared and go out and do the job."[10]

The Orioles got out of the gate fast, winning their first five games, and never looked back. On June 26, Robinson hit grand slam home runs in consecutive at-bats in a 12–2 win over the Washington Senators, his only grand slams as an Oriole.

It was an unusual 24-hour cycle for Robby. The night before, nursing a sore back from an encounter with a right field wall, he played in a 14-inning game against the Red Sox and got the only bunt single of his major league career. It was get-away day, and because of the length of the game, the Orioles got away late and back to Baltimore early in the morning. When he arrived home, he got little sleep because his seven-year-old son, Frank Jr. (who was called Kevin) had a high fever and was up most of the night.

Later that day, the sleep-deprived, bone-aching Robinson made the trip over to Washington for a night game with the Senators. He came up with the bases loaded in the fifth inning, facing Joe Coleman. With two strikes on him, Robby got a good swing on a pitch and drove it over the right field wall for an opposite-field grand slammer. It was almost an accident. "With two strikes, I was just looking to hit the ball," he said.[11]

The next inning, he once again came up with the bases loaded, this time against lefty Joe Grzenda. And again, he hit it out of the park, this time to left field. "The count was 2-and-0 so I had a pretty good idea of what was coming," he said.[12]

He became the seventh major leaguer to hit two grand slams in one game and the third to do it on back-to-back plate appearances. On both of Robby's homers, the same three men were on base and got there the same way—McNally on a walk, Buford with a single and Blair with a walk.[13]

On October 1, they ended the season by hanging Washington with its

14th consecutive loss by a score of 3–2. It was also the Orioles' 11th straight win, a club record. Robinson hit the 475th home run of his career, tying him with Stan Musial for 12th on the all-time list.

The Orioles won 108 games, one fewer than in the previous year, and lost 54, cruising to their second straight American League East championship. Powell was the league MVP with 35 home runs and 114 runs batted in to go along with a .297 average. Robby hit .306 with 25 homers and 78 RBI. His average was right where it usually was but his power numbers were once again down. Brooks Robinson hit .276 with 18 homers and 94 RBI.

One scary moment occurred early in the season when Blair was beaned by a sidearm fastball from the Angels' Ken Tatum in Anaheim. Robby watched from the on-deck circle as Blair went down in a heap, much like he had done earlier in his career when he couldn't get out of the way of fastballs at his head from Ruben Gomez and Camilo Pascual. Blair was out for three weeks. Merv Rettenmund, getting a chance to play, appeared in more than 100 games and hit .322.

Once again, the pitching was solid. Cuellar was 24–8, McNally was 24–9 and Palmer was 20–10 to lead the dominant starting pitching. The Orioles also got Moe Drabowsky back in mid-season. He had gone to Kansas City the year before in the expansion draft but was back now to go along with Hall, Watt and Pete Richert in the bullpen. Richert, a starter most of his career with several ballclubs who once struck out four batters in an inning, led the Orioles in saves with 13.

For the second straight year, the Birds played the Minnesota Twins in the League Championship Series and disposed of them once again in a three-game sweep. Cuellar, McNally and Palmer were the winning pitchers, with Cuellar hitting a grand slam home run to help his own cause in the opener. The Orioles would have loved to have another crack at the Mets in the World Series, but it wasn't to be. New York finished third in its division, won by the Cincinnati Reds, who then swept the Pittsburgh Pirates in their League Championship Series.

That meant Robinson would be facing his former team in the World Series, but two of the people closely associated with the ill-fated (for Cincinnati) trade of Robinson in 1965 were long gone. Bill DeWitt sold the Reds at the end of the 1966 season. Milt Pappas, the key acquisition in the deal for Cincinnati, was traded to Atlanta in 1968 and sold to the Chicago Cubs in 1970.[14]

The Reds were loaded with talent—the beginning of what would come to be known as the "Big Red Machine" of the 1970s. Catcher Johnny Bench hit 45 homers and drove in 148 runs to go along with a .293 batting average. Third baseman Tony Perez had 40 homers, 129 RBI and a .317 average. First baseman Lee May hit 34 home runs and had 94 runs batted in, though hitting only .253. Getting on base for the big boppers were Pete Rose, whom Robinson had mentored eight years earlier, and speedster Bobby Tolan, both of whom hit .316.

The pitching staff was led by Jim Merritt, 20–12, who developed arm trouble at the end of the year, Gary Nolan, who went 18–7, Wayne Simpson, who was 14–3, and Don Gullett, a fireballing left-hander. Rose said Gullett was so fast, he could throw a ball through a car wash without it getting wet.

The World Series had some unusual aspects to it. The games at Riverfront Stadium in Cincinnati were the first World Series games played on artificial turf. The Series was the last one played entirely with day games. The Reds jumped out to 3–0 leads in three games—and lost all three. The star of the Series was Robinson—Brooks, not Frank, who hit .429 with two home runs and made numerous spectacular plays in the field. The Orioles won the series in five games. But Frank did all right. He hit two home runs and drove in four runs.

Robby said a play Brooks made in the first game set the tone for the rest of the series. Lee May crushed a ground ball down the third base line that looked like a sure double. Robinson lunged for it and his momentum took him into foul territory. He got the ball and threw it across his body to first base, where Powell scooped it up a fraction before May hit the bag. Frank Robinson said it was one of the best plays he ever saw, considering Brooks was three steps into foul territory and didn't have time to measure his throw—he just did it by instinct.

One of the most unusual plays in World Series history occurred in that same game. With the Reds' Bernie Carbo on third and Tommy Helms on first, pinch-hitter Ty Cline hit a high chopper in front of the plate. Carbo sped for the plate as Elrod Hendricks, the Baltimore catcher, snatched the ball and reached out to tag him.

Home plate umpire Ken Burkhart had moved out and straddled the foul line when the ball was hit to get in position to call it fair or foul. As Carbo slid around Burkhart and Hendricks whirled around to try to tag him, the action took place behind Burkhart, who could not see the errant slide or attempted tag with any clarity. Hendricks tagged Carbo with his glove—but he had the ball in his other hand. Burkhart saw Hendricks tap Carbo with his glove, and called him out. Reds manager Sparky Anderson argued but to no avail. Burkhart had to call something, so he called what he thought he saw.

Casey Stengel, who was attending the Series, was asked later what he thought of the play. He said, "It was a dead heat. Hendricks missed the tag, Carbo missed the plate and Burkhart missed the call."[15]

At baseball's winter meetings, the big buzz was the possibility of the Orioles trading Robinson. On the surface of it, it seemed absurd. But the Orioles were well stocked in outfielders with Robinson, Buford, Blair and Merv Rettenmund, who was a reserve who led the team in hitting with a .322 average. Plus the Orioles had a hot prospect in the minors, Don Baylor who had been hitting the cover off the ball and was ready for the big leagues. Robinson was obviously marketable, and he would be 36 next year.

Yankees manager Ralph Houk was ecstatic at the possibility of landing Robinson. The Yankees had dangled left-handed pitcher Fritz Peterson as possible trade bait. "I'd give anything to have Frank Robinson," he said. "I've never seen him make a mistake. He knows when to run, when not to run. You'd be surprised what the S.O.B. does to beat you—steal a base, get a hit, make a play—and he's a leader."[16]

As so often happens at the winter meetings, the possible deal made for great anticipation and great press but never came about.

After the World Series, Robby returned to Santurce for his third season of managing in the winter leagues. This time he had a prize pupil on his team—Reggie Jackson, a 24-year-old outfielder for the Oakland A's who had great potential but had a penchant for striking out. A's owner Charlie Finley wanted him to go to Puerto Rico to get himself straightened out.

He struck out 14 times in the first week he was there. Then two things happened. He went back to the states and got fitted for eyeglasses, and he returned to be under the guidance of Frank Robinson. Both moves paid off. Jackson hit 20 home runs to help the ballclub to the semi-finals of the Caribbean League championship. There they defeated a San Juan team managed by Roberto Clemente before losing to Licey of the Dominican Republic in the overall championship series.

Robinson worked with Jackson on cutting down on his swing and being selective at the plate. The results were obvious. "He's just not striking out anymore," said Robby. "He's made up his mind just to make contact and with his power, the results have been something else."[17]

Back in the states. the Orioles made one key acquisition in the off-season and it didn't involve Robinson. On December 1, they traded pitchers Tom Phoebus and Fred Beene and two other players to the San Diego Padres for pitcher Pat Dobson and relief pitcher Tom Dukes. The key player in the deal for the Orioles was Dobson, a young pitcher who they expected to pitch better than Phoebus.

Dobson broke in with the Detroit Tigers in 1967 and won 11 games and lost 20 in three seasons with them. He was traded to the San Diego Padres, where he had a 14–15 record on a team that won only 63 and lost 99. At the respective points in their careers, the Orioles saw more potential in Dobson than they did in Phoebus.

As the 1971 season began, the Orioles were a confident bunch, having won 217 games in the past two years, sweeping two League Championship Series and capturing their second World Series championship in the past five years. Sometimes confidence can become overconfidence and trouble can occur.

Billy Southworth, the last manager to have three straight 100-win seasons with the St. Louis Cardinals in the 1940s, always maintained that the second championship is harder to achieve than the first, and the third is hardest of all. You are the toast of the town, he said, and you are told so often how good you are that you begin to think you are invincible.

He said he warned his 1944 Cardinals ballclub about the obstacles they faced after winning in 1942 and 1943. "I tried to impress upon them they were farther out of condition, both mentally and physically, especially mentally, because they had all been invited here and there. They had been put on a pedestal. They had been wined and dined," he said.[18]

The Orioles began the 1971 season sluggishly, compared to recent years, as if they were expecting their reputation to carry them. Boston first baseman George Scott had said in winter ball in 1970 that the Mets proved that the Orioles weren't unbeatable. Now it was as if his Red Sox were out to prove it. Baltimore won seven of its first eight games but then won only five games the rest of April. May was practically a repeat of April and by month's end, the Orioles had a respectable 27–19 record—but respectable was well below expectations. Not only that, they trailed the Red Sox by a game and a half in the standings. Palmer, Cuellar and McNally were carrying the load with 21 of the 27 wins. Dobson was struggling with his new team, having won only two games in the first two months of the season while losing three. Robby, now 35 years old, had just four home runs.

In May, Robby talked to reporters before a ballgame about a belief he had held ever since he got into organized ball—the danger of fraternizing with opposing players. "There's no way you can go barreling into second base and dump a guy, like you should do, when you've been fraternizing with him before the game," said Robby. "How can a pitcher throw a guy tight and move him off the plate if they were out to dinner the night before?"[19]

If there was a turning point in the season, it occurred in a Memorial Day doubleheader with the White Sox. The Orioles lost the first game, 1–0. In the nightcap, Don Buford hit home runs in two of three at-bats off Joel Horlen and Bart Johnson. Buford's next time up, Johnson hit him with a pitch at his head and Buford charged the mound. (Horlen had pegged Buford with a pitch earlier in the game, so Buford's reaction to another beaning seems understandable.) There was no fight, but the incident seemed to wake up the Orioles. They won nine straight, moved into first place in mid–June, and hardly looked back.

Dobson, who had trouble getting on track at the start of the year, made eight starts in July and had eight wins, all complete games. By season's end, the Orioles had won 101 games and had four 20-game winners—McNally 21–5, Dobson 20–8, and Palmer and Cuellar both 20–9. The Orioles were the first club in 51 years to have four 20-game winners and only the second team in all of baseball history to do it. (As of 2013, no team had done it since then.) They were also the first team since Southworth's teams of 1942–1944 to have three consecutive 100-win seasons.[20]

Robinson picked up the pace and had a decent year with 28 homers and 99 runs batted in. Interestingly, just as George Scott of the Red Sox looked at the Orioles' loss to the Mets in 1969 as motivation, so did Robinson, but in a different way. "It was still the '69 series paying a dividend," he said. After that, we didn't take anything for granted. We wanted to come back and win it and win it and win it as often as we could. We had learned a lesson."[21]

On July 13, Robby was one of six future Hall of Famers to homer in the All-Star Game in Detroit, won by the American League, 6–4. The other homers were hit by Henry Aaron, Johnny Bench, Roberto Clemente, Harmon Killebrew and Reggie Jackson. Jackson's homer hit the lights above the upper deck. Robinson became the only player in baseball history to hit a home run for the National League in one All-Star Game and for the American League in another. He was named the Most Valuable Player in the game, making him the only player to be MVP in both leagues and in an All-Star Game.

On July 30, Robinson hit the 493rd home run of his career against the Kansas City Royals, tying him with Lou Gehrig for 11th place on the all-time list. The homer broke up a no-hit bid by the Royals' Dick Drago and was the only run in a 1–0 Orioles victory in a game cut short by rain in the fifth inning.

On September 13, Robby connected in both games of a twi-night doubleheader against the Tigers. His homer in the second game was the 500th of his career. He remained 11th on the all-time list, a distinction he had achieved with his 494th, surpassing Lou Gehrig. His 500th went practically unheralded in the morning papers because he hit it, almost literally in the middle of the night.

Arthur Daley, in his column in the *New York Times* a week later, tried to give Robby his just due. "His timing hardly could have been worse," he wrote. "The homer was struck just before midnight in the ninth inning of the finale of a twilight-night double header and therefore news of it missed most of the morning editions."[22]

Robby had hit number 499 in the first game and admitted that between games, he thought about number 500. When he led off the eighth inning of the second game and flied out, he figured his night at the plate was over. But the Orioles got a couple of base runners in the eighth and ninth, and Robinson got another chance to swing. He said he watched it go—and it wasn't pretty, not one of his best swings—but the ball went out of the park.

It was a big moment, even if most of the nation was asleep, but he told Arthur Daley it wasn't his most memorable homer. That distinction, he said, went to the homer he hit in 1966, after he had just joined the Orioles—the one he hit off Luis Tiant, who had thrown three straight shutouts, the one that went clear out of Memorial Stadium. He got a standing ovation from the crowd. "It meant a lot to me," he said. "I was with a new team in a new league. They seemed to say to me: You are one of us. You have made it."[23]

The Orioles' opponent in the League Championship Series was the Oakland A's, who were a lot like the Orioles of 1968—loaded with young talent and being right on the cusp of being a great team. They had Jackson, of course, Joe Rudi and Sal Bando. Their starting lineup had one player, second baseman Dick Green, who was 30 years old. The rest were 29 or under.

Their pitching staff was led by 21-year-old sensation Vida Blue, who went 24–8 during the regular season. Jim "Catfish" Hunter, age 25, was 21–11. The other two starters were Chuck Dobson, 15–5 age 27, and John "Blue Moon" Odom, who was 26 and was 10–12 on the year. They were young, they were good, they were confident. Nonetheless, Baltimore disposed of them in three games—left them weeping, Robinson said—as Earl Weaver improved his League Championship Series record to 9–0 over the past three seasons.

The next task was to take on the Pittsburgh Pirates in the World Series. The Bucs had a powerful lineup led by Willie Stargell, who hit 48 home runs, and Roberto Clemente, who was Pittsburgh's counterpart to Robby. He could do everything well and he played with intensity. The Pirates had a young pitching staff led by Steve Blass and Nelson Briles along with the "Fireman of the Year" in the bullpen in Dave Giusti.

The first two games were at Memorial Stadium in Baltimore. In the opener, the Orioles rallied from a 3–0 deficit, Robinson homered and McNally pitched well enough to come away with a 5–3 Orioles victory.

In the second game, Baltimore gave Palmer enough run support for him to win easily, 11–3. The victory marked the 16th consecutive win for the Orioles, 11 to end the season, three against Oakland in the playoffs, and now two in a row against the Pirates in the World Series. They seemed unbeatable to everyone except the Pirates.

The scene shifted to Three Rivers Stadium in Pittsburgh for Game Three. The Pirates needed a gem and they got one from Blass, who handcuffed the Orioles on three hits. One of them was Robby's second home run of the Series.

Game Four was the first night game in World Series history. Pirates manager Danny Murtaugh took a chance and started rookie Luke Walker. He gave up singles to the first three batters and walked two others before he was pulled in favor of Bruce Kison. The Orioles had a history of overcoming 3–0 leads in World Series games. In this one, they had a 3–0 lead before the Pirates came to bat—and they couldn't hold it. Kison pitched brilliantly in relief and the Bucs won, 4–3, to tie the Series at two games apiece.

The Pirates won the next one, 4–0, behind the pitching of Briles and had the chance to end the series in six games—including four straight after losing the first two games—when the series returned to Baltimore. But the Orioles prevailed, 3–2, in ten innings behind McNally, prompting a seventh game.

The final game was a classic pitching duel between Cuellar for the Orioles and Blass for the Pirates. Clemente homered off Cuellar, a solo shot, and Pittsburgh managed to get only one more run, but it was enough to win because Blass stymied the Orioles for the second straight time, this time a four-hitter in a 2–1 Pirates victory.

Blass, a largely unheralded hurler outside of Pittsburgh, could easily have been the Series MVP. But that honor went to Clemente, who hit .414 with 12 hits in 29 at-bats, including two doubles, a triple, two home runs and four runs batted in. He also made some spectacular plays in right field.

Writer Roger Angell described it this way: "It was the kind of baseball that none of us had ever seen before—throwing and running and hitting at something close to the level of absolute perfection."[24]

After the World Series, the Orioles went on a long-planned trip to Japan during which they played 18 games and won 16 of them. That prevented Robby from going to Puerto Rico to manage Santurce again in the winter league. Ruben Gomez took his place. While Robinson was playing baseball halfway around the world, he was well aware of the rumors flying around the baseball world back in the states, the same ones that had swirled the previous winter.

Phil Jackman, sports writer for the *Baltimore Sun*, reported on December 11 that the cover of the Orioles yearbook for the past season had action photos of Brooks Robinson, Boog Powell, Mike Cuellar, Dave McNally and Jim Palmer. One person was conspicuously absent from the cover—Frank Robinson.

"An oversight?" asked Jackman, who answered his own question. "Hardly. The Birds went into the interleague trading period, spring training and the start of the 1971 season perfectly willing to make a trade for their leader if the price was right," he wrote.

That was last winter. As for this winter? Jackman wrote, "Chance are if the Oriole yearbook were going to press again tomorrow, once again F. Robinson's visage wouldn't be on the front page."[25]

CHAPTER 11

Another Transition

On December 2, 1971, the Orioles traded Robinson and pitcher Pete Richert to the Los Angeles Dodgers for pitcher Doyle Alexander and three prospects—Bob O'Brien, Sergio Robles and Royle Stillman.

Ballplayers understand that baseball is a business and that trades are a part of that business. They have pride, too, so when two players such as Robinson and Richert are traded for four players, it gives them a sense of their worth to the team to which they are headed—depending on the caliber of the players.

In exchange for Robinson and Richert, the Orioles got Alexander, who was 6–6 as a rookie pitcher; O'Brien, a pitcher who was 2–2 with the Dodgers and who never appeared in another major league game; Robles, a catcher who was to have 18 at-bats in two years with the O's; and Stillman, an outfielder who managed to get 36 at-bats in two years, played another year in Chicago and was out of the big leagues after that.

While the Orioles were playing in Japan, Harry Dalton, the front office man who helped build the Baltimore dynasty, felt motivated to try to do it somewhere else. He took a job as general manager of the Los Angeles Angels, who had been in the league for ten years without making the play-offs. He was replaced by Frank Cashen, the club's executive vice president, and one of Cashen's first moves was to trade Robinson.

Robby knew he was going to be traded. Cashen talked to him about it on the trip to Japan. The Orioles had to make room for Baylor, who had the same potential for stardom as Robinson had in 1956 when the Reds found a place for him on their roster. Robinson told Cashen that if a trade was inevitable, he would prefer to go to a west coast team so he could be close to his home in suburban Los Angeles. Cashen pulled it off.

Many of the Orioles reacted to the Robinson trade as if it were a death in the family. Weaver said he hated it but he also hated to have to tell Baylor to spend another year in the minor leagues when he was ready for the major leagues. He later said if the designated hitter concept, which took effect in 1972 after Robinson was gone, had been adopted a year earlier, Robby would have been the Orioles' DH and he and Baylor would have been in the same lineup.

Paul Blair said the trading of Robinson made no sense. "Why would you send this man out?" he asked. "He was the center of our ball club. When we needed a big hit or run, Frank got it for us. There was just no reason to trade him."[1]

In Los Angeles. Robby was considered by many teammates as a "quiet leader," which amused him when he heard about it because he said he didn't have a reputation for being too quiet.

In fact, when he arrived, he immediately had a disagreement with Dodgers general manager Al Campanis, who greeted him by giving him a book called *The Dodger Way to Play Baseball* and told him he wasn't going to get a pay raise. Robinson was shocked. He felt that after playing 16 years in the major leagues, winning MVP awards in both leagues as well as in the All-Star Game and in World Series competition, it was more than a little insulting for his new general manager to offer him a book on how to play baseball.

More insulting to Robinson was getting no pay raise. Campanis knew what he was making with the Orioles. His $135,000 salary was hardly a secret. Robby thought it was customary, as it is in the ordinary working world, that if a man takes a new job, the new employer pays him more than he had been making at the old one.

But Campanis didn't budge. Robinson left his office fuming but had a commitment to appear on a television show called *Sports Challenge* in which athletes competed against one another in a sports trivia contest. Two of the other contestants on the show were Jim Kiick and Larry Csonka, running backs for the Miami Dolphins football team. With them was their agent, Ed Keating.

Robby struck up a conversation with Keating and told him about his discussions with Campanis. Keating offered to negotiate for Robinson for five percent of any increase he could get for Robby. Robinson signed on, Keating went to meet with Campanis and came away with a $17,000 pay raise for him.

Dodgers teammates picked up right away on Robinson's leadership skills. "He gets the big hit when we need it," said Bill Buckner. "When there's a man on third and one out, you know the run will score," he said. Wes

Parker said, "He's a definite leader. He's helped to bring this team together just by being here."[2]

On May 23, in a game against the Giants, Robinson hit two home runs but was forced to leave the game when he crashed into the right field wall making a catch. His new manager, Walter Alston, said after the game, "Robby showed what he means to us. He has an intense competitive spirit."[3]

Robinson, who now had several years' experience of managing winter ball and who had the desire to be a big league manager some day, had long been an observer of managers. He knew how Birdie Tebbetts mentored young players like himself, how Fred Hutchinson liked to scare you into playing up to your ability, how Hank Bauer liked a set lineup with few changes, and how Earl Weaver was always making changes as he thought three innings ahead.

So Robby was excited to be playing on a team managed by the legendary Walter Alston, who had signed one-year contracts with the Dodgers every year since 1954 and was one of the most respected managers in the game.

Alston's major league playing career consisted of one at-bat with the St. Louis Cardinals in 1936 in which he made an out. But he excelled as a manager, winning the pennant and the World Series with the Brooklyn Dodgers in 1955, his second year at the helm; winning the National League flag again in 1956; and winning the pennant and the World Series with the transplanted Los Angeles Dodgers in 1959, 1963, and 1965. His 1966 Dodgers club also made it to the World Series but lost to Robinson's Orioles.

So Robby was excited to be playing for a legend, but his excitement soon turned to disappointment. He had always heard that the Dodgers were sticklers for executing the fundamentals—the type of baseball that was probably espoused in the book Campanis tried to get Robby to read. Bunt, hit behind the runner, run everything out, slide hard, hit the cutoff man, play the hitters properly in the field—and practice, practice, practice. That's what he expected.

In spring training with the Orioles, Earl Weaver used to get out on the field and demonstrate exactly how he wanted things done. Then his players would keep at it until Weaver was satisfied. One drill could take an hour or two.

Not so with the Dodgers. Robinson said one day in spring training, Alston told the outfielders he wanted them to practice hitting the cutoff man. So all the outfielders trotted out on the field for the drill. It lasted 15 minutes, said Robby, and it was the only time all spring they practiced hitting the cutoff man.

The Dodgers had fleet-footed Willie Davis in center field. He had a good glove, his three-error performance against the Orioles in the 1966 World Series notwithstanding. And he could really run. Not many balls got by him. But he was lax on fundamentals. Robinson noticed that right away but of course said nothing. That was the job of the manager and coaches. Time and again in spring training and during the season when there was a man on base, Davis would scamper after a ball and come up throwing, consistently missing the cutoff man. It happened all year, said Robby. In one game, Alston shook his head and said, "What's wrong with Willie?" and one of his coaches said, "Why does he keep doing that?" But nobody ever talked to him about it, said Robby.

Robinson saw many instances where the Dodgers failed to execute routine plays, ones that should have been drilled into them in spring training and for which they should have been chewed out or benched for failing to execute.

Robinson's assessment of Alston was similar to what he thought of Mayo Smith years earlier during Smith's brief tenure with the Reds. "Walter Alston didn't do much of anything as a manager beyond making out the lineup card," said Robby. "He had two favorite moves, and he made them every chance he had—sending Manny Mota up to pinch-hit and bringing Jim Brewer in from the bullpen."[4]

Robinson's frustration with Alston making out the lineup card may have been because Robby's name wasn't on that card often enough to suit him. He appeared in just 103 games and hit .251 with 19 home runs and 59 runs batted in. Part of the reason for that was injuries early in the season that limited his playing time. But in the second half, when he was healthy, Alston used him sparingly.

The Dodgers hoped Robinson would do for them what he had done for the Orioles—provide enough pop to bring them a championship. But LA finished third in a strike-shortened season. Campanis determined that with Robinson, at age 37, the law of diminishing returns was probably setting in. On November 29, 1973, the Dodgers traded him cross-town to the Los Angeles Angels, reuniting him with Harry Dalton, his GM in Baltimore during the glory years.

"The important thing about playing for Dalton," said Robinson, "is that he knows what I can do and what I can't do. I don't have to prove myself to him."[5]

Robby said things just didn't work out in his one year with the Dodgers and he wasn't looking forward to another year with them—another reason he was okay be close to home. "I couldn't have gone through another year," he said. "I'm not the type to sit around. If it hadn't been for the trade, I would have sought my release or pushed for a trade."[6]

The Dodgers traded Robinson along with Bill Singer, Bobby Valentine, Bill Grabarkewitz and Mike Strahler to the Angels. In return, the Angels sent pitcher Andy Messersmith and Ken McMullen, a veteran infielder, to the Dodgers.

Robby returned to Puerto Rico in the winter after his one-year hiatus from managing Santurce because of the trip to Japan with the Orioles. When he returned, he went to spring training with his third team in the last three years. He had at least one old friend on the team. Vada Pinson, his constant companion when he and Robinson were teammates in Cincinnati, was now with the Angels.

Given the chance to play regularly, Robinson showed he still had some zing in his bat. Though his average dropped to .266, he hit 30 home runs and drove in 97 runs, leading the Angels in both categories. On July 1, his homer was the only hit off of the Twins' Jim Kaat in a 2–1 loss to Minnesota. It was the second time in his career that he homered to prevent a no-hitter, the other coming on July 30, 1971, against Dick Drago of Kansas City. On September 19, 1973, when he hit one out of the park against the Texas Rangers in Arlington, it marked the 32nd big league ballpark in which he had hit a home run, a major league record.

Though he was producing on the field, circumstances in the dugout and clubhouse created turmoil on the ballclub. Robby, carrying a salary of more than $150,000 with well-publicized aspirations of becoming a manager some day, arrived on the Angels at about the same time as they promoted one of their coaches, Bobby Winkles, to be the manager at $28,000 a year.

Winkles played eight years of minor league ball before turning to coaching in the college ranks. He was the head coach of the Arizona State Sun Devils from 1959 to 1971. His ballclubs won the College World Series championships in 1965, 1967 and 1969. Sun Devils players who made it to the major leagues included Reggie Jackson, Risk Monday and Sal Bando.

Angels owner Gene Autry hoped to bring Winkles' winning spirit to the Angels when he hired him as a coach in 1972. In 1973, he took over as manager. He brought with him his college coaching philosophy and techniques, and Robinson said it was different but it wasn't all bad.

"Bobby Winkles had a lot of new ideas that he introduced in spring training," said Robinson. "One that proved to be very beneficial to all of us resulted in the Angels not having a muscle pull all season, which was virtually unheard of in baseball," he said. His method was to have players do daily calisthenics—not the jumping jack calisthenics more suitable for gym classes, but muscle stretching exercises where one player would slowly apply pressure to another player's outstretched leg. Robby said he had never been able to do the exercise of reaching forward from the ground and touching his toes but he was able to do it after one week of Winkles' calisthenics.[7]

It is hard to pinpoint exactly when the relationship between Winkles and Robinson fell apart, but when it did, it affected the entire team. When Robinson joined the Angels, he was encouraged to be a mentor to the younger players on the team who could benefit from his experience. That situation started to deteriorate late in the 1973 season when the Angels were struggling. Winkles began to think that Robinson's mentoring had led to circumstances in which players unhappy with Winkles were coming to Robby not just for advice but for sympathy and support.

Perhaps the differences could have been worked out if the Angels were winning consistently and contending for first place. That was their purpose in acquiring Robinson. But his supporting cast was weak. Bob Oliver hit 18 homers and drove in 89 runs. No other Angel drove in more than 57.

The Angels had two reliable starting pitchers in Nolan Ryan, 21–16, and Bill Singer, 20–14, but couldn't count on any other starter. Clyde Wright was 11–19 and Rudy May was 7–17. So even with two 20-game winners, the Angels' starting rotation had an overall record of 59–66. The Angels finished fourth in their division with a 79–83 record.

By 1974, the friction between Robinson and Winkles escalated and became part of the media's coverage of the Angels. The *Los Angeles Times* reported in July of 1974, "Bitterness between the veteran outfielder and second-year

Angels manager Bobby Winkles and Frank Robinson didn't get along, and their differences led to Winkles being fired (author's collection).

manager developed late last year, leading Winkles to demand last winter that Robinson be traded and Robinson telling Dalton he would play only one more season for the Angels."[8]

Winkles said he tried to talk with Robby to work things out, and he held several clubhouse meetings with the team to try to curtail dissention that was building. It didn't help when Robinson was quoted in the press as saying, "Damn it, I'll do it my way."[9]

As columnist Dick Young pointed out in the *New York Daily News,* "What Frank Robinson fails to realize here is that Bobby Winkles is his boss. When a difference of opinion occurs between boss and employee, we must defer to the boss. That's what the word boss means. He has the final say."

Young also mentioned Robby's well-known aspirations of being a manager and noted that if he were to succeed, he would have to learn that the club owner is the boss and learn to live with it.[10]

Early in the 1973 season, Winkles and Robinson would often confer in the dugout and discuss strategy, how to pitch to certain hitters, how to position outfielders against certain hitters and that sort of thing. By the end of the season, they were hardly speaking and often sat at opposite ends of the dugout. Other players would gravitate to one end of the dugout or the other, magnifying the problem.

Nolan Ryan, who was then a young pitcher on the ballclub, wrote about the rift in a book he co-authored, and he was not sympathetic to Robby. "Robinson tried to manage the Angels while he was playing with them and he was a disruptive factor on the team. You were either Robby's player or you were Bobby's," said Ryan.[11]

Robinson's explanation: "I tried to show my teammates how to win, show the younger players what it takes to win, how you had to do that little extra, give yourself up for the team. But when players have never won, it's very difficult."

Robby liked to needle players, to get under their skin a little bit, to motivate them, a carryover perhaps from the kangaroo court that had been so successful in Baltimore. Winkles didn't like him getting on the other players; he was more of a "rah-rah" kind of leader, that had served him so well at Arizona State. He also told Robby to quit getting on the umpires so much.[12]

On June 28, 1974, Winkles was fired. Third base coach Whitey Herzog managed the team for four games. Then Dick Williams, who had managed the Boston Red Sox American League champions of 1967 and the Oakland

A's championship teams of 1972 and 1973, took over. Robinson was never under consideration for the job. Dalton, well aware of the tension on the team, had tried to trade Robby to the Yankees earlier in the year, but the deal fell through.

In reacting to being let go, Winkles told the press he was fired because he couldn't handle Frank Robinson. Robby said Winkles was fired because he couldn't handle major league ballplayers.

One of Williams' first actions as the new manager was to name Robinson the captain of the team. The Angels had never had a captain. It was a good move by Williams because it not only gave Robby the respect he thought he deserved but also demonstrated to the rest of the team the harmonious relationship the manager wanted to cultivate with his star player.

Nolan Ryan, a young pitcher for the Angels when Frank Robinson came over in a trade, said Robinson caused dissent because players often sought him out instead of manager Bobby Winkles when they wanted advice (author's collection).

Williams told the press that Robby had unwittingly helped him win championships in Oakland by working with Reggie Jackson on his hitting when Jackson played winter ball for Robinson in Puerto Rico. Jackson came back a better hitter, and the A's won five straight division championships and three straight World Series championships.

"I'm glad Dick has this much faith in me," said Robinson. "Now I can give advice to someone without thinking: Am I doing the right thing?"[13]

Good intentions prevailed but the talent wasn't there and the spirit had been drained out of the ballclub with all of the friction that had developed over the past two years. "There was little Robinson or Williams could do to stop the Angels' tailspin. The season's pattern had been set. Too many players had stopped caring. Too many had been injured. There was no relief—either in the bullpen or the farm system."[14]

The Angels had been plodding along with a 30–44 record when Winkles was fired. Herzog won two and lost two in his brief interim period. Williams came aboard with a great track record and high hopes, but the Angels lost ten in a row from the time he took over—the longest losing streak he had ever experienced as a manager. By the time he got his first win, California was 32–56, in last place, 17½ games behind first-place Oakland and eight games behind fifth-place Minnesota.

It didn't take long for Robinson to have problems with his new manager. When Williams named Robinson as team captain, it was with the understanding that he would be paid a $500 bonus. Williams said if the club wouldn't pay it, he would. When Robby approached Dalton about it, Dalton told him the club had never had a team captain and was certainly not going to pay for one.

Robinson went to Williams, explained the situation to him, and reminded him that he had agreed to pay the $500 if the club didn't. Williams denied ever making that agreement. So Robinson found himself stuck on a last-place team with players who were hard to motivate and with a manager he didn't trust.

He talked it over with his wife. He was not ready to retire, but if the Angels released him or put him on waivers, he would sign with any team that agreed to give him a contract for 1975. When California put him on waivers, the Orioles claimed him but only wanted him for the stretch drive of the pennant race. They did not intend to sign him to a new contract, so Robby nixed the deal.

On September 12, the Angels traded him to the Cleveland Indians for catcher Ken Suarez and outfielder Rusty Torres. The Indians gave him a raise and agreed to give him a contract for 1975. At age 39, this figured to be his last stop. But it had vestiges of his first stop, for the Indians general manager was Phil Seghi, who had been assistant general manager at Cincinnati when Robby played there.

Robby got there in time to appear in 15 games. He got to the plate 61 times, hit two home runs and drove in five runs. He had only eight other hits and his batting average was .200. He was there long enough to see that the Indians were a team with some large egos and small expectations. Gaylord Perry, their ace pitcher, accounted for about one-fourth of their total victories.

Ken Aspromonte was in his third year as Indians manager. He was a former major league infielder who played for six teams in seven years before getting into coaching and managing. His record in Cleveland was fairly consistent but the ballclub was never in contention past the first couple of months of the season. His 1972 team was 72–84, finishing fifth. In 1973, the Tribe slipped to 71–91, a sixth-place finish. In 1974, they were headed to a 77–85 record for fourth place, Aspromonte's best year. But in late September, he called a team meeting and announced he had resigned, effective at the end of the season.

When Robinson was obtained by the Indians, there was the suspicion among many in the press and throughout baseball that he would be the next Indians manager, the same type of talk that was generated when he was traded to the Angels. Seghi denied it, saying he was interested in Robinson's bat being in the lineup. But Robinson had been saying for years he wanted to be a manager someday, and had spent his winters in Puerto Rico training for it. Aspromonte had lost the respect of some of his players. Outfielder George Hendrick left the ballpark on the last day of the season and went home, even though Aspromonte had penciled him in the starting lineup. Asked who would start in place of Hendrick, Aspromonte replied, "I don't know. Ask No. 20 [Robinson]."

Robinson also denied any pre-arranged deal to elevate him to be the manager. "As far as I know, I was brought to Cleveland as a player, period," he said. "On the first day, I went to Aspromonte and told him I was glad to be there and would help him any way I could. He seemed fine. Then, the next thing I knew, Gaylord went off in the papers and Aspromonte quit. It was as if the Bronx Zoo had moved to Cleveland."[15]

Gaylord was Gaylord Perry, the veteran pitcher, future Hall of Famer, and Southerner. All of those factors may have contributed to him being upset at the money the Indians had been reported to have given Robinson. He told reporters he wanted to be paid at least one dollar more than Frank Robinson. Robby read it and confronted Perry in the locker room before the next game. He told him he could say whatever he wanted to say in negotiations with the Indians but not to drag Robby's name into it in the press. By all accounts, it was an ugly scene with Aspromonte coming out of his office to step between the two men.[16]

While there was growing sentiment in some quarters that the time had come for major league baseball to have a black manager, a view shared publicly by Commissioner Bowie Kuhn, the feeling was not universal.

A former major league infielder, Bill Werber, who was once a teammate of Babe Ruth's and played in the era in which blacks were excluded for the big league, took exception to Kuhn's views. In an open letter to Kuhn, published in the *New York Times* on September 8, four days before the Indians acquired Robinson, Werber wrote, "Inasmuch as you distinguish players by race, will not the Jews ask for representation on the management level? What do you propose to say if the Italians demand an Italian manager and the Puerto Ricans demand a Puerto Rican manager?"[17]

Werber pointed out Hank Aaron expressed interest in someday managing the Atlanta Braves and questioned whether his race was enough of a qualification. "How well does Aaron read and write and how lucid is he in expressing himself?" asked Werber.[18]

Then he zeroed in on Robby.

"Frank Robinson is yet another black whose name is sometimes mentioned as managerial material. Do you recall his arrest and conviction in Cincinnati some ten years back for assault with a deadly weapon in a beer dive late at night?[19]

"Are you of the opinion that a black who carries a knife or a gun and threatens to use it is qualified to manage? If you had a choice to make between Frank Robinson and Bobby Richardson to manage your ballclub, would you choose Robinson because he is black?"[20]

A smiling Frank Robinson talks with the press shortly after being named the first black manager in Major League baseball, on October 3, 1974 (National Baseball Hall of Fame and Library, Cooperstown, New York).

Werber, in his obvious disdain for Robinson, greatly exaggerated the incident with the gun. Robby's arrest was for having no gun permit, not assault with a deadly weapon, and the altercation occurred at a hamburger stand, not a "beer joint"—factual errors that the newspaper did not acknowledge or correct.

It published Kuhn's response on the same page as Werber's letter appeared. It said, in part, "I have never suggested that being black by itself was enough of a qualification. A black manager would obviously have to be as qualified as any other manager. I am satisfied there are qualified men available and it is only simple justice for baseball to recognize that fact."[21]

And so it was, in this environment of a mediocre ballclub, disharmony in the clubhouse and a society not entirely enthusiastic about breaking the color line in baseball management, that on October 3, 1974, Frank Robinson was named as new manager of the Cleveland Indians.

CHAPTER 12

Cleveland

Cleveland was a city with a rich industrial history and a proud sports legacy, a community that was not immune to racial unrest that gripped much of the country in the 1950s and 1960s. It is the city in which the Sherwin Williams paint company was founded in 1866. John D. Rockefeller began to make his fortune there with the start-up of his Standard Oil Company in 1870. In 1933, two Cleveland men, Jerry Siegel and Joe Schuster, put their creative heads together and came up with the Superman comic book.

The city had its share of firsts in sports and politics, and broke racial barriers in both areas. In 1936, Jesse Owens, a black man from Cleveland, went to Berlin and won four gold medals in the Olympic Games. In 1947, Larry Doby became the first black baseball player in the American League when he played for the Cleveland Indians. Jim Brown, another black athlete, was an outstanding running back for the Cleveland Browns in the National Football League in the 1950s and 1960s. In 1967, Carl Stokes became the first black person to be mayor of a major American city when the citizens of Cleveland elected him as their mayor. And now Frank Robinson was to add to that legacy, becoming the manager of the Cleveland Indians in 1975.

Robinson was proud to be the first black manager in baseball but he was hoping in time that he would be evaluated and respected as a manager and that "black" would not always be attached to his position as if part of the title.

The press conference announcing his hiring was the first example of the pedestal on which he was being placed. Managerial changes had been a part of baseball ever since the sport was organized a century earlier, and most transitions had been made without much fanfare. In Cleveland, on October 3, Indians general manager Phil Seghi announced Robinson's appointment while Commissioner Bowie Kuhn and other baseball officials looked on.

Robby received something no other new manager ever received—a telegram from the president of the United States. President Gerald Ford congratulated him, saying his hiring was "welcome news" and was a tribute to Robinson "personally, to your athletic skills and your unsurpassed leadership."[1]

Robinson said he appreciated all the attention he was getting and the good wishes of so many people all over the country, but he hoped ultimately to be judged by the way his team performed and not by the color of his skin.

The press acknowledged the accolades he had received but also mentioned the challenges he faced. The Associated Press put it this way:

> "The elevation of Robinson ended a years-long struggle by blacks to be elevated to a meaningful management position in baseball. It places Robinson in charge of a team which has a top white pitcher who has publicly criticized him and a black centerfielder who has been accused of being hard to handle."[2]

In addition to its main story, the *Cleveland Plain Dealer* published eight related stories in the same edition as the announcement. In one of them, columnist Hal Lebovitz wrote, "He will be the first black manager at the start of the season—perhaps the first half—but after that, he'll no longer be unique. He'll be Frank Robinson the manager. And he'll rise or fall, not on the color of his skin but on his ability or lack of it."[3]

Robby was a hot commodity on the luncheon and banquet circuit. He told a group of boosters in Youngstown in January that his starting pitchers would include the two Perry brothers, Gaylord and Jim, and Fritz Peterson would also be part of the rotation. The other slots were still open. Charlie Spikes and George Hendricks, the "hard to handle" center fielder, would fill two of the outfield positions, with left field up for grabs. Buddy Bell, son of Gus Bell, Robby's old teammate with the Reds, would be the third baseman, Frank Duffy would start at short, Jack Brohamer would be at second, and there could be a revolving door at first involving catchers Dave Duncan and John Ellis, both of whom had experience at first base, and Robinson himself from time to time.

That scenario changed on February 25 when the Indians traded Duncan to the Baltimore Orioles for Robby's old teammate, first baseman Boog Powell. The trade gave the Indians a left-handed power hitter in the lineup, provided a left-handed designated hitter to go along with right-handed DH Rico Carty, and gave Ellis free rein to be the number one catcher. Robby also intended to use himself from time to time as a first baseman or designated hitter.

In the Youngstown interview, Robinson also talked about his expectations of the club as a whole and of the individual players. He said he thought the Indians could surprise a lot of people but it was important for them to get off to a good start. "I intend to be honest with the players and I expect the same of them," he said. "I will stress fundamentals in the spring," he said. "This is one place all major league clubs are weak."[4]

He revealed some of his managerial philosophy in an article he wrote for *Guideposts* magazine. "I want my players to know I care about them as people," he wrote. "And people who care about one another support one another. They work, hope and dream together. The Bible says love is kind and patient, full of hope and trust. If you believe that, then Birdie was a guy who really loved his players."[5]

On February 27, pitchers and catchers reported for spring training in Tucson, Arizona, and sports writers from all over the country were there to report on the Indians' new manager. He held a meeting with players in which he told them there would be no curfew in spring training but he expected everyone to be back at the hotel by 2 a.m. He told reporters that Gaylord Perry would be his Opening Day pitcher April 8 in Cleveland against the Yankees and thought Doc Medich, rather than New York ace Jim "Catfish" Hunter, would start for New York. The reason: Robby believed the Yankees would save Hunter for their home opener a few days later.

Robinson took some swings in the batting cage that first day and also did some running in the outfield. "It's the first time I ever saw a manager sweat," said pitcher Fritz Peterson.[6]

He and Gaylord Perry met early on and agreed to put their clubhouse dispute of the year before behind them. But it wasn't long before another flare-up occurred. Robby had running drills he wanted all his pitchers to do and, when called in to pitch during a game, he wanted them to run in, and to run off, when they were removed from the game.

Perry told Robby he had his own running drill that he wanted to continue, but Robinson said it was important for team unity that everyone followed the same rules. Perry complied reluctantly. Then, in an exhibition game, Perry strolled in when he was called on to pitch and strolled off when he was removed. He and Robinson had another confrontation after the game in which Robby told him he didn't like his attitude. Perry said he had won 21 games last year and he'd win 20 this year. "No individual is bigger than the ballclub," said Robinson. "Everybody will be treated the same."[7]

When Robinson joined the Indians in September of 1974, he noticed an obvious division among the players in the dugout. The white players and coaches sat at one end of the dugout near Aspromonte. The black players and coaches sat at the other end, where coach Larry Doby sat. Robinson always sat in the middle. He thought the separation of the players represented a lack of loyalty to the manager and that Doby wasn't doing anything to correct it.

When Robinson was hired, he decided to pick his own coaches, so all of Aspromonte's coaches, including Doby, were let go. Doby was part of Cleveland's baseball history, being the American League's first black player in 1947 and playing for the Indians in their last two World Series appearances, in 1948 and 1954. He probably considered himself managerial material and, a few years later, managed the Chicago White Sox for a short time.

Robinson was aware of his legacy but did not want him on his coaching staff. "When it came time to name my coaches, I wanted coaches who backed the manager, and I didn't see Doby do that with Aspromonte," said Robinson.[8]

An incident occurred in spring training that might have been a tip-off to some of the bizarre events that would occur in the upcoming season. On a close play at the plate, catcher Ellis swung around but missed the sliding base runner. As the runner trotted to the dugout, Robby and others on the Cleveland bench yelled at Ellis that the runner missed the plate.

Robinson said Ellis had a peculiar quality in that he knew players by their uniform numbers but didn't remember their faces too well. So he went to opponents' dugout and began tagging everyone on the bench. The guilty party finally got up and started to run toward home plate. By this time, the Cleveland pitcher was at home plate. Ellis threw him the ball, and a rundown began between the dugout and the plate in which the runner was eventually tagged out.

Robinson said it was probably a baseball "first" and the runner was probably out anyway for being out of the baseline, but it made for some spring training merriment. Afterward, Robby asked coach Jeff Torborg, "Do you think John Ellis heard my speech about playing smart baseball this year?"[9]

On Opening Day, 56,204 spectators packed Cleveland Stadium, including Robby's wife and two children and Rachel Robinson, widow of Jackie Robinson. General manager Seghi and team owner Ted Bonda had to be thrilled with the attendance and the excitement of the day. Seghi, who liked to orchestrate events and envision great things, told Robby before the game, "Hit a home run in your first at-bat." Robby had correctly predicted that Doc Medich would be the Yankees starter.

Robinson and Cleveland general manager Phil Seghi share a laugh as they examine Robby's bat in this publicity photograph. Seghi kiddingly asked Robinson to hit a home run in his first at-bat as player-manager—and he did (National Baseball Hall of Fame and Library, Cooperstown, New York).

Perry set the Yankees down in the top of the first. After Oscar Gamble popped out for the Indians in the bottom of the first, Robinson, the designated hitter, came to the plate to thunderous applause. Photographers had been allowed on the field and they had their cameras poised between the dugouts and on-deck circles.

Medich quickly got two strikes by Robby, and he fouled off the next pitch. Medich, pitching carefully, missed on the next two pitches. Trying to get a third strike past him on the outside corner, Medich threw a fastball low and away. Robby turned on it and hit the ball into the left field seats. It was truly a magical moment, one that could not have been predicted— although general manager Seghi had come close. Gaylord Perry was the first one out of the dugout to greet Robby after he crossed the plate. The Indians went on to win the game, 5–3.

The game story was the top story on page one of the *Cleveland Plain*

Dealer the next day. "Only Jackie Robinson would have been happier—and prouder—than Frank Robinson yesterday," wrote Russell Schneider. "It was the kind of debut that even Hollywood wouldn't dare manufacture."[10]

These were eventful times for a mediocre baseball team, but not everyone was thrilled with what was happening. Robinson received racist hate mail on a regular basis that included threats against his life. Twenty-eight years after Jackie Robinson broke the color line in baseball, Frank Robinson was experiencing the same type of taunts.

Robby hoped the Indians would get off to a fast start, but it was not to be. They were 7–8 in April and Robinson continued to have problems in trying to get along with Gaylord Perry, his best pitcher. Both men were superstars, stubborn and used to having things pretty much their own way. Gaylord's oldest brother, Jim, was also on the team, and he too didn't see eye to eye with his manager.

The Perry brothers grew up in North Carolina, sons of a tenant farmer, and they learned the meaning of hard work and being tough at an early age. Before they were teenagers, both had learned to plow a field with a mule. But both excelled in sports and their father encouraged them to play as much as they could when their chores were done.

They were three-sport athletes in high school. Gaylord was an all-state football player and averaged 30 points a game in his high school basketball career. But for both brothers, baseball was the sport they loved the most, and each was a star pitcher.

Jim signed with the Cleveland Indians and Gaylord hoped to do the same. But the Indians didn't show as much interest as the San Francisco Giants. He pitched for the Giants for ten years and in 1971 was traded with infielder Frank Duffy to the Indians for pitcher Sam McDowell. In his first three years with Cleveland, he won 24, 19 and 21 games.

Jim broke in with Cleveland and pitched four years with the Indians, but is best remembered for ten years he spent with the Minnesota Twins, helping them to the World Series in 1965. After spending a year with Detroit, he came back to the Indians, where he and his brother became a tandem for the first time since their high school years.

On April 18, just ten days after the hoopla of Opening Day, Jim Perry was pitching a good game, losing 1–0 to the Milwaukee Brewers after eight innings. With the bases loaded in the Brewers ninth, Robby sent pitching coach Harvey Haddix out to remove Perry and bring in a relief pitcher. Perry demonstrably kicked the dirt on the pitching mound as he was removed.

In the locker room after the game, Robinson told Haddix to have Perry see him in his office. Robby waited about ten minutes and then decided to wait until the next day to talk with Perry—time for the manager to cool down. The next morning, he discovered what kept Perry from seeing him the night before. Perry had been criticizing Robinson to sports writers who published his comments in the morning papers.

As Robby had demonstrated throughout his career, he did not tolerate being disrespected. On May 20, Jim Perry, sporting a 1–6 record, was traded to the Oakland A's for pitcher John "Blue Moon" Odom. Gaylord Perry's reaction: "I'm next."[11]

On May 17, Robinson had his first serious run-in as manager with an umpire. In a game in Chicago in which the Indians were down 8–0 in the sixth inning, Jorge Orta hit a triple off the right field wall, driving in two more runs. Robinson claimed a fan touched the ball in play and that Orta should be awarded a ground-rule double. First base umpire Jerry Neudecker disagreed, and in the ensuing argument, Robby pushed Neudecker. For that action, American League president Lee MacPhail suspended Robby for three games. The honeymoon for the new manager was definitely over.

Robinson said he anticipated having problems from time to time with umpires and having to deal with the press on a daily basis. What he hadn't anticipated was the issues with individual ballplayers. He had worked for some tough, gruff managers over the years, such as Fred Hutchinson in Cincinnati and Earl Weaver in Baltimore, who often were dictatorial. But players treated them with respect and understood they were the boss.

In describing how a manager should be, he liked to tell the story about his first manager, Birdie Tebbetts, who removed him from a game for a pinch-hitter in his rookie year. Robby came back to the dugout and slammed his bat down in disgust. Tebbetts walked over to him and quietly asked him if he was mad because Tebbetts had taken him out of the game. No, said Robby, he was mad because he was removed because he wasn't hitting very well. "Good," said Tebbetts, "because I just wanted you to know who's managing this team." That was a message that stuck with Robinson for 20 years and one that he wished some of his players understood.[12]

Odom, acquired from the A's to work in long relief, wanted to be a starter and was unhappy from the time he arrived in Cleveland. On June 4, Robby needed Odom to start a game. Odom's reaction was a reflection of his attitude. He asked, if he did well, would that hurt his chances of being traded. Odom threw a two-hit shutout. Three days later he was traded to Atlanta for Roric Harrison.

On June 13, Gaylord Perry's prediction came true. He was traded to Texas for three pitchers—Jim Bibby, Jackie Brown and Rick Waits.

In an effort to try to create some unity and keep the players focused on fundamental baseball—and yet have a little fun with it—Robby decided to institute a kangaroo court like the one he oversaw in Baltimore in which players were held accountable for what their teammates thought were miscues. Oscar Gamble was voted in as judge. But to Robinson's dismay, players were being found guilty and being fined for having ugly girlfriends and things of that nature—far removed from focusing on baseball. The atmosphere in Cleveland, where losing was a way of life, was totally different from the winning attitude Robby had experienced and contributed to in Baltimore.

Another player whom Robinson had problems with was catcher John Ellis. He had been Gaylord Perry's catcher and sided with the pitcher in his disputes with Robinson. He also lacked the attention to detail that Robby demanded of his players. For example, Ellis was fined numerous times for missing signs.

In June, in a game broadcast on national television, Robby sent up a pinch-hitter for Ellis, who reacted by returning to the dugout and throwing some equipment around. Robinson confronted him and they had harsh words for one another, as a national television audience watched. Ellis was soon relegated to the role of backup catcher and was traded away in the off-season.

The season full of oddities continued in July. On July 11, general manager Seghi told reporters in Cleveland that umpires were being unfair to Robinson and holding him to a tougher standard than other managers. On the same day, Robby, in Oakland with the ballclub, didn't help his cause any when he told the press his assessment of individual American League umpires. He rated as "not bad" Larry Barnett, Nestor Chylak, Bill Deegan, Don Denkinger, Jim Evans, Richard Garcia, and Bill Kunkel. He said Jim McKean and Dave Phillips were good umpires but were in bad crews, and Marty Springstead could be good but that his temper got the best of him.[13]

Assessing umpires publicly was not a great public relations move on the part of Robby, particularly on a day when his general manager was defending him, but it was just another example of Robinson's intensity, his compulsion to do things his way, and his lifelong propensity of crowding the plate in most everything he did.

On the field, as his team continued to flounder, Robinson decided to go with a youth movement and give some of the youngsters the opportunity to see what they could do. It paid off so well that Robby said at the end of the year he wished he had done it earlier.

He moved Dennis Eckersley into the starting rotation on May 25 and he shut out Oakland, 6–0. (The losing pitcher was Jim Perry.) Eckersley won his first three starts and had won a game previously in relief. The 20-year-old finished the season with a 13–7 record to lead the staff.

Rick Manning, also age 20, got a shot at playing every day in the out-field and quickly became a fan favorite because of his hustle in the field and on the base paths. Duane Kuiper, age 25, was inserted into the starting lineup at second base. He hit just one home run in his entire career but he was a good contact hitter and hit .292. Rick Waits, who was 23 and thought to be a thrown-in in the deal that brought Jim Bibby to Cleveland, had a better year than Bibby, winning six and losing two with an earned run aver-age of 2.94.

On August 16, the Indians were 52–65 and going nowhere. Propelled by Robby's youth movement, Cleveland went 27–15 the rest of the way to finish at one game below .500—its best record since 1968.

Kuiper, the young second baseman, said Robinson was a stickler for executing the fundamentals and could be cruel and crude in his locker room tirades when the team didn't execute. But Kuiper said he, Eckersley, Manning, and other younger players liked playing for Robinson. "If you tried to break up double plays and hustled, he left you alone," he said. "If you got the bunt sign and laid down a great bunt and moved the runner along, you probably wouldn't get a compliment from Frank. He wasn't going to pat you on the back for doing your job."[14]

On September 23, Indians management rewarded Robinson for the team's second-half surge by signing him to a new one-year contract. At the winter meetings, Cleveland did some wheeling and dealing, trading John Ellis, Jack Brohamer and Oscar Gamble in a series of deals and acquiring pitcher Pat Dobson, Robby's team mate in Baltimore, catcher Ray Fosse, and infielder Larvell Blanks, among others.

Robinson believed Dobson would provide a veteran presence on the pitching staff, Fosse would compete with Alan Ashby for the starting catch-ing job, and Blanks would share time with Duffy at shortstop. As for Robin-son' status, he had shoulder surgery in the off-season and said he didn't expect to play except to pinch-hit and be an occasional designated hitter. But he pointed out the Indians already had a good designated hitter in Rico Carty, a consistent .300 hitter.

"All's Quiet with Frank Robinson" was the headline over Garry Brown's column in a Springfield, Massachusetts, newspaper as the 1976 season got under way. Robby told the writer that the hoopla from 1975 was over with and that he hoped everyone could just focus on baseball. "The second time around is going to be a lot easier for me," he said.[15]

Cleveland played respectably and the kids continued to come through. Eckersley, now 21, won 13 games again and Manning hit .292. Fosse was a pleasant surprise taking over as the number one catcher and hitting .301. Kuiper was rock solid at second base and contributed a .263 batting average. The newly-acquired Dobson won 16 games and Bibby won 13. The Indians finished with an 81–78 record, their first winning season in eight years.

But things were anything but "all quiet" with Robinson. He continued to have bad relationships with some of his players, and in 1976 it got ugly. On April 25, Seghi, Robinson and several players attended a Wahoo Club luncheon, an event sponsored by Indians boosters in which awards are presented. Rico Carty, the hard- hitting designated hitter, received an award as the Indians "player of the year" in 1975. In his acceptance speech, Carty blasted Robinson, who was sitting three feet from him, claiming the Indians desperately needed leadership and they were not getting it from Robby. It was a verbal ambush, a surprise attack, and Robinson was stunned at being publicly humiliated by one of his own ballplayers.

Robinson had had problems with Carty ever since Robby joined the Indians, perhaps because Carty thought the new guy was going to take his designated hitter job away from him. When Carty was in the dugout, Robinson overheard him second-guessing him on some of his managerial moves. But all of that was inside-the-clubhouse stuff. Carty's rebuke at the Wahoo Club was public and intentional. Seghi, who was there, said simply that Carty was entitled to his opinion which Robby didn't think was much of a vote of confidence for him.

Another problem developed when Larvell Blanks, the new infielder, became unhappy with his lack of playing time and found sympathetic comrade in Carty. Blanks was a better hitter than Frank Duffy, but Robinson believed that for every run Blanks drove in, he gave two away with his shoddy fielding at shortstop. He talked to Blanks about the possibility of playing in the outfield, and Blanks was indifferent about it. On one day when Blanks saw his name was not in the starting lineup, he took his equipment out of his locker and threw it in a garbage can. When Robinson talked to him about his attitude before a game, he showed up in the dugout with a piece of tape over his mouth.

Sometimes, Robinson clearly brought on his own problems. On June 30, the Indians played an exhibition game against the Toledo Mud Hens, one of their farm teams. The game was at Toledo. The Mud Hens promoted the game by saying Robinson and Cleveland coach Rocky Colavito would each bat at least once.

Bob Reynolds came into pitch for the Mud Hens in the fourth inning. He was a former major leaguer whom the Indians had picked up on waivers from Detroit but who was cut from the squad at the end of spring training. "Bullet Bob," as he was called because of his fastball, thought Robinson handled his situation poorly.

In the fifth inning, Colavito came to bat and singled. Robinson stepped into the batters' box to the cheers of the crowd. Reynolds' first pitch whistled behind Robby's head. Robinson yelled at him, "You're gutless—if you're going to throw at someone, at least knock him down." Robinson flied out. As he was returning to the dugout, he passed Reynolds and again chided him for throwing at him in an exhibition game. Reynolds reportedly replied, "At least you're talking to me now." Then Robby decked him—some say with one punch, others say with two—but Reynolds went down in a heap. Robinson was ejected from the game. Robinson apologized to the Mud Hens, to the Indians organization, to the people of Toledo and to the fans.

Third base coach Jeff Torborg said several players heard Reynolds say before the game that if he had the chance, he'd bean Robinson. Also, Torborg said he was standing near Robinson and Reynolds just before the fight broke out and heard Reynolds say, "I should take care of you right now."[16]

Not long after that, Joe Tait, the Indians' radio play-by-play announcer, was a substitute host on a sports talk call-in show. When a caller asked Tait if Robinson should remain as the Indians' manager, Tait said, "If I were the GM, Frank wouldn't have been back this year because I don't think he's good for a young team." Tait went on to say he didn't think Robby should be fired in mid-season.

Robinson, of course, was infuriated at being publicly humiliated again. Tait was entitled to his opinion and was not employed by the Indians, but had been approved by Indians management to be their play-by-play radio announcer. When Robby confronted Tait later and asked him why he would say such things, Tait replied, "Because, Frank, I think you're a lousy manager."[17]

Despite all of the bumps in the road, on October 4, Seghi offered and Robinson accepted a contract to manage the Indians for a third year. It was no secret that Seghi was not happy with some of Robby's personnel problems and how he handled them, nor was Robinson satisfied with the lack of support he felt from the front office when things were going tough.

But at the press conference announcing the signing, they both said their past problems were behind them. Seghi said, "There is always a certain amount of give and take between a manager and a general manager. But there has never been a rift between Frank and me, though there are times I question his judgment and I am sure there are times when he questions mine."[18]

The 1977 season started much like Robinson's first two years, with the Indians playing near-.500 ball and in the middle of the pack of the American League East. Before a game in June, Seghi and Bonda met with Robinson in his office, and Seghi asked Robby to bring his coaches in. When they had all gathered, Seghi began criticizing them about things he had noticed while watching the games from his perch near the pressbox. He said the Indians weren't playing good baseball, and among other things, the coaches were telling the players to take bigger leads off of first base.

Seghi had been a minor league manager in the 1950s before he got into front office work, but he never lost the manager mentality, and this was just another example of it, Robby thought. But this time it was different. Even though he was the general manager, he was overstepping his bounds by this obvious display of micromanaging.

Robinson became angry that Seghi was berating his coaches when the responsibility for running the team was Robby's. He and Seghi got into such a hot argument that Bonda felt the need to intervene. After he calmed both men down, he left the office and Seghi followed him. Robby figured Seghi probably staged the argument in front of Bonda and that his days with the Indians were numbered.

On June 18, the Indians won their second straight game from the Detroit Tigers. After the game, Robinson got a call from Seghi that he wanted to see him the next morning in his office. The next day was Sunday and Seghi was never ordinarily in his office on Sunday morning. Robby knew why he was being summoned.

The first black manager ever hired in the major leagues was about to be the first black manager fired. When he got the news officially Sunday morning, Seghi told him there would be a press conference in a few hours and that Jeff Torborg, Robinson's third base coach, would be named as new manager. Robinson told him Torborg was a good choice.

Prior to that day's game, Robby went to the clubhouse to say his good-byes. He congratulated Torborg, shook hands with his players and wished them well. Then he cleared out his office and flew home to Los Angeles, unemployed for the first time in 24 years.

He was experiencing what life is like as a big league manager and the fate that rests with most of them sooner or later. As one pundit said, "There are two kinds of managers—those that have been fired and those that are gonna be."

In 1990, 13 years after Robinson had departed, Tait met up with Carty at an old-timers game in Cleveland. Carty hugged him and said, "Hey, Joe, we got rid of that son of a bitch Robinson, didn't we!"[19]

CHAPTER 13

San Francisco

Frank Robinson was unemployed for exactly 22 days. On July 11, he got a call from Dave Garcia, one of his coaches, who had left the Indians to take a coaching job with Norm Sherry and the California Angels. When Sherry was fired, Garcia was named as his successor, and he invited Robby to be his hitting coach.

His main project was Don Baylor—the same Don Baylor who was the Orioles' hot prospect in 1971 that caused the Baltimore Orioles to trade Robby. Baylor played parts of two seasons and then four full seasons with the Orioles before being traded to the Oakland Athletics. He played one year there and signed as a free agent with California in a multi-year contract for big bucks. But he was in a year-long slump with the Angels.

Robinson looked at some tapes of Baylor at the plate when he was hitting well and compared with the most recent tapes of him. Robby noticed that Baylor had changed the way he held the bat in the batter's box and worked with him to return to his old form. But Robinson told Baylor his biggest problem was that he was trying to live up to the hype of his big salary and told him he just needed to be himself.

Baylor appreciated the attention. "Frank made an extraordinary attempt to help me," he said. "He lived 40 miles away. He'd get to Anaheim by 3 p.m. for 7:30 games just so we could work. The first thing he did was knock some sense into me. Frank hammered away at my beliefs that I could carry a team all by myself, that I could earn millions of dollars on every swing."[1]

He relaxed, went back to holding the bat the way he used to, and regained some of his old form. The next year, Baylor led the American League in runs batted in with 139.

Robinson wanted to go back to Puerto Rico again in the winter but the owners decided to go in a different direction and Robby wasn't part of the plan. He'd had a good run there and the parting was amicable. But Robinson wanted a winter managing job to keep his resume fresh in case another major league opening came up. So he signed on to manage a team in the Mexican League.

It was a winter of four-hour bus rides on rocky roads, being careful about what he ate, drinking almost nothing besides 7-Up, and having a ballclub filled with players who spoke no English, with two or three exceptions. It was similar in some ways to his days back in Ogden, Utah, when he was first starting out, where the days and nights were long and his roommate didn't speak English. The other similarity was that each place in its own way represented a potential stepping stone in Robinson's career.

He was in Mexico when he received a call from the Angels that he would not be rehired for the next season. As it turned out, neither was Garcia. Robby called Hank Peters, still the general manager in Baltimore, and asked him to keep him in mind if a coaching opening came up. A month later, Peters called him and told him Earl Weaver wanted him on his coaching staff. Weaver created a position for Robby—outfield coach.

Robinson went to spring training and loved the opportunity to teach young ballplayers, showing them how to position themselves against certain hitters, drilling them on how to hit the cutoff man with their throws and, above all, schooling them on the "Weaver way" of doing things. For instance, Weaver wanted all of his outfielders to play deep. He never wanted a ball to go over their heads. Robby preferred to have them play a little further in, believing more balls were hit to medium depth or less than hit deep. But that was not the Weaver way, so Robby taught it the way the manager wanted it done.

When the season started, Robinson sat on the bench next to Weaver and they would talk about how the outfielders should be positioned. Weaver would look out on the field and tell Robby the left fielder needed to move more toward left center or the center fielder needed to move back or the right fielder was too close to the line. And before Robinson could do anything, Weaver was on his feet, letting out a shrill whistle and waving his arms to get his outfielders positioned the way he wanted them. Robby was more amused than offended but he realized there wasn't much for him to do in his new job.

In May, Ken Boyer, the former St. Louis Cardinal third baseman who was now managing the Orioles' Triple A team in Rochester, New York, was hired to manage the Cardinals. Robinson was offered the Rochester job.

He had mixed emotions about taking it. He would be leaving a major league job for a minor league one—but it would give him the chance to manage again, this time in the U.S., and might lead to another shot at being a major league manager. He agreed to take the job on the condition that if things didn't work out, he could return to the Orioles.

He took over a team that was 10–8 and went 58–64 under Robinson's direction, failing to make the playoffs. Toward the end of the season, he indicated he would like to come back if he didn't get a major league offer. But he learned that his job had been offered to Fred Hatfield, a former major leaguer who had been managing in the minor leagues. Hatfield turned down the offer to take a job in the Detroit Tigers organization.

Robinson was furious that Hatfield had been offered his job without him being told he was being replaced. It was an example of a situation that was an affront to his pride, one in which he was disrespected—and any time that happened, Robby was unforgiving.

"No matter what happens, there's no way I'd come back to Rochester now," he told the press. "I want the fans and everyone to know that I would have loved to come back. But there's no way, under any circumstances."[2]

As per the agreement with the Orioles, Robby returned to Baltimore as Weaver's "defensive coordinator," similar to what he had been doing before he went to Rochester. Perhaps recalling his days with the Dodgers and how Walter Alston paid little attention to fundamentals in spring training, Robby did just the opposite. Veteran pitcher Jim Palmer had complained about how many games poor outfield play had cost the Orioles in 1978 and Robinson wanted to make sure that didn't happen again. So starting in spring training, Orioles outfielders spent a lot of time in the field, reacting over and over again to simulated circumstances so they would know what to do instinctively in game situations.

The outfield play was superb in 1979, and the hitting and pitching were pretty good too. Led by a pitching staff featuring Palmer, Scott McGregor and Cy Young Award winner Mike Flanagan, the Orioles won the American League championship.

They faced the California Angels in the only League Championship Series from 1971 to 1981 that didn't feature the Kansas City Royals or the Oakland A's. In an exciting series, the Orioles won the opener 6–3 on a pinch-hit, walk-off home run by John Lowenstein in the tenth inning. In the second game, Baltimore took a 9–1 lead after three innings and held on for a 9–8 win.

The O's were within two outs of a series sweep when Al Bumbry dropped a routine fly ball in the ninth inning, allowing the tying run to score, followed by Larry Harlow's double that brought home the game-winner in a 4–3 Angels victory. In Game Four, Scott McGregor took care of business, tossing a six-hit shutout as the Orioles advanced to the World Series with an 8–0 victory.

Their next opponent was the Pittsburgh Pirates in the World Series. Baltimore took a three games to one World Series lead over the Pirates but could not get the fourth win, even with Palmer, McGregor and Flanagan taking the mound. Robinson said the World Series loss was as disheartening to him as the 1969 loss to the Mets, except in this case, he was a coach, not a player, and could not contribute anything with his bat.

In 1980, Jim Frey, the Orioles' first base coach, left to manage the Kansas City Royals and won a championship in his first year there. Robby was happy for Frey but was becoming increasingly frustrated at how major league owners were passing up opportunities to hire blacks as managers. In San Diego, for example, the Padres filled a managerial vacancy by hiring their radio broadcaster, Jerry Coleman, a former ballplayer with no managerial or coaching experience. In Robby's view, they hired a white radio announcer over many more qualified black men.

Weaver named Robinson to be his first base coach in 1980. Robby enjoyed being back on the field and being part of the action. And the Orioles had a good team. They won 100 games but finished second in their division to the New York Yankees.

In December, the San Francisco Giants fired their manager, Dave Bristol. A few days later, Hank Peters called Robinson and told him the Giants had asked permission to talk to Robby about the open position. Peters gave them the okay. Robinson met with owner Bob Lurie and general manager Spec Richardson, and on January 14, 1981, signed a two-year contract to manage the Giants. In so doing, he became the first black manager in the National League.

The Giants were much like Cleveland team that Robinson inherited when he took over—one that had become so accustomed to losing that it was part of the culture. Robby's challenge was to take a mediocre team, try to find players in the farm system or through trades to fill some gaps, and inject the "Let's go" attitude that he brought to the Orioles a decade earlier.

The San Francisco pitching staff was anchored by Vida Blue, a left-hander who had helped the Oakland A's to some championships in previous years, and Doyle Alexander, acquired in an off-season trade. Ed Whitson, another veteran, as well as Tom Griffin and Allen Ripley, rounded out the starting rotation. The Giants had a solid bullpen with Greg Minton, Gary Lavelle and Al Holland getting most of the work.

Their big hitters were first baseman Jack Clark, who was moody off the field but hit line drives on the field, and outfielder Larry Herndon. Both of them could be counted on for 20-plus home runs and 80-plus RBI. Milt May and Bob Brenly shared catching duties. Darrell Evans and Jerry Martin joined Herndon in the outfield along with Billy North, a speedster. A key acquisition was Joe Morgan, part of "The Big Red Machine" on the great Cincinnati ballclubs of the 1970s. Morgan was in the twilight of his career but Robinson thought he would bring a winning attitude and influence in the clubhouse that might be far more important than anything he did on the field.

The region's sports writers were frank in assessing Robby's challenges in taking over the Giants. "The New Zookeeper," proclaimed a headline in the *Orange County Register.* The subhead said, "Frank Robinson brought in to tame a team with giant-size problems."

Register staffer John Strege attempted to outline the problems. "Two years ago, Vida Blue threatened to shoot a sports writer. Last year, manager Dave Bristol shined an eye of one of his pitchers, John Montefusco. Mike Ivie increased his major league record for retirements to three. The fourth is a certainty. He's playing again."

In addition to all of that, there was the "God Squad"—a nickname given to a group of players whose religious beliefs led them to conduct chapel meetings in the clubhouse and putting up a shelf filled with spiritual materials. "Welcome, Frank Robinson, to the San Francisco Zoo," wrote Strege.[3]

Robinson's beliefs on how to produce a good ballclub hadn't changed in 25 years. It began with fundamentals. If a ballclub didn't execute the basics of baseball, they would never be a winner, he thought.

Robinson said one difference in the players of the 1980s from those when he was breaking in 30 years earlier was that they made the jump to the major leagues much faster. "They never really have the chance to learn the game properly in the minors," he said. "You expect kids to guess up here and not make mistakes. And the only way to do that is to carry the fundamentals you work on in spring training right into the regular season."[4]

He said the ability to bunt is a good example. If a player is able to lay down a bunt and move a teammate into scoring position, and that player later scores, that could be the difference in a one-run game. Over the course of a season, a good bunt could lead to winning a lot of games. Robinson said a lot of things can happen when you force a fielder to act quickly, such as bobbling the ball or making a wild throw.

The same holds true for fundamentals in fielding the ball, he said. "Teams that don't give up a lot of runs obviously have a better chance of winning than teams that do. I've found the offense will generally take care of itself."[5]

Robinson did not have the usual privilege of a manager of hiring his own coaches. The Giants were financially strapped and not in a position to pay two sets of coaches—paying off the salaries of the fired coaches and taking on the payroll of new ones.

March 16, 1981, is not a date that is etched in the memory of many baseball fans, but it has some historic significance. On that day, the Giants played the Seattle Mariners in an exhibition game. Ex-Dodger Maury Wills was managing the Mariners. So when the two teams took the field, it was the first time in major league history that both teams were managed by black men.

The Giants opened the season with Vida Blue on the mound, Milt May behind the plate, an infield of Jack Clark, Joe Morgan, Johnny LeMaster and Enos Cabell, and an outfield of Larry Herndon, Jerry Martin and Darrell Evans. As the season progressed, catcher Bob Brenly would get a lot of playing time, particularly against left-handed pitchers, and outfielder Billy North, with his exceptional speed, would see a lot of action as well.

An unprecedented complication occurred during the 1981 season that changed the pennant races as well as the relationships among the front office, the players and the fans. Players went on strike on June 12 and did not return to play until August 10. The issue was free agency. The owners wanted to be compensated with a player of similar value if one of their players signed as a free agent with another team. The players contended that this would dilute the value of free agency. In the end, a system was worked out in which a free agent draft system was developed, which lasted for about four years.

But the mid-season strike posed a problem as to how to determine league championships. It was decided that each division would have first-half and second-half champions who would engage in a playoff to determine who would advance to the regular post-season series.

Free agency had become a part of life in major league baseball. Many teams were willing to spend big bucks to sign players who they thought would fill a void and perhaps bring them a championship. The Giants always had trouble signing free agents because of players' reluctance to play all of their home games in chilly, windy Candlestick Park with its rock-hard infield and weather conditions that could change from balmy to wintry in the span of a couple of hours.

Spec Richardson's venture into the free agent market was the signing of Rennie Stennett, once a standout player with the Pirates but whose best days were behind him. Two years before signing with the Giants, Stennett hit .336 for Pittsburgh. In two years with the Giants, he never hit higher than .244. As a free agent, he was a bust.[6]

Robinson said the Stennett signing might have been the beginning of the end for Richardson, who was fired as general manager during the strike and replaced by player personnel director Tom Haller, a former Giants catcher.

Haller played the first seven years of his 12-year career with San Francisco and played on the Giants' last World Series team in 1962. He played four years with the Los Angeles Dodgers before finishing his career with Detroit.

Like any new manager, Robby hoped the Giants would get off to a fast start, but it didn't happen. They lost 15 out of their first 25 games and didn't show signs of getting any better. Robinson, candid as always, said, "Good teams don't make the mistakes we're making. I'm like the kid who sticks his finger in the dike. You plug up one hole and there's a break another place."[7]

During a stretch in which they lost six out of seven to San Diego and Atlanta, Cabell was picked off twice in one game and in another, the veteran Morgan, on third base with one out, inexplicably broke for home on a routine grounder to third and was thrown out easily.

Those kinds of mistakes were killers for a team that wasn't hitting. And the Giants weren't hitting. Following three straight losses to the Phillies on May 2–4, the Giants were hitting .228 as a team, 16 points lower than their team batting average of .244 in 1980, which was last in the National League. After 25 games, Clark was batting .195, Evans was at .233, North at .215 and LeMaster at .225.

When the players' strike hit, creating what became the first part of a two-part season, the Giants were in fifth place in their six-team division, ten games behind the front-running Dodgers. As the second half got under way, Robby was the victim of a surprise attack by one of his best players, Jack Clark, reminiscent of what Rico Carty had done to him in Cleveland.

Clark, hitting .224 at the break, told the press, "Robinson isn't perfect.

He's made lots of mistakes. He criticizes me but his managing hasn't been all that great. I think he's more concerned about himself. He hasn't spoken to me five or ten minutes all year."[8]

Robby was shocked by the outburst. He chose to handle it by having a meeting with Clark in which he apologized for not being more communicative with him, and the two men agreed to put it behind them and move forward.

In the second half of the season, the Giants began to hit better, with Clark and Evans in particular getting some clutch hits. San Francisco also benefited from the contributions of two newcomers—catcher Bob Brenly, brought up from the minors, and outfielder Jeffrey Leonard, acquired from Houston in April along with Dave Bergman in exchange for Mike Ivie. Brenly provided good backup to Milt May and gave Robby a lefty-righty hitting combination behind the plate. Leonard had good power with the potential of becoming a star.

The Giants finished the second half in third place with a 29–23 record, 3½ games behind Houston. Their combined record for the two halves was 56–55, which was inconsequential in terms of the pennant race but a huge improvement over the previous two seasons under Dave Bristol.

But another problem had developed. Robby and general manager Tom Haller didn't see eye to eye on a lot of matters involving player development and transactions, to the point where Haller was making player moves without consulting his manager. There was never a close working relationship between the two men, and the club suffered because of it.

There was some good news in the off-season for Robinson and the team. On January 13, 1982, Robby was elected to the Hall of Fame in his first year of eligibility, along with Henry Aaron, former commissioner A. B. "Happy" Chandler and former New York Giants infielder Travis Jackson.

For Robinson and his team, more good news came a month later when the Giants signed free agent Reggie Smith. Like Morgan, Smith was a veteran with experience at being a winner, having played in the World Series once with the Boston Red Sox and three times with the Los Angeles Dodgers. Though he was 37, Smith could still hit and Robby thought his work ethic and leadership, to go along with Morgan's, would be a great influence in the clubhouse.

The rift between Robinson and Haller caused its first big bump in the road in November. Haller had a chance to acquire Duane Kuiper from Cleveland. The Indians wanted pitcher Ed Whitson in return. Haller talked to Robinson about it, and while Robby liked Kuiper and knew him well from his days at Cleveland, he nixed the deal because the Giants were well stocked in infielders. He also didn't like the idea of giving up a pitcher without getting one in return.

At least, he thought he had nixed the deal. So he was surprised to learn on November 14 that Haller had indeed traded Whitson to the Indians for Kuiper. Robinson learned about it from the media and was furious. He now had two left-handed hitting second basemen who were going to want to play every day and he was shy one starting pitcher.

In 1982, Clark continued his carping about Robinson in the press but he and several other Giants put together good years. Morgan hit .289 with 14 home runs and 61 runs batted in. Smith hit .284 with 18 home runs and 56 RBI. Clark batted .274 with 27 homers and 103 runs batted in. A youngster named Chili Davis played a sparkling center field and hit .261 with 19 home runs and 76 runs batted in. On July 30, the Giants were 48–52 and then went on a second-half tear, similar to what Robinson's Indians teams did. San Francisco went 39–23 the rest of the way, including 20–7 in September, and went into the last weekend of the season in a three-way race for first place with the Dodgers and the Braves. The Giants ended the season with a three-game series against the Dodgers. They lost the first two games, eliminating them from the race. On the final day of the season, Morgan hit a three-run homer that was the key blow in a 5–3 win which eliminated the Dodgers and allowed the Braves to win the division title.

The club's starting pitching was spotty and fairly new. Bill Laskey, obtained from Kansas City in the off-season, led the staff with 13 wins. Lefty Atlee Hammaker, obtained in March in a deal that sent Vida Blue to Kansas City, went 12–8. No other starter was in double figures. But the bullpen was sensational. Minton went 10–4 with 30 saves. Gary Lavelle went 10–7, Al Holland 7–3, and Fred Breining, used as a spot starter and a reliever, 11–6.

The Giants as a whole went 87–75, their best record in four years, and Robinson was named National League "Manager of the Year" by United Press International. "It all goes back to the players and the way they responded," said Robby, when informed he had won the award.[9]

The 1983 season started to fall apart before it even began. Haller and Morgan were at odds on Morgan's contract for the coming year. Also, Haller was actively seeking to sign Steve Garvey, the Dodgers' fine first baseman, as a free agent. In pursuing Garvey, he paid little attention to Reggie Smith, who became a free agent.

When he couldn't come to terms with Morgan, Haller traded him to the Philadelphia Phillies along with pitcher Al Holland for pitchers Mark Davis and Mike Krukow and minor leaguer Charles Penigar. Garvey decided to sign with the San Diego Padres and Smith, feeling snubbed, left the Giants to play for Tokyo in 1983.

In the space of about 30 days, Robinson had lost two veterans who had hit .289 and .284 and brought a winning attitude to the clubhouse, much as Robby had done for the Orioles back in 1966.

In the college draft, the Giants had the chance to sign Barry Bonds, a slugging outfielder from Arizona State, son of former Giants outfielder Bobby Bonds. Barry Bonds wanted $75,000. Haller offered $40,000. Bonds did not budge from the $75,000 figure. Haller gradually upped his offers to $70,000 but would go no further. Bonds continued his college career and eventually signed with the Pittsburgh Pirates.[10]

When the Giants got off to a 5–13 start in 1983, Hal Bodley assessed the damage in *USA Today.* "Last season, Robinson had veterans such as Joe Morgan and Reggie Smith to turn to when the going got tough," he wrote. "People close to the Giants say the rift between Robinson and Haller has widened."

When Bodley talked to Robinson about the changes, Robby was his usual candid self. "There's no doubt you miss a Morgan and a Smith, guys who could get you the big hit when you needed it. They could certainly do some things for you that we're missing. They were a very important part of the team," he said.[11]

One concession Haller did make to Robinson was allowing him to pick a third base coach to replace Jim Davenport. Robby liked Danny Ozark, whom he watched coach when he was with the Dodgers, and hired Ozark to join him in San Francisco.

What he didn't like was coming into the clubhouse before ballgames and seeing Haller and Ozark conferring—at a time when Haller was hardly speaking to Robby. Robinson respected Ozark as a third base coach but began to wonder whether he could trust him.

The Giants continued to flounder. They made 94 errors in their first 83 games. Chili Davis, who had been so productive in his rookie year, somehow lost his bat speed and was hitting below .200 when he was sent down to Phoenix to regain his stroke. Laskey was once again their top pitcher at 13–10. Krukow, who came over in the Morgan deal, went 11–11. The bullpen wasn't as strong as it had been the year before, but part of the reason for that was that Holland was gone, part of the Morgan trade.

The Giants rallied in the second half of the season, as they had in pre-vious years, but still fell short of the .500 mark at 79–83, a fifth-place finish in a field of six. It was a disappointing year after having come so close to a championship in 1982.

Giant's management went to some bizarre extremes to try to right the ship, including the hiring of a team psychologist, Dr. Joel Kirsch, in mid-season, who offered to work with the players at no charge for the remainder of the year. If Lurie and Haller liked the results, they could hire him for a fee for the following season.

Robinson was not thrilled with the arrangement but had no choice but to put up with it. He did, to an extent. It started out with Kirsch talking with players in the clubhouse. Then he began going on road trips and talking with players on the plane and at the hotel. Then he began coming on the field with them before games. Robby drew the line when he caught Dr. Kirsch working with a reserve catcher on his throws to second base. From that point on, he was prohibited from being directly involved in player performance activities.

The 1984 season began like other recent seasons had, with the Giants struggling to put a string of wins together. Only this time, there was no late-season surge. They lost nine games in a row in late April and early May, and lost seven in a row in June. A headline in the *San Francisco Chronicle* read, "The Sad Truth Is, the Giants Simply Stink." Columnist Glenn Dickey wrote, "If the Giants continue to lose, pressure will build to fire Frank Robinson. It is always easier to fire a manager than to fire 25 players."[12]

Jack Clark, the team captain, was the only regular having a decent year, and in June he suffered a season-ending knee injury. Johnny LeMaster was in an 0-for-36 slump and was complaining about being dropped to eighth in the batting order.

In August, the Giants were in Atlanta, sporting a 42–64 record, in last place in the National League West, but had just beaten the Braves twice. Robin-son was in his hotel room feeling pretty good about a modest two-game win-ning streak when his phone rang at 12:30 a.m. It was Bob Lurie, informing him that he was in town and that he would like to see him right away.

Robbie went to Lurie's room at the hotel, knowing there could be only one reason why the owner would want to see the manager after midnight on the road. It was not unlike Phil Seghi in Cleveland wanting to see him in his office on a Sunday morning. "I think it's time to make a change," said Lurie.

Danny Ozark was named interim manager for the remainder of the year. Jim Davenport, Haller's friend and former teammate, was named man-ager for the 1985 season.

CHAPTER 14

Back to Baltimore

Frank Robinson flew home to Los Angeles Sunday afternoon, after he had stopped by the ballpark to say goodbye to his players and coaches and to wish them well.

As he was unpacking, his telephone rang. It was Harry Dalton, now general manager of the Milwaukee Brewers. He told Robinson he needed a hitting coach and asked if Robby would be interested. Robby told him he needed a chance to catch his breath but he would meet the club when it arrived in Chicago for a series in three days.

So he was unemployed for less than 24 hours. But he had some concerns. The Brewers were struggling, about 20 games out of first place. He knew from his own experience that Milwaukee's manager, Rene Lachemann, had to be under tremendous pressure. He also knew from his own experience that when a club brings in a new man as a coach, someone with managerial experience or managerial aspirations, it makes for an uneasy relationship with the manager. He remembered how Bobby Winkles felt when he joined the Angels, how Ken Aspromonte felt when he joined the Indians, and how he felt when Danny Ozark came aboard with the Giants. He accepted the job but he purposely tried to keep a low profile in deference to Lachemann.

At the end of the season, Dalton contacted Robinson again. He told him Lachemann would not be returning and that George Bamberger would be the new manager. Bamberger would be allowed to hire his own coaches—a time-honored tradition in baseball that Robinson was not afforded by Tom Haller in San Francisco. Dalton offered Robby a job as his special assistant, an opportunity for Robinson to gain experience in the front office. In the major leagues, Henry Aaron was the only black to have a similar position. It was a great offer. The only sticking point was that Dalton also wanted Robinson to be the club's minor league hitting instructor.

Robinson wanted the experience of being an assistant to a general manager but he did want to have to hit the minor league circuit as part of his job. He had hoped those days were behind him. He accepted the offer tentatively but asked Dalton to hold off any announcement until after baseball's winter meetings.

While he was contemplating the Milwaukee job offer, Edward Bennett Williams, owner of the Orioles, called and offered him a job as bench coach and outfield coach for Baltimore. Robinson saw it as a chance to return to the organization that had done so much for him and to a community where he was appreciated and respected. He accepted the job and contacted Dalton to inform of his decision.

Robby realized in returning to Baltimore that he faced the same kind of situation that he guarded against when he took the job in Milwaukee. Just as Lachemann's job was in jeopardy there, Joe Altobelli might be walking a tightrope in Baltimore. Even though he had led the Orioles to the World Series in 1983, the club had slumped to fifth place in 1984 and there were reports that some players were complaining about a lack of communication with their manager. All of that had a familiar ring to Robby, who was "Manager of the Year" with the Giants in 1982 and looking for work less than two years later.

As it happened, he developed a great relationship with Altobelli but the club just could not get going in 1985. In June, the Orioles were three games above .500 at 29–26 when Williams fired Altobelli and brought Earl Weaver out of retirement to take the helm once again. The ballclub was 53–52 the rest of the way, faring about the same as it did under Altobelli.

The 1986 Orioles were pennant contenders in the early part of the season but lost 42 of their last 56 games, despite the best efforts of the best manager they ever had. Robinson said, "Earl tried everything he could, including 141 different lineups, but we went from bad to worse. And you could see the old fire dwindle in Earl." They finished at 73–89, Weaver's first and only losing season in the major leagues.[1]

Weaver resigned at the end of the season. Robinson and Cal Ripken, Sr., a longtime Orioles coach whose sons, Cal Jr. and Billy, were infielders on the team, were both interviewed for the job. Robby and Ripken Sr. were good friends and they agreed that if either of them was hired, the other would be hired as a coach. The Orioles chose Ripken, who followed through on the promise and hired Robby as one of his coaches.

The Orioles got off to a good start in 1987 and were 26–20, in third place on May 28, but just four games out of first place. From that point on, they went 41–75, despite an 11-game winning streak between July 12–25. That was not enough to offset what happened in September when they won only 7 and lost 24, including a stretch in which they lost 17 out of 18. From a potential contender in May, the club dropped to sixth place.

It was a team in flux. Several of the veteran players said Orioles management seemed to hedge between an attitude of thinking they were one or two players away from being a contender to admitting they needed to rebuild. The result was a team with aging players whose best years were behind them, with not much help coming from trades or the minor league system. They still had Eddie Murray, the two Ripkens and Fred Lynn. But they had a pitching staff that produced a team ERA of 5.01 for the season.

The goal in spring training of 1988 was to forget about 1987. Baltimore had a new general manager, Roland Hemond, who had helped guide the Chicago White Sox to a division championship in 1983 (they eventually lost to the Orioles in the League Championship Series). Hemond replaced Hank Peters, general manager since 1975, who was fired after the disastrous 1987 season.

Club owner Edward Bennett Williams had another change in mind. He asked Robby to join the club's front office as an assistant to Hemond. It would be the first time in his baseball career that he wouldn't be somewhere on the field. But Robinson loved the opportunity it presented. "It was a great opportunity for me to help turn around an organization I love," he said. "The first black manager in baseball may just, in years to come, become the first black general manager."[2]

The senior Ripken was optimistic in spring training, as all managers are, saying his team would be a contender this year. They lost on opening day at home to Milwaukee, 12–0, then lost another one to the Brewers before heading off to Cleveland to play the only team that finished below them in 1987. There, they lost four more. Ripken had been in baseball all his life and had seen many teams come out of slumps and have great years. On the flight back home from Cleveland, he told catcher Terry Kennedy, "we might be 12–12 soon."[3]

He went to the ballpark the next day and began making out his lineup card when he learned that management wanted to see him. He was fired. Ripken had been a loyal Oriole, through good times and bad, and his name was revered in Baltimore as it still is today. But ultimately, popularity is fickle in baseball. Winning is the date to the prom. Still, managers have been known to quit early on in a season but no manager in history had been fired after just six games.

Hemond said he just felt a change was necessary—and the decision was made easier knowing a man with Robinson's experience and capabilities was available. He offered him the job of replacing Ripken. Robby had been looking forward to getting some front office experience. That lasted six months. When he was offered the chance to manage again, he said the word "yes" came out of his mouth before he had a chance to think about it. His only regret was replacing as fine as man as Ripken.

The Orioles became the fifth major league team to hire a black manager—and Robinson had held three of the five jobs. The other black managers were Larry Doby for 87 games with the Chicago White Sox in 1978 and Maury Wills for 82 games with the Seattle Mariners in 1980 and 1981.

In taking over the Orioles, he asked the fans and the media not to expect miracles. "I don't profess to be a superman or anything like that," he said. "I do have ideas about the way things should be done." Then he touched on a familiar theme of his. "I think the players will be more fundamentally sound and execute the fundamentals better. If they don't, we'll be out there working on them."[4]

But the losses just kept piling up. They dropped the first two games under Robby's direction to extend the losing streak to eight. It looked like it might end when Mike Boddicker struck out ten batters and retired 18 Kansas City Royals in a row in a game at Memorial Stadium. With the score tied and two out in the ninth inning, Jim Eisenreich singled for the Royals. Frank White hit a fly ball to left that left fielder Jeff Stone lost in the lights. The ball dropped and Eisenreich scored all the way from first with what turned out to be the winning run.

The Orioles took on Cleveland next. Scott McGregor lost a tough one when the Indians erased a 2–1 Baltimore lead with two runs in the eighth inning to earn a 3–2 victory. In the next game, Mike Morgan didn't allow a run, but the Orioles didn't score any and the game remained scoreless until Cleveland pushed across a run in the 11th inning. In the bottom of the 11th, with Jim Traber on first, Eddie Murray smacked a long drive that missed being a game-winning homer by inches. It went off the top of the wall. Murray had a double—but somehow Traber advanced only from first to third. The Orioles didn't score and the game was over.

As the team continued to lose, the pressure on them to win became greater and greater. Loyal fans, instead of calling them the O's, started calling them the "ZerO's." They became the butt of jokes on late-night television. As the losing streak inched towards 20, CNN started covering them as a news rather than a sports story.

Through it all, Robinson tried to put on a good front for the media, though nobody hated to lose more than he did. He opened one post-game press conference by saying, "The answer to the first question is 'I don't know.'" At another post-gamer, he said, "The hell with the Gipper; win one for me."[5]

Mercifully, the streak ended after 21 straight losses with a 9–0 win over Chicago. That night, a half-continent away, at the Los Angeles Forum where the Lakers were playing, public address announcer Lawrence Tanter periodically gave the crowd scores of other games. He included one baseball score: Baltimore 9, Chicago 0. One fan in particular, season-ticket holder Barbara Robinson, let out a cheer. "I had been calling him after every loss," she told the press. "But I had to stop. It was getting too expensive. He's been so strong—stronger than I've been."[6]

The Orioles dropped the next two games to the White Sox. Robinson obviously knew he was managing a team that wasn't very good but, contrary to one of the raps against him in the past, he enjoyed working with young ballplayers to help them develop. And he never criticized individuals or a team that gave it all to try to win.

Reporters who met with him before a game in June were astonished by what some described as the new Frank Robinson. His team had won only 18 games and was on a pace to lose 118. Yet Robinson seemed relaxed, even jovial, as he met with the press. Someone mentioned that an Oriole hit a three-run homer the night before, the first three-run homer of the year for Baltimore. "We can't count on that," Robinson said with a grin. "We don't get two men on that often."[7]

Robby, now 53 years old, had obviously mellowed. He wasn't the belligerent, intimidating man who cursed his way through managerial tenures in Cleveland and San Francisco. Some speculated that in both those cities, as the first black manager in the major leagues, he felt the pressure to succeed. The Orioles represented stability in his life. He had arrived there as a player 22 years earlier and had led them to four league championships. The organization had been good to him as well, providing him with a minor league managing job, big league coaching jobs and a brief stint in the front office. Even with the worst team in baseball, he felt secure—and the only way to go was up.

"I would not have taken this job under these conditions anywhere else," said Robinson. "This organization is in trouble right now. It has given me an awful lot. It gave me recognition nationally as a player. Whenever I was out of work or needed a job, I was hired here."[8]

One of the first things he did upon becoming manager was to meet with Cal Ripken, Jr., and his brother, Billy, who were devastated by the firing of their father. "He didn't have to do it," said Cal Jr. "It meant something to me and Billy. As time went on, that meeting may have had more meaning, just for the fact that it happened."[9]

The Orioles continued to flounder. They didn't have the talent to put together a sustained winning streak, and they didn't have any luck to help them turn things around. By the time the long season ended, they were 54–107, in last place, 34½ games out of first. Their fate was sealed in the first month of the season when they were 15 games behind before they won their first game.

Robinson went to spring training in 1989 with an edict for his players: he didn't want to hear a word about 1988. That season was gone—dead and buried. It was time for a fresh start. The Orioles had some fresh talent. Eddie Murray, one of the links to the 1983 championship team and a future Hall of Famer, was traded to the Dodgers in the off-season. He was one of the Orioles all-time greats but he had become disenchanted in recent years and wanted out. The Orioles accommodated him.

The opening day lineup in 1989, with the exception of Ripken, was filled with players whose names were unfamiliar to most baseball fans who were not ardent followers of the Orioles—Brady Anderson in center field, Phil Bradley in left, Steve Finley in right, Craig Worthington at third base, Ripken at short, Rene Gonzalez at second and Bill Traber at first. Mickey Tettleton was behind the plate. The opening day starter was David Schmidt. Larry Sheets was the designated hitter. As the season progressed, Billy Ripken, Joe Orsulak, and Mike Devereaux would work their way into the starting lineup.

On paper, it did not appear to be a team of destiny. Rather, it was the nucleus of the team that lost 107 games the year before. But Robinson and his coaches instilled the old "Let's go" attitude that had served Robby so well in the Orioles' glory days. The Orioles beat Boston on opening day, slamming the door on any comparisons to how the season started in 1988. As the season progressed, the Orioles gelled, much like the 1969 Mets had done.

Baltimore was 12–12 in April, no great shakes, but a marked improvement from their starts in the recent past. Doing nothing spectacular but playing good fundamental baseball—the Robinson trademark—they entered July at ten games over .500 with a 43–33 record, in first place, 5½ games ahead of the second-place Yankees.

In the midst of all of their success, Robinson became increasingly frustrated with his relationship with umpires. It came to a head in a game on Sunday, July 9, the last game before the All-Star Game break. The Orioles lost to the Milwaukee Brewers, 7–2. In the fifth inning, Bradley singled and was called for interference as he slid hard into second, trying to break up a double play. It was exactly the kind of baseball Robby taught his team to play, but the umpire ruled Bradley had interfered with second baseman Jim Gantner's throw to first. When Robinson went out on the field to protest, he was told to sit down or be thrown out of the game.

His reaction after the game was to threaten to resign for the good of the team. "I can't manage this ballclub the way things are going," he said. "I can't go out and defend my team. I can't question a call. It's not fair to these players and it's not fair to the people I work for."[10]

Some interpreted Robby's complaints as him thinking he was being treated unfairly because of his race. "That never entered my mind," he said. He just wanted to be treated with the same respect as other managers.

His comments did not fall on deaf ears. During the All-Star break he was summoned to a meeting, along with Orioles front office personnel, with Bobby Brown, president of the American League. When the meeting concluded, Robinson said he was satisfied his complaints had been heard and he was ready to move on.

His upstart Orioles, devoid of names like Robinson, Powell, Palmer and Murray, now depended on Joe Orsulak, Mike Devereaux, Jeff Ballard and Bob Milacki. They still had Cal Ripken but he was having a below average year, hitting around .250 most of the time. Still, the Orioles prevailed, and on July 19 had a 7½ game lead over second-place New York.

But the magic vanished just as quickly as it had appeared. Between July 19–27, Baltimore lost eight in a row, then won once, then lost five more in a row. On August 1, they still were in first place, but only by a game over the Boston Red Sox. The Brewers and Blue Jays were both 2½ back, Cleveland was three behind and the Yankees were five games out. Not only had the Orioles lead shrunk by 6½ games in 12 days, but now it was a five-team race.

The O's managed to right the ship and went 33–26 the rest of the way, but fell one game behind the Blue Jays as they headed to Toronto for a pennant-deciding three-game series. In the opener, Ballard and Todd Stottlemyre locked up in a gem. Phil Bradley hit the first pitch of the ballgame out of the park to give the Orioles a 1–0 lead. Ballard made that hold up and took the 1–0 lead into the eighth inning.

When Toronto's Tom Lawless reached base with one out, Robby decided Ballard had done his job and turned the game over to his ace reliever, Gregg Olson. Lawless stole second and went to third on an infield ground out. Then Olson uncorked a curve ball that was a foot beyond the outstretched glove of catcher Jamie Quirk. The tying run scored. Toronto eventually won it, 2–1, in 11 innings and won 4–3 the next day to clinch the championship.

"After that loss, I told them to hold their heads high," said Robby. "It was hard to feel too bad but I sure would love to have won that year. We were just a bunch of misfits, a bunch of guys who came together as a team."[11]

Tettleton, the catcher, hit 26 home runs. His previous high in home runs was 11. Ballard, who won 18 and lost only 8, had gone 2–8 and 8–12 in 1987 and 1988. Milacki had appeared in only three major league games prior to 1989, when he went 14–12. Relief pitcher Mark Williamson had a lifetime record of 13–17 prior to 1989, when he went 10–5. Olson, the relief specialist, had appeared in ten games with no saves in 1988. He pitched in 64 games and had 27 saves in 1989.

When several players have "career years" all in the same year, great things can happen—and the Orioles' improvement from 54 wins to 87 wins from one year to the next was the second biggest turnaround in major league history. It earned Robinson the American League "Manager of the Year" Award, a sign of the respect that he craved ever since he began his managerial career.

But success was fleeting for his Orioles and in 1990 and 1991, it fled. Ballard, the ace of the 1989 staff with an 18–8 record, went 2–11 in 1990. Milacki, 14–12 in 1989, won just five games in 1990 while losing eight. Dave Johnson led the staff with 13 wins. No one else won more than 11 games. A big part of the problem was anemic hitting. Tettleton went from 26 homers to 15, drove in only 51 runs and hit just .223. Ripken had 21 home runs and 84 runs batted in but hit only .250. No one else on the club had more than 60 RBI. The result was a 76–85 record and a fifth-place finish in the division.

In 1991, when the O's began the season by losing 24 of their first 37 games, Robinson became the scapegoat for his team's ineptitude and he was fired, replaced by coach Johnny Oates.

General manager Roland Hemond acknowledged the downturn was not Robinson's fault—a trademark phrase when general managers fire a manager. The team had probably overachieved in 1989, he said, and some deals that were made to try to strengthen the team hadn't worked out. Something needed to happen to change the direction, and this was it.

The Orioles rewarded their tireless, loyal warrior with a job in the front office, "kicked upstairs" in a business sense, as they named him an assistant to Hemond.

"Assistant general manager" had a nice ring to it and Robinson, while disappointed in what he was not able to accomplish on the field, saw the appointment as a step in the next direction he had eventually wanted to take in baseball.

No matter what position he held in baseball, it seemed, he was either a trailblazer or hell-bent on becoming one.

CHAPTER 15

The Front Office

For the first time in more than 30 years, Frank Robinson went to work without wearing a uniform. Sporting a coat and tie, he came to the Baltimore Orioles offices each day prepared to assist Roland Hemond in any way he could. At the same time, he wanted to learn as much as he could about front office work because he hoped to be a general manager himself someday.

His goal was not to be the first black general manager, but he hoped to see the day when the word "black" was not used in reference to any job title in baseball. But he became increasingly frustrated when he saw black friends of his in baseball being passed up for jobs they were qualified for, sometimes for the flimsiest excuses.

On April 6, 1987, Dodgers general manager Al Campanis appeared on *Nightline*, hosted by Ted Koppel. The program was intended to be a recognition of the upcoming 40th anniversary of Jackie Robinson breaking the color line in major league baseball. At one point, Koppel asked Campanis why there weren't more black managers and general managers. His answer stunned Koppel and millions watching on television. Campanis said blacks "lacked the necessities" to be successful in management positions.

Robinson said afterward that Campanis had revealed baseball's dirty secret—that white baseball owners didn't think blacks were smart enough to manage or be in the front office. Robby had been reluctant to speak out on racial issues over the years except occasionally when he thought he was personally victimized. When he joined the Cincinnati Reds in 1956, Gabe Paul paid his membership dues to get him into the NAACP. Robby agreed to it as long as he didn't have to be a spokesman. Among others, Jackie Robinson had also urged him to be an advocate.

Campanis's statement came at a time when Robby was working with writer Barry Stainback on a book about his life. Robinson used the book as his opportunity to lash out at the injustice of blacks being prevented from moving up in the baseball hierarchy.

He said one of the standard answers given to black former players who want to manage or coach is that they don't have the experience as minor league managers. When Gabe Paul was general manager of the Yankees, he told Robinson he would love to hire him as a manager if he just had some minor league managing experience—even though Robby had won championships for several years managing major league players in Puerto Rico. The next two Yankees managers, Dick Howser and Lou Piniella, were both white with no minor league managing experience.

Bobby Tolan played in the major leagues for 14 years and hooked on with the San Diego Padres as a coach. Tolan, who was black, had managerial aspirations. When the Padres looked for a new manager, they bypassed Tolan and hired their radio announcer, Jerry Coleman, a white former ballplayer with no coaching or managerial experience.[1]

Robinson held the position of assistant general manager through the 1995 season. During that time, the Orioles always seemed to be in a state of flux. They underwent ownership changes and manager changes but nothing seemed to improve their performance on the field. Johnny Oates, who succeeded Robinson as manager, lasted 3½ seasons. In 1995, the club named Phil Regan, a former pitcher and pitching coach, to replace Oates. He lasted one year. Regan was replaced by Davey Johnson, Robinson's old teammate in the glory years. Late in the 1995 season, as the Orioles were finishing out of the playoffs for the 12th straight year, Hemond resigned as general manager, probably recognizing that his position was in jeopardy with all the other changes taking place.

General managers are often remembered—and vilified—for deals they made that didn't work out, and Hemond was no exception. Just as Bill DeWitt is remembered for trading Frank Robinson in Cincinnati and Spec Richardson in San Francisco spent a bundle on Rennie Stennett, who turned out to be a free agent bust, Hemond traded three young players, outfielder Steve Finley and pitchers Curt Schilling and Pete Harnisch, to the Houston Astros for their slugging first baseman, Glenn Davis.

Over a five-year period, Davis had averaged close to 30 home runs and 95 runs batted in per season for the Astros. In his first season with Baltimore, he was injured part of the year, hit ten home runs and drove in just 28 runs. The next year, he hit 13 home runs with just 48 RBI. In 1993, after 30 games in which he had one homer and nine RBI, he was released. Meanwhile Harnisch, Schilling and Finley had successful careers with several other teams, Harnisch winning more than 100, Schilling winning more than 200 and Finley compiling more than 2,500 hits.

When Hemond left, it opened the door for Robby, who had been his assistant for four years. But it closed just as quickly when Johnson was hired as manager and the Orioles went outside the organization to hire Pat Gillick as general manager.

The whole situation was a frustrating one for Robby. When he was relieved of his duties as manager in 1991 and brought in to the front office, he thought it might be a stepping stone to becoming a general manger some day. But it wasn't long before he discovered that being an assistant to a general manager left him, as he called it, "out of the loop." He got up in the morning, put on his coat and tie, went to his office, got caught up on the latest baseball news through newspapers and other resources, and waited for the phone to ring. It hardly ever did. Later on, he was given the responsibility of participating in salary negotiations with players, but there was really no negotiating, he said, because owner Peter Angelos set specific limits on what the Orioles would pay. "We weren't negotiators. We were messengers," said Robinson.[2]

When Hemond left, Robinson went to Angelos and told him he was ready to be the general manager. He had been in the Orioles organization for 30 years as a player, coach, manager and, for the past four years, assistant general manager. He was well experienced and well prepared for the next step. But Angelos told him he was too old for all the running around a general manager had to do. Pat Gillick had had the experience of being general manager at Toronto and building championship teams there. And apparently, in Angelos' thinking, he wasn't too old to be running around. He was two years younger than Robby.

When Gillick arrived, he arranged for Robinson to sit in on a conference call with others in the Orioles organization. He told everyone he wasn't a hatchet man and for them not to worry about their jobs. They would go through the next season and then evaluate everything. When the conference call was over, Joe Foss, an Orioles executive who handled primarily business matters, asked Robinson to come to his office to meet with him and Gillick. When Robby arrived, he was told he was not being rehired. There was no job for him in the organization.

Robinson left Foss's office in disbelief. A few minutes later he went to Gillick's office to find out what happened to cause the change of heart. In the conference call just a few minutes earlier, Gillick had said everyone's job was safe. What happened? "That wasn't meant for you," said Gillick.[3]

It was a sobering moment for a man who had spent 40 years in baseball, a man who had been independent enough to do things his own way, crowding the plate, not only in the batter's box in 21 years as a player, but in trailblazing as a manager and as a spokesman for black athletes trying to climb the ladder of success. Time and again, blacks had been passed over for promotions because they were told they lacked the experience to move up. Now, Robinson had spent four years in a job that did not offer the challenges and workload he desired, but at least it was providing experience to get to the next level. But in the end, it wasn't enough. He flew home to Los Angeles feeling shunned by the organization he loved.

In April of 1997, near the 50th anniversary of Jackie Robinson's debut in the major leagues, Murray Chass wrote in the *New York Times,* "While one Robinson is honored, another Robinson can't even get a job. At the time baseball celebrates the 50th anniversary of its integration by Jackie Robinson, Frank Robinson sits at home in Bel Air, California, unable to find employment in the game that has been his life."[4]

Tom Keegan, writing in the *New York Post,* proposed a job for Robby that he thought he would be well suited for: commissioner of baseball. At the time, Bud Selig, owner of the Milwaukee Brewers, was serving as acting commissioner while owners searched for a permanent leader. Keegan wrote, "This is a big hire for the owners, who need to be smart enough to choose a man who will act in the best interest of baseball, not a yes man.... What's needed by baseball is an authoritative commissioner whose face symbolizes success in the game. Someone like Frank Robinson."[5]

As it turned out, the owners chose Selig to be the full-time commissioner—and that turned out to be a break for Robby. Selig saw the value of having someone with Robinson's experience in his office. In May of 1997, Robinson was hired to be a consultant to Selig and was also hired by the two league presidents to oversee baseball's Arizona Fall League.

"I'm excited to be back in baseball," said Robinson. "This is something I know. This is something I spent 42 years in. You feel comfortable. It's like going to sleep. You know it's something you can do."[6]

More good news headed his way when in 1998, the Cincinnati Reds decided to honor Robinson 32 years after they traded him. On May 21, at Cinergy Field, the Reds officially retired his uniform number—20—joining his old manager Fred Hutchinson (No. 1) and Johnny Bench (No. 5) as the only people in Reds history to be given that honor.

Robinson agreed to attend the ceremony, before a Reds-Rockies ballgame, but it was evident he was still hurt by how he had been disposed of by Bill DeWitt and never, until now, given the recognition he felt he deserved. "A lot of people never knew I was a Red," said Robby. "That's hard for me to believe. I tell them I played ten years in Cincinnati and they say, 'You did?' I have to remind people."[7]

He noted that the Orioles retired his number the year they traded him to the Dodgers, the first number they ever retired. Robinson was hurt and disappointed that the Reds never acknowledged his achievements and was still angry that it ignored his induction into the Hall of Fame. But he always said he never had anything against the people of Cincinnati who rooted for him at the ballpark and gave him free food at the boarding house where he lived whenever he hit a home run.

So he was pleased that the Reds finally were going to honor him and happy to return to the city where he got his start. He arrived in town the day before the festivities and took his daughter, Nichelle, who was now 33, for a drive through the Silverton area where the Robinsons lived when she was born.

The next night, on hand for the retiring of the number were Robby's wife, Barbara, daughter Nichelle, former teammates Chuck Harmon, Brooks Lawrence and Joe Black, and National League president Len Coleman. Unable to attend was 85-year-old Birdie Tebbetts, Robby's first big league manager. In a newspaper interview from his home in Florida, Tebbetts, who died less than a year later, said of Robinson, "He's the greatest under-rated player maybe ever. Most people start naming names, Frank's on the next page, but that's not right. He made me. When Frank Robinson came to our ballclub, it began an era of great young players and he had everything to do with it."[8]

In addition to his work as an assistant to Selig, Robby was also an analyst for the ESPN television network with its baseball coverage. He had to take break from both because of a health scare in 1999. He had gone for his annual physical examination, feeling pretty good and physically fit. A routine blood test determined that he had prostate cancer. On August 10, he underwent surgery at U.S.C. Norris Comprehensive Cancer Center and Hospital for removal of the cancerous prostate gland. The surgery was successful and he was released from the hospital two days later.

When Selig hired Robinson, he promised that his role in the commissioner's office would be more than ceremonial, and he followed through on that over the next few years. Robby was involved in many projects but none was more meaningful than in 2000, when he was named vice president in charge of on-field operations. More than anything else, this made him baseball's disciplinarian.

Many in the media thought Robby was ideally suited for his new role. Peter Schmuck, writing in the *Baltimore Sun,* said, "Robinson was not only a great player and groundbreaking manager, but he was also a hard- nosed and sometime volatile competitor who had his share of experiences with baseball's disciplinary system. That history should give him added credibility with the players."[9]

Will Clark, a former San Francisco Giant (in an era after Robinson's tenure) and a current first baseman for the Orioles, thought Robinson was a good choice for the job because of his experience. "That's the one thing that athletes respect the most—that the guy has been on the field and done it," said Clark. "But he's been a superstar doing it. He, more than anyone, knows what it's like to be under special scrutiny."[10]

It didn't take long for Robinson to exercise his authority. On April 22, a brawl broke out between the Chicago White Sox and Detroit Tigers. Troubles began in the sixth inning when Detroit pitcher Jeff Weaver hit Chicago's Carlos Lee with a pitch. Weaver was removed from the game and exchanged words with Lee as he walked to the dugout. In the seventh inning, Chicago pitcher Jim Parque plunked Detroit's Dean Palmer, who charged the mound and threw his helmet at Parque. Both benches emptied, some punches were thrown, some kicking occurred and several players were bloodied before umpires could restore order. Later in the game, after another hit batsman, the benches started to empty again but no fights erupted. In all, 11 players were ejected.

Robinson went further. After receiving a report from the umpires and reviewing videotapes, he suspended 16 players, the biggest punishment ever levied in baseball history over a fight on the field.

A little less than a month later, a more bizarre incident occurred. On May 16, in a game between the Dodgers and the Cubs at Wrigley Field, a fan directly behind the Dodgers bullpen down the right field line reached out and swiped the cap of reliever Chad Kreuter, striking him in the head in the process. As he ran off, several Dodgers bolted over the short wall in pursuit of the thief, all of which resulted in a melee in the stands. Robinson received a full report on the matter and suspended 16 players and three coaches, saying it was totally unacceptable for them to leave the field and go after spectators. In suspending 19 players and coaches, he broke his own record for punishments in the space of 24 days.

Some players, managers and coaches, who weeks earlier had praised Robinson's appointment, now saw him as power hungry and insensitive, relishing the role of disciplinarian, Robinson took it in stride. He said with a laugh, "I called my wife and she said I could come home but I couldn't come out of the house, We have no friends now. Everyone's mad at us."[11]

Surprisingly, Robby, as one of the game's greatest hitters, put much of the blame for baseball's melees on the hitters. He said in his day, a pitcher could hit a batter five times in a game and it was treated as just part of the game. He said Don Drysdale would sometimes smile when he plunked him. Robby was totally against head-hunting but he and players of his era understood the pitcher had the right to pitch inside, "Why do you think they called Sal Maglie 'The Barber?' Because he knew how to shave you," said Robby.[12]

Robinson was baseball's "dean of discipline" for two years when Commissioner Selig had another special assignment for him.

When Robby's days on the field were over as player, coach and manager, Commissioner Bud Selig hired him for many jobs in baseball's front office (National Baseball Hall of Fame and Library, Cooperstown, New York).

The Montreal Expos had been a struggling franchise for years. In 1994, they were on the brink of winning their division championship when a players' strike ended the season, forcing cancellation of the playoffs and the World Series. In subsequent years, debt mounted and attendance started to fall. The Expos began unloading many of their high-priced stars—Larry Walker, Randy Johnson and others—in order to deal with the debt. The fans reacted by staying home. Attempts to get financing for a new ballpark fell through. By 2001, attendance at Expos games was often less than 10,000.

While the powers that be in major league baseball looked for a solution, including trying to find a city in which to relocate the Expos, the club's owner, Jeffrey Loria, purchased the Florida Marlins and took his entire staff with him, including manager

Jeff Torborg. The Expos were in limbo, a bankrupt, rudderless ship, yet still a franchise in the National League. It was up to Selig and his staff to come up with a short-term solution until a new home could be found for the Expos.

They decided that the office of Major League Baseball would operate the team so that it could function and the players would have a team and a paycheck. That would take care of the front office mess, at least temporarily. But someone was going to have to manage the team, to be a leader in this time of stress, and keep the team competitive. The man they chose was Frank Robinson.

CHAPTER 16

Back in Uniform

Montreal came into the National League in 1969 as one of the league's two expansion teams, along with the San Diego Padres. They were called the Expos, a takeoff from the Montreal Exposition of 1967, one of the most popular, well-attended World's Fairs ever held. Like all expansion teams, the Expos were stocked with youngsters getting a chance to play in the big leagues as well as old-timers trying to hang on. The one thing young and old had in common, for the most part, was that established teams didn't want them.

Not surprisingly, the Expos struggled in the early years but gradually developed a good farm system and made some good draft choices and some good trades. By the 1980s, they were a legitimate contender for a division title. In the split-season year of 1981, the Expos made it to the National League Championship Series with stars such as pitcher Steve Rogers and a batting order that included future Hall of Famers Gary Carter and Andre Dawson, as well as speedster Tim Raines. They played the Los Angeles Dodgers in the championship series. In the decisive fifth game, Rick Monday hit a ninth-inning homer off Rogers to give the Dodgers a 2–1 victory.

The Expos remained competitive in the 1980s and early 1990s. In 1994, they had their best shot at getting into the World Series. Managed by Felipe Alou, Montreal had a 74–40 record, the best in all of baseball, when a players' strike ended the season in August. The Expos were led by outfielders Moises Alou, Felipe's son, who was hitting .339 with 22 homers and 78 runs batted in, and Larry Walker, who had a .322 average with 19 home runs and 86 RBI. Ken Hill led the hurlers with a 16–5 record while 22-year-old Pedro Martinez went 11–5, foreshadowing the stellar career ahead of him.

Nothing was quite the same after that. The ballclub went on a downhill slide both on and off the field. Financial woes led to the unloading of star players, and that led to fans beginning to lose interest, adding to the financial woes. Owner Jeffrey Loria wanted to build a new stadium in downtown Montreal and hoped to get the support of local taxpayers to help finance it, which didn't happen.

They also showed little support at the box office. In 2001, the Expos finished in last place at 68–94 and were last in the National League in attendance, drawing 642,745, an average of about 7,800 a game. After 53 games, Felipe Alou was fired and was replaced by coach Jeff Torborg, the same Jeff Torborg who had replaced Robby in Cleveland 24 years earlier.

The situation was so bad that the Expos and the Minnesota Twins in the American League, another struggling franchise, were put on notice for "contraction," meaning dissolving of the franchises after the 2001 season. But a court ruling in Minnesota, coupled with the Twins' lease of the Metrodome, which had one more year to go, staved off contraction for both teams. In early 2002, the owners and the Players Association signed an agreement that put off any considerations of contraction until after the 2006 season.

Meanwhile, Loria and his partners wanted to divest themselves of the Expos so they could purchase the Florida Marlins. To save the Montreal franchise, the other 29 owners approved the sale of the Marlins to Loria and agreed to take over control of the Expos. In other words, in a bizarre arrangement, the ballclub was to be owned by Major League Baseball.

When Loria took ownership of the Marlins, he took his front office, his manager and his coaches with him. So Major League Baseball and Commissioner Bud Selig had a team but didn't have a manager. Selig didn't look beyond his own office to solve that problem. He asked Frank Robinson to help him out, and Robinson agreed.

Robinson was accustomed to taking over under-achieving teams but these circumstances were far different from anything he had encountered in Cleveland, San Francisco, Baltimore or Puerto Rico. At his age, 66, and with his unusual role, he narrowed his scope and objectives quite a bit from his previous managerial experiences.

"I didn't have the desire to get back into managing long-term," he said at the time. My desire and enthusiasm are short-term. My thinking is, it's a challenge. I want to do it because I think I can be successful. I look at it as giving something back to baseball. I'll give it my best shot."[1]

It didn't take long for the competitive juices to kick in. The Expos played .500 ball early in the season, winning one, losing one, then winning two, losing two. But they put together a six-game winning streak at the end of April. On April 25, Robby's Expos climbed to a 14–8 record with a

5–1 win over Milwaukee in which Jose Vidro, their exciting young shortstop, hit his tenth double of the young season. Montreal astonished the baseball world by taking over first place in the National League East, two games ahead of the New York Mets.

On May 1, the Expos defeated Houston, 5–4, as Tony Armas, Jr., picked up his fourth win and Vladimir Guerrero hit his ninth home run. Robby's team was 17–10, now tied with the Mets for first place. The seven games above .500 was the high-water mark of the year for the Expos.

Soon they lost six in a row and sputtered to a 31–33 record by June 11. Then, led by the hitting of Guerrero, Vidro and Lee Stevens, they won eight in a row and nine out of ten. They were 40–34 on June 23, in second place, 5½ games behind the Atlanta Braves, who were on the verge of running away with the division title.

Tony Armas, Jr., was 7–7. Javier Vazquez was 5–3. Tomo Ohka, a Japanese pitcher whom the Expos had picked up from the Red Sox with a lifetime record of 7–17 in three previous seasons, was turning out to be a pleasant surprise. He was tied for the team lead in wins with seven and had lost only three.

On June 27, general manager Omar Minaya, who had been pressed into service just as Robinson had, pulled off a major deal. He traded young prospects Grady Sizemore, Cliff Lee, and Brandon Phillips as well as first baseman Lee Stevens to the Cleveland Indians for veteran right-handed pitcher Bartolo Colon and pitcher Tim Drew. Key players in the deal were Colon, Sizemore and Lee. All three played extremely well for their new teams and went on to have successful major league careers.

In Canada, reaction was mixed to the trade. Some called Colon a stunning acquisition while others called the trading of so many young prospects shocking. "Combine a bold GM, a franchise in peril and a division title within reach and you'll see some surprising developments," wrote Ben Nicholson-Smith in his baseball blog.[2]

Colon pitched well. He was 10–4 with a 3.31 earned run average in 117 innings. Combined with his record at Cleveland, he was 20–8 for the season. But the Expos fell into their pattern of playing at .500 or below in July and August—and then they did what Frank Robinson-led teams seemed to do wherever he managed. They put on a late-season surge that included a seven-game winning streak in September to finish with an 83–79 record, good for second place in the National League East.

The Expos had "rented" Colon for half a season to try to win the division crown. Failing that, the ownership (the other major league owners) were not about to put up big bucks on a franchise that was in limbo at best. On January 15, 2003, Colon was traded to the Chicago White Sox for Rocky Biddle, Orlando Hernandez and Jeff Liefer.[3]

Robinson signed on to manage the Expos for another season. "When I came and took the job, I thought Major League Baseball would have this team for one year and it would be either contracted or sold to someone," he said. "That's what was attractive for me to come back. I enjoyed it. And when we finished, I just felt like the job wasn't complete."[4]

He said he had been assured the team would not be stripped of top players so that he would forced to field a Triple-A caliber team the next year. Not long after that, the Colon trade was made, but the Expos did pick up a quality starter in Livan Hernandez in another deal.

Also, the Expos agreed to play 22 "home games" in Puerto Rico during the 2003 season, showcasing major league baseball in Latin America and hopefully providing an attendance boost. Robinson, who had managed nine years in Puerto Rico in the winter leagues, had no problem with the scheduling, saying the fans down there were knowledgeable and enthusiastic.

The Expos exceeded expectations again in 2003 and were in the playoff hunt much of the year before fading late. They finished with an 83–79 record, the same as the years before, only this time it was good for only fourth place in the division. Hernandez was their leading pitcher with a 15–10 record. Biddle contributed 34 saves. Shortstop Orlando Cabrera led the club with 80 RBI. Guerrero had his typical good year, hitting .330 with 25 homers and 79 runs batted in. Vidro hit .310 with 15 home runs and 65 RBI.

But the franchise was still an enigma, a team without true ownership or a true home, and a dwindling fan base that was becoming increasingly resentful. As negotiations continued on a place for them to move, the Expos remained in Montreal for the 2004 season. But they lost two more of their star players, Javier Vazquez in a trade to the New York Yankees and Vladimir Guerrero to free agency.

It was left to Robinson, who agreed to stay on, to try once again to field a competitive team. But with Guerrero gone, it was as if the air had been let out of the balloon. The Expos lost 11 of their first 13 games and ended April with a 5–19 record. Robby hadn't experienced such futility since 1988, when the Orioles lost their first 21 games. After a sluggish May, they picked up the pace a little in June and July but, as was the case with the 1988 Orioles, the disastrous start prevented them from making any meaningful headway. At least in Baltimore, the team had thousands of fans who loved them. Such was not the case in Montreal.

On September 29, a few hours before their last home game of the season, it was announced at a press conference in Washington that the Expos would move to the nation's capital the next season. That night, a season-high attendance of 31,395 said goodbye as they watched the Expos drop a 9–1 decision to the Florida Marlins. In their final year in Montreal the team went 67–95.

Just as a ballclub moving into a new stadium is often an energizing time for both players and fans, the move to a new city carries that same kind of anticipation. Robinson talked about it in spring training in Viera, Florida. As he met with reporters in his office, there was a barrage of laughter coming from his coaches, who were in the locker room getting ready for an exhibition game. "You'd think they had just won the pennant out there," said Robby. "See what a change in uniforms can do for you?"[5]

One of the things the players looked forward to hopefully was playing before large crowds in their home ballpark—now RFK Stadium—something that was missing in Montreal for several years but that every other team experienced year after year.

"When you go into other cities—you go into Philly, you go into Atlanta—you see these guys with a full house every night," said catcher Brian Schneider. "The crowd can get you a little more pumped up for the game or keep the momentum going for you. And we haven't had that."[6]

The Nationals opened the 2005 season with nine road games and came home with a 5-4 record. Their first home game, on the night of April 14, drew a crowd of 45,596—about what they drew in a week the previous year—and they were treated to a thrilling game. The Nationals beat the Arizona Diamondbacks, 5–3, as third baseman Vinny Castilla hit a double, triple and homer and drove in four of the five runs.

The Nationals were competitive but didn't draw much attention outside of Washington after their first swing to the other cities around the National League. On June 2, they were 27–26—average—but way above expectations considering their recent past. That night, Gary Bennett, a backup catcher to Schneider, hit his first home run of the season as well as a double with the bases loaded to lead an improbable comeback victory against the Atlanta Braves.[7]

That victory seemed to ignite the Nationals. They went on a ten-game winning streak, lost once, then won two more to make it 12 out of 13 en route to a 20-6 record for the month.

Even as well as things seemed to be going, there were a couple of lively flare-ups and, not surprisingly, Robby was in the middle of both of them.

On June 5, the Nationals defeated the Florida Marlins, 7–3. In the fourth inning. Robinson went to the mound to remove Tomo Ohka. As he reached the mound, Ohka turned his back on him and did not give him the ball. Robinson had to reach over to Ohka's hand and grab it from him. The next day, the Nationals' front office fined Ohka an undisclosed amount for showing disrespect for the manager.

Robinson said it was an unfortunate incident, particularly when the team was just starting to gel. "The other players see. The fans see it. Opposing teams see it. It just sets a bad example," he said.[8]

Robinson said Ohka, a veteran on the ballclub, expressed displeasure from time to time when he felt Robby had lost confidence in him. As a gesture of showing it was time to move on, Robinson got Ohka into the next day's game as a pinch-runner.

That skirmish was minor compared to what occurred nine days later in Anaheim, the game after the Nationals' ten-game winning streak ended. The Nationals had a brash outfielder, Jose Guillen who had been with the Angels the year before. He had been suspended by Angels manager Mike Scioscia for insubordination and later dealt to the Nationals. On June 14, in the seventh inning of a tight ballgame with the Angels, Guillen told Robby he was familiar with Angels pitcher Brendan Donnelly from being his teammate the year before—and that he knew Donnelly doctored the ball. Robinson came out of the dugout and asked the umpires to check the glove of Donnelly for a foreign substance. They checked the glove, found pine tar, and kicked Donnelly out of the game.

Scioscia came out of his dugout and, in the process of displaying his anger, walked over and began shouting in Robinson's face. As the 46-year-old Scioscia confronted Robinson, who was approaching his 70th birthday, both benches emptied—the Nationals coming out to defend their manager, the Angels coming out to join in whatever was going on.

Tom Boswell of the *Washington Post* reported it this way: "Apparently, Scioscia thought it was safe to get in this senior citizen's grill and try to show up one of the game's fiercest players. Luckily, for Scioscia, four umps were just barely enough to keep Robinson out of roundhouse range."[9]

Peter Schmuck wrote in the *Baltimore Sun*, "No one can doubt that Robinson still has some fire in his belly with the Nationals on a roll and his latest mood swing plastered all over ESPN. The guy didn't hit 586 home runs and make history as the first black manager in both leagues by being a shrinking violet."[10]

Robinson was still hot about it the next day. "He had no reason to come over to me," he said. "He had no right to walk over there and say what he said to me. I wasn't going to let him intimidate me; I'm the intimidator."[11]

Both Robinson and Scioscia were fined $1,000 and suspended for one game. It was a bit of irony that the former chief of discipline for Major League Baseball was now being disciplined, but Robby didn't see it that way. "I'm a manager now. What am I supposed to do, not do anything to be suspended or fined just because I used to have that position?"[12]

After umpires restored order, Guillen hit a three-run homer to help seal the win for Washington, and he gestured toward Scioscia as he ran around the bases.

On July 2, the halfway point in the season the amazing Nationals were 50–31, in first place, with a 5½-game lead over Atlanta. Livan Hernandez was 12–2 and seemed headed for a Cy Young Award.

But the season slowly started to unravel. Nick Johnson and Ryan Church both went on the disabled list with injuries. Hernandez had a sore knee but stayed in the rotation as he tried to play through the pain. Vinny Castilla had been playing with sore knees since spring training and by July he was hobbling. Also in July, Guillen, always the firecracker, got into a dugout argument with pitcher Esteban Loaiza because Loaiza didn't retaliate after Pedro Martinez, now with the Mets, drilled Guillen with a pitch.

The Nationals lost 16 of their next 22 games. On July 26 they fell out of first place and would never regain the top spot.

"It was like someone turned a switch off," said Robinson. "It was like someone changed the personnel. We just were not the same team, didn't do the same things, didn't play the same way, didn't have the same attitude."[13]

From being 50–31 the first half of the season, the division's best, the Nationals were 31–50 the second half, the division's worst, to finish in fourth place with an 81–81 record. Hernandez, 12–2 at mid-season, finished at 15–10. Loaiza went 12–10. Chad Cardero was the ace of the bullpen with 47 saves, most in the major leagues.

While the club on the field had a disappointing finish, the front office was beginning to stabilize for the first time in several years. In 2006, the Lerner family, headed by real estate mogul Ted Lerner, became principal owners of the team. Stan Kasten became team president and Jim Bowden was named general manager. All had high hopes for 2006.

In November of 2005, Robinson received an honor more distinguished than any of the Most Valuable Player. Rookie of the Year, World Series MVP or Manager of the Year awards. In a ceremony at the White House, President

George W. Bush presented him with the Presidential Medal of Freedom for his 50 years in baseball as player, coach, manager and executive, and for setting an example of character in athletics.

It wasn't long into the 2006 season before Robby was once again involved in controversy on the field—before the Nationals had even played their home opener. In a game against the Mets at Shea Stadium, five batters were hit by pitches, including Jose Guillen, who was restrained from charging the mound after he was hit in consecutive at-bats by Martinez. Pitchers on both teams were culprits. Robby was suspended for one game and fined, his relief pitcher Felix Rodriguez was suspended for three games and fined, and Guillen was fined.

On April 20, Washington jumped on the Philadelphia Phillies early, scoring nine runs in the first two innings en route to a 10–4 win, marking Robinson's 1,000th victory as a big league manager. He became the 53rd manager to reach that milestone, but shrugged it off, saying it just meant he had been around a long time. He said he was more impressed that his team had a 4–2 road trip.

On May 25, Robinson did something he had never done before as a manager, and he was emotional about it after the game. He removed catcher Matt LeCroy in the seventh inning of a game against the Houston Astros, having him suffer the indignity of walking off the field during an inning instead of removing him between innings, which is baseball etiquette.

The circumstances were unique. LeCroy was filling in because regular catcher Brian Schneider was on the disabled list. The Astros were running wild on him. In the first six innings, they had seven stolen bases and had forced him into two throwing errors. The Nationals had jumped off to a 7–1 lead early in the game but Astros were clawing their way back, due in part to LeCroy's inefficiencies. When Houston had runners on first and third and were threatening to tie the game, Robinson pulled LeCroy and put in Robert Fick to replace him. The Nationals won the game, 8–5.

Afterwards, in his post-game press conference, Robby wiped away tears. "I've never had that happen before," he said. "And I don't like someone having to go through what he had to go through today. I feel for people who have to go through something like that. But I couldn't do anything about it. I feel for him, and I hope the fans understand."[14]

For his part, rather than feeling sorry for himself, LeCroy sympathized with his manager. "He had to do something to get them to stop running," he said. "I'm man enough to take it. I don't think he should get that emotional about it. He's doing his job, just like I would do it if I was in his position."[15]

Some in the press wondered if the 70-year-old manager was mellowing. They would get their answer soon enough. In June, he fired pitching coach John Wetteland without consulting general manager Jim Bowden, who had hired him. Robinson was concerned about a lack of discipline in the bullpen as evidenced by some horseplay that included vandalism.

Bowden publicly backed Robinson but the firing was one of many personnel issues in which Robby and his general manager disagreed. It was a familiar pattern in Robinson's history as a player and manager, and it led to the same result whether it was with Bill DeWitt in Cincinnati, Phil Seghi in Cleveland, Tom Haller in San Francisco or Jim Bowden in Washington.

Robinson was having less and less say in what was happening with his team. Between 2005 and 2006, four of his coaches were let go and replaced by men hired by Bowden. Then Bowden sold utility player Jamey Carroll, whom Robinson liked, to the Colorado Rockies for $300,000 because Bowden thought Royce Clayton and Damien Jackson provided enough infield backup.

In June, Bowden hired former Mets and Baltimore manager Davey Johnson as a special consultant. As Mark Zuckerman reported in the *Washington Times*, "Conspiracy theorists didn't have to use much energy to conclude Johnson would ultimately replace Robinson."[16]

The turn of events surely was not lost on Robby, given his experience at seeing how Bobby Winkles felt when Robinson joined the Angels, how Ken Aspromonte felt when he joined the Indians, how Hank Bauer felt when Earl Weaver was hired as an Orioles coach, and how Robby felt when Danny Ozark joined the Giants' coaching staff. It was an old song in baseball.

While all of this was going on off the field, the Nationals sputtered on the field. The opened the season by losing 9 of their first 11 games and had a pattern of putting together small winning streaks followed by longer losing streaks. They were 8–17 at the end of April but rallied in late May and early June, winning 9 of 11 to pull within four games of .500 at 30–34. Then they lost 14 of their next 17 and ended the season with a 71–91 record. First baseman Nick Johnson led the team in hitting with a .290 average, third baseman Ryan Zimmerman was the top RBI man with 110, but the main hitting star was Alfonso Soriano, playing his first year in Washington after tenures with the Yankees and Rangers. Soriano hit 46 home runs, a team record and drove in 95 runs.

Robinson's contract with the Nationals was up at the end of the year.

During the season, Robby had lobbied for a three-year extension. He wanted to help build the franchise into a contender and talked publicly about his contract hopes while privately still having differences with Kasten and Bowden. In the last week of the season, Robinson met privately with Kasten and Bowden. They each told him the same thing, that he would not be back to manage the ballclub in 2007.

The decision was announced at a press conference on Saturday, September 30, the next to last day of the season and prior to the Nationals' game with the New York Mets. Before the press conference, Robby met with his players to inform them of the decision. He was stoic and kept his emotions in check. After thanking them for their efforts, he told them, "Now don't try to get on my good side. I still have two more games to manage. That's not going to get you into the lineup."[17]

He and Bowden stood side by side at the press conference. Bowden talked about the anxiety he felt in his decision to release Robinson. "It's the most difficult because of who Frank Robinson is and what he means to the game of baseball, not just in Washington, not just in Baltimore, not just in Cincinnati, for all of baseball. Frank represents playing the game the way it's supposed to be played," he said.[18]

> "It has been a good ride for me," said Robinson. "It has been 51 years. The old saying is, when you take a manager's job, if you stay around long enough, you are going to be fired. I have no bitter feelings about the situation. It has happened before and it would happen again if I was going to manage again."[19]

That night, the Nationals lost to the Mets 13–0.

The Nationals had announced on Saturday that they would honor Robinson on Sunday for his years of service to the club. The *New York Times* put it this way: "The Washington Nationals announced they would honor Frank Robinson on the same day they would fire him. Such is the delicate nature of dismissing a 71-year-old baseball legend."[20]

CHAPTER 17

Been There, Done That

Frank Robinson has had a baseball life in which, from very early on, he had nothing to prove, yet lived his life as if he had something to prove every day. He expected the same dedication and intensity from his players and, more often than not, their attitudes caused them more problems with their manager than any fielding errors or 0-for-4s at the plate.

His problems with baseball management often had to do with not seeing eye to eye on personnel decisions and with Robby's reluctance to accept that fact that the boss may not always be right, but he's always the boss— as with Bill DeWitt in Cincinnati; Phil Seghi in Cleveland; Tom Haller in San Francisco; Pat Gillick in Baltimore and Jim Bowden in Washington.

His baseball accomplishments are indisputable and, in many ways, unmatched by any other ballplayer if, for no other reason, the sheer volume of them.

1956—National League Rookie of the Year.
1961—National League Most Valuable Player.
1966—American League Triple Crown winner.
1966—American League Most Valuable Player.
1966—World Series Most Valuable Player.
1971—All-Star Game Most Valuable Player.
1981—National League Manager of the Year (UPI).
1982—Elected to Hall of Fame.
1989—American League Manager of the Year (Baseball Writers' Association of America).

He hit three home runs in a game once, on August 22, 1959, and hit two home runs in a game 53 times. He hit for the cycle once, on May 2, 1959. He had five hits in a game three times in his career and four hits in a game 30 times. On May 9, 1963, he had his best game, going 5-for-5 with two home runs and seven RBI. He also picked up a Gold Glove Award, in 1958.

There are no statistics available for the number of times he broke up double plays with aggressive slides, but there is some data that attests to his tenacity as a player and manager. Robinson was hit by pitches 198 times in his career and was ejected from ballgames as a player, coach and manager 39 times.

From the time he was a kid in Oakland, when George Powles taught him how to tuck his head in and spin away from inside pitches, to his days as a manager and baseball executive speaking out on baseball's failure to hire blacks as managers and front office personnel, Frank Robinson knew to crowd the plate. Despite all of his other accomplishments, that is certainly a part of his legacy.

As his friend and teammate Brooks Robinson said about him, "Frank was not out to make friends but to knock someone on his tail."[1]

After the Nationals fired Robby, Tom Boswell wrote in the *Washington Post*, "In 2005, the fiery yet venerable Robinson was the face of the franchise. Now, he's the 71-year-old legend who's been shunted aside because, apparently, he is simply considered too big a pain in the neck, too large and ego."[2]

Boswell, who covered Robinson for more than 30 years, said he was one of the smartest baseball men he had ever known, a natural-born leader with great insights into the game. But he said Robinson was often candid in his comments, perhaps too candid, and could be indifferent to hurting the feelings of others. "He tends to force everybody into a friend-or-foe stance. Nobody in the game demands more respect for himself. Yet he is thin-skinned and often on the lookout for slights. He dishes it out but hates to take it."[3]

Indeed, he felt he was slighted in 1966 after he won the Triple Crown and didn't think he got the endorsement opportunities he deserved; in 1982 when nobody from the Cincinnati Reds organization attended his Hall of Fame induction; or in 2000, when he thought the Cleveland Indians should have commemorated the 25th anniversary of him becoming baseball's first black manager.

Baseball Commissioner Bud Selig recognized Robby's value as an ambassador of the game and as an advisor in many capacities, to the point of virtually creating jobs for him to keep him in the game. He was a special assistant to the commissioner; a member of the commissioner's Special Committee for On-Field Matters; vice president of on-field operations from 2000 to 2002 (when he was the "dean of discipline"); manager of the Montreal

Expos and Washington Nationals, at first serving in an emergency situation at the request of the commissioner; special advisor to the executive vice president of baseball operations, 2007–2009; special assistant to the commissioner, 2009–2010; senior vice president for major league operations, 2010–2011; executive vice president of baseball development, 2012–present.

In the spring of 2011, Baltimore Orioles manager Buck Showalter invited Robinson to spring training to give a pep talk to his young ballplayers, and he said his players were impressed by what they saw and heard.

> "He obviously can command a room," said Showalter. "He's been in front of players for quite a while.
> "I've got to tell you, looking at them today when he was talking and seeing the 20 over his shoulder [on a plaque mounted on the clubhouse wall] and putting HOF next to his name when he signed it—they understood."[4]

Luke Scott, one of the ballplayers in the locker room that day, said it was a moment to remember. "The guy's been there, done that, a Hall of Famer," said Scott. "Obviously it's a good idea to listen and to take to heart what he says."

Scott said he was a little surprised and motivated by Robby's talk to the players because it went beyond baseball, what Scott referred to as Godly principles, American principles, rather than just baseball principles.

Robby might have been thinking back 60 years to his days as an American Legion player in Oakland under the guidance of George Powles or to his rookie year in Cincinnati with Birdie Tebbetts as a mentor, for it is easy to picture them saying the same things he told the young Orioles that day:

"Be prepared, don't make excuses. Work hard. Be a person of honor and integrity. Be a person that's honest. Think about this game and how special it is. Live in the moment and be thankful and try to be in it as long as you can."[5]

Chapter Notes

Introduction

1. In *The Sporting News Chronicle of Baseball*, published in 1993, there is a two-page spread on the 1966 baseball season but no mention of Robinson winning the Triple Crown.

2. *Washington Post*, October 1, 2005.

3. Bill Corum, "Bu Coming and Going, He's a Good Manager," *New York Journal-American*, August 17, 1949. Corum's reference was to Billy Southworth but could easily be applied to any big league manager.

Chapter 1

1. Robinson made the comment when he was looking back on his career, speaking at the Major League Baseball Beacon Awards banquet on June 20, 2009.

2. John C. Skipper, *Umpires: Classic Baseball Stories from the Men Who Made the Calls* (Jefferson, N.C.: McFarland, 1997), 10.

3. "Frank Robinson: Hawk Among Orioles," *Ebony*, September 1966, 88.

4. Bob Maisel, "Baltimore Loves You, Frank," *Baltimore Sun*, August 2, 1982.

5. Albert B. "Happy" Chandler was a United States senator from Kentucky when he was named as baseball's second commissioner, replacing Kenesaw Mountain Landis, who had died. Chandler was also a two-time governor of Kentucky, serving from 1935 to 1939 and from 1955 to 1959. He is credited with making it possible for blacks to play Major League baseball, going against the wishes of the owners, for whom he worked. In 1951, when his contract was up, he was not rehired. He died in 1991 at the age of 92.

6. Dennis Corcoran, *Induction Day at Cooperstown: A History of the Baseball Hall of Fame Ceremony* (Jefferson, N.C.: McFarland, 2011), 137–138.

7. Robinson Hall of Fame speech, delivered August 1, 1982, in Cooperstown, New York.

8. Henry Hecht, "Robinson Never Ducked a Fight," *New York Post*, July 30, 1982, 89.

9. Don McGrath, "Robinson in the Hall," *San Francisco Chronicle*, August 2, 1982, 41.

10. Ibid.

11. Hecht, "Robinson Never Ducked a Fight."

12. Danny Peary, *We Played the Game* (New York: Hyperion, 1994), 486.

13. Daniel Okrent and Harris Lewine, *The Ultimate Baseball Book* (Boston: Houghton Mifflin, 1991), 294.

14. Ken Nigro, "Cooperstown Welcomes Favorite Oriole," *Baltimore Sun*, August 2, 1982, C1.

15. Ibid.

16. Bill Madden, "F. Robinson, Aaron, Chandler Join Hall," *New York Daily News*, August 2, 1982, C27.

17. Maisel, "Baltimore Loves You, Frank." Hagy became such an institution at Orioles games in Memorial Stadium that the club had a "Wild Bill Hagy T-shirt Night" in his honor and had a moment of silence prior to a game on the day he died in 2007.

18. Nigro, "Cooperstown Welcomes Favorite Oriole."

19. Frank Robinson and Barry Stainback, *Extra Innings* (New York: McGraw Hill, 1988), 204.

20. Robinson Hall of Fame speech, delivered August 1, 1982, in Cooperstown, New York.

Chapter 2

1. Art Rosenbaum, "Ex-Bad Boy of Oakland," *San Francisco Chronicle*, August 30, 1962.

2. Originally published in 1937, *Everybody's Autobiography* was reprinted by Exact Change Publishers in 2007. The city of Oakland has two sculptures commemorating its "notoriety." One simply has the word "There" spelled out in capital letters. Another has the words "Here" and "There" spelled out with a bridge in between.

3. Robinson and Stainback, *Extra Innings*, 23.

4. Robinson Hall of Fame speech, delivered August 1, 1982, in Cooperstown, New York.

5. Rosenbaum, "Ex-Bad Boy of Oakland."

6. Ibid.

7. Other McClymonds athletes over the years include Curt Roberts, the first black player signed by the Pittsburgh Pirates; Willie Tasby and Lee Lacy, major league ballplayers; and Joe Ellis and Paul Silas, NBA players.

8. Robinson and Stainback, *Extra Innings*, 35.

9. Rosenbaum, "Ex-Bad Boy of Oakland."

10. Ibid.

11. From 1945 to 1975, Mattick was a scout for nine different major league teams. He signed Robinson, Curt Flood, Vada Pinson, Rusty Staub, Don Baylor, and Gorman Thomas, among many others. He later served as manager and in the front office of the Toronto Blue Jays and is credited with helping build and develop their championship teams.

12. Interview with the author on August 5, 2013. Porter, 2½ years older than Robinson, never lived up to the potential Mattick saw in him. He played parts of eight years in the major leagues, for the St. Louis Browns, Detroit Tigers, Cleveland Indians, Washington Senators and St. Louis Cardinals. He then coached and managed in the minor leagues for several years.

13. Robinson and Stainback, *Extra Innings*, 26.

14. Ibid.

15. Ibid.

16. Ibid., 27–28

17. John Erardi, "1956: Merging Forces," *Cincinnati Enquirer*, March 30, 1998.

18. Ibid.

Chapter 3

1. Lew Moore, "Coney Island Segregation Ended 40 Years Ago," *Cincinnati Enquirer*, May 27, 2001.

2. Peary, *We Played the Game*, 513.

3. Mark Sheldon, "Robinson Impacted Cincinnati Amid Segregation," mlb.com, February 3, 2012.

4. Robinson speaking at the Major League Baseball Beacon Awards banquet on June 20, 2009.

5. Doug Wilson, *Fred Hutchinson and the 1964 Cincinnati Reds* (Jefferson, N.C.: McFarland, 2010), 136.

6. Ibid., 135.

7. Robinson and Stainback, *Extra Innings*, 31.

8. Tom Swope, "Reds Will Go Down Line with Robinson," *Cincinnati Post*, April 18, 1956.

9. For several years in the 1950s, during the so-called "McCarthy era," the Reds changed their name to "Redlegs" because many individuals and organizations in the United States were suspected of or accused of having Communist ties. U.S. Senator Joseph McCarthy of Wisconsin was the chief culprit in what was most often nothing more than character assassination. Since Communists were commonly referred to as Reds, the ballclub started calling itself the Redlegs to avoid any controversy.

10. Earl Lawson, "Robinson Always Stars in Debut," *Cincinnati Times-Star*, April 19, 1956.

11. Ibid.

12. Robinson and Stainback, *Extra Innings*, 37.

13. Peary, *We Played the Game*, 334.

14. Ibid., 336.

15. Jim Feldman, "Apple Pie, Ice Cream Man," *Cincinnati Post*, August 8, 1956.

16. Three years later, the Braves were involved in another game in which they were held hitless for nine innings and eventually won the game. On May 26, 1959, Harvey Haddix of the Pirates threw a perfect game for 12 innings. He lost the perfect game in the 13th when Henry Aaron reached on an error. Joe Adcock followed with the Braves' first hit, a ball that sailed over the fence and should have been a home run. But Aaron, thinking the game was over, started to trot off and was

called out for being out of the baseline. Adcock was credited with a double.

17. William A. Cook, *Big Klu: The Baseball Life of Ted Kluszewski* (Jefferson, N.C.: McFarland, 2010), 94.

18. SABR Biography Project, George Crowe, sabr.org/bioproj/person/7226fd06.

19. Frank Graham, Jr., "Cincinnati's Million Dollar Baby," *Sport*, October 1957.

20. Ibid.

Chapter 4

1. Joe King, "Tebbetts Charges Bias in Robinson Beaning," *Cincinnati Times-Star*, July 17, 1957.

2. Earl Lawson, "Birdie Charges Rival Hurlers Pick on Robby," *Cincinnati Times-Star*, July 17, 1957.

3. Joe King, "Tebbetts Backs Down After Prod from Giles," *Cincinnati Times-Star*, July 18, 1957.

4. Ibid.

5. *Cincinnati Times-Star*, November 13, 1957.

6. Robinson and Stainback, *Extra Innings*, 47.

7. Bill Ford, "Reds Frankie Robinson Admits to Having Batting Weakness," *Cincinnati Enquirer*, March 11, 1958.

8. Earl Lawson, "Robby's Beaning Poses Questions," *Cincinnati Times-Star*, April 10, 1958.

9. Ibid.

10. Robinson and Stainback, *Extra Innings*, 36.

11. Ibid., 37–38.

12. Mayo Smith proved he could manage when he had a good ballclub. His 1968 Detroit Tigers team has a pitching tandem of Mickey Lolich and Denny McLain and a lineup that featured Al Kaline, Bill Freehan and Norm Cash. That was the year McLain won 31 games, but Lolich was the pitching star of the World Series in which the Tigers defeated the St. Louis Cardinals.

13. Peary, *We Played the Game*, 513.

14. Ibid., 606.

15. Stan Musial and Bob Broeg, *Stan Musial: The Man's Own Story* (New York: Doubleday, 1964), 286–287.

16. Okrent and Levine, *The Ultimate Baseball Book*, 294.

17. Carl Cannon, "Prime Time with Frank

Robinson," *The Washingtonian*, August 1, 2006.

18. Bill Ford, "Names Called Before Fight, Robbie Says," *Cincinnati Enquirer*, August 16, 1960.

19. Ibid.

20. Robinson and Stainback, *Extra Innings*, 35.

21. Earl Lawson, "Gabe Tells How Ace Might Have Been Lost," *Cincinnati Post & Times-Star*, August 11, 1961.

Chapter 5

1. Robinson and Stainback, *Extra Innings*, 49.

2. Ibid.

3. "Robinson Is Arrrested on Weapons Charge," *Cincinnati Post & Times-Star*, August 9, 1961.

4. "Robinson Fined on Gun Charge," *Cincinnati Post & Times-Star*, March 20, 1961.

5. Robinson and Stainback, *Extra Innings*, 51.

6. Emmett Watson, "In Sunshine and in Shadow," *Sports Illustrated*, August 26, 1957.

7. Ibid.

8. Robinson and Stainback, *Extra Innings*, 40–41. Stories of Hutchinson's behavior often show not only his temper but his sense of humor. When he was managing Detroit, he got in an argument with umpire Bill McKinley, who threw him out of the game. Hutchinson told reporters, "They shot the wrong McKinley."

9. Peary, *We Played the Game*, 513.

10. Robinson and Stainback, *Extra Innings*, 64–65.

11. Larry Merchant, "Two Strikes, Then Pow," *Philadelphia Daily News*, August 10, 1961.

12. Milton Gross, "Robinson Had to Grow Up," *New York Post*, October 4, 1961.

13. Jim Brosnan, as quoted in "Two Strikes, Then Pow," Larry Merchant column in *Philadelphia Daily News*, August 10, 1961.

14. Larry Merchant, "Two Strikes, Then Pow," *Philadelphia Daily News*, August 10, 1961.

15. Ibid.

16. Ibid.

17. Robinson and Stainback, *Extra Innings*, 52.

18. "A.L. Wouldn't Stand for Robby's Stance," *New York Times*, October 9, 1961.

19. Sandy Grady, "Bad Winter Spurs Robinson's Fine Summer," *Philadelphia Bulletin*, August 10, 1961.

20. Frank Robinson and Dave Anderson, "How a Pennant Race Tests Your Guts," *Sport*, September 1965.

Chapter 6

1. Earl Lawson, "Robinson Plans to Quit. Baseball," *Cincinnati Post & Times-Star*, September 29, 1962.

2. Ibid.

3. Ibid.

4. Robinson and Stainback, *Extra Innings*, 53–54.

5. William A. Cook, *Pete Rose: Baseball All-Time Hit King* (Jefferson, N.C.: McFarland, 2004), 22.

6. Ibid.

7. Dick Young, "Young Ideas," *New York Daily News*, September 8, 1963.

8. Bob Hertzel, "Another Look," *Baseball Prospectus*, April 20, 2010.

9. Robinson and Stainback, *Extra Innings*, 56–57.

10. Robinson and Anderson, "How a Pennant a Pennant Race Tests Your Guts."

11. Michael Sokolove, *Hustle: The Myth, Life and Lies of Pete Rose* (New York: Simon & Schuster, 2005), 59–61.

12. Ruiz played six seasons for the Reds, compiling a batting average of .239. In 1969 he was traded to the California Angels, where he was better known for his clubhouse fights than anything he did on the field. On February 9, 1972, he was killed when his car ran into a post. He was 33 years old.

Chapter 7

1. The reference to the trade is at the end of a long narrative by Sarandon's character in which she is professing allegiance to the "Church of Baseball," saying she's tried all the other religions and they haven't worked for her. But she admits not everything is perfect in baseball either. After all, the Reds traded Frank Robinson for Milt Pappas.

2. ESPN.com's rankings of the most lopsided trades in sports history appeared online in 2001. The rankings, with the worst being first, were as follows: 1. The Yankees' sale of Babe Ruth to the Red Sox in 1920. 2. The Bal-

timore Colts trading the draft rights to John Elway to the Denver Broncos in 1984 for quarterback Mark Herman, offensive tackle Chris Hinton and a first-round draft choice. 3. The New York Nets' sale of Julius Erving to the Philadelphia 76ers in 1976. 4. The Boston Celtics getting both Robert Parrish and a draft choice (which turned out to be Kevin McHale) from Golden State in exchange for Joe Barry Carroll in 1980. 5. The Los Angeles Dodgers trading pitcher Pedro Martinez to the Montreal Expos for Delino Deshields in 1994. 6. The New York Mets and California Angels making a multi-player trade in 1971 in which the principals were Nolan Ryan going to California and Jim Fregosi going to the Mets. 7. The Robinson-Pappas deal.

3. The phrase that made DeWitt infamous has been twisted by many, including Robinson. DeWitt said he was "not a young 30." While the meaning is the same, he has been widely misquoted as calling Robinson "an old 30."

4. Earl Lawson, "Tears and Cheers as Robby Bids Reds a Fond Adieu," *Cincinnati Post & Times-Star*, February 12, 1966.

5. "Robinson Blasts Reds," *Philadephia Bulletin*, April 4, 1966.

6. Ibid.

7. John Eisenberg, *From 33rd Street to Camden Yards* (New York: McGraw-Hill, 2001), 147–148.

8. Ibid., 163

9. Ibid.

10. "Catching Up with Milt Pappas," *Baltimore Sun*, June 16, 2009.

11. Dean Hanley, "The Frank Robinson for Milt Pappas Trade Was Not Illogical," DeansCards.com, August 24, 2010.

12. Bill James, *The Politics of Glory: How Baseball's Hall of Fame Really Works* (New York: Macmillan, 1994), 76–77.

Chapter 8

1. Baseball is a game filled with strange developments that make it intriguing. Larsen, possessing one of the worst records in the history of the game, 3–21 in 1954, pitched one of the greatest games in baseball history two years later. On October 8, 1956, Larsen threw a perfect game for the New York Yankees against the Brooklyn Dodgers in the World

Series. It remains not only the only perfect game but the only no-hitter in World Series history.

2. Robinson and Stainback, *Extra Innings*, 60.

3. Jimmy Cannon, "The Spokesman," *New York Journal-American*, March 24, 1966.

4. Ibid.

5. Phil Pepe, "Hope for the Orioles," *Sporting News*, March 7, 1966.

6. Mark Kram, "Discord Defied and Deified, *Sport*, October 5, 1970.

7. Ibid.

8. Eisenberg, *From 33rd Street to Camden Yards*, 162.

9. Ibid.

10. Robinson's blast off Tiant remains the only ball hit over the roof of Memorial Stadium.

11. Eisenberg, *From 33rd Street to Camden Yards*, 164.

12. "Rescue Revealed: When Robby Nearly Died," *New York World Journal Tribune*, October 11, 1966.

13. Ibid.

14. Johnson gave his account of the incident in a story published in the *Washington Times* on May 18, 2012. The occasion was the first visit of Johnson's team, the Washington Nationals, to Baltimore since Johnson had become the skipper in Washington. He was asked to recall his days with the Orioles and he recounted the Robinson incident at the pool. Though several players were undoubtedly involved in pulling Robby out of the pool, the original story of the episode, published in October of 1966, mentions only Etchebarren. Robinson's account of the near drowning in his autobiography, *Extra Innings*, published in 1988, mentions only Etchebarren. Also, Johnson said the party occurred after the World Series. Some leeway should be given to a man recalling something that happened 46 years ago.

15. As of 2013, he is still the only player to win the Most Valuable Player Award in both leagues. He was the first Triple Crown winner since Mickey Mantle in 1956. Carl Yazstremski achieved it with the Boston Red Sox the year after Robinson, and no one accomplished it after that until Miguel Cabrera with the Detroit Tigers in 2012. Nobody has won it in the National League since Joe Medwick of the St. Louis Cardinals in 1937.

16. Eisenberg, *From 33rd Street to Camden Yards*, 171.

17. The only other team to have tossed three consecutive shutouts in a World Series was the 1905 Giants. In fact, it was 46 years before consecutive shutouts were recorded. The San Francisco Giants did it to the Detroit Tigers in the 2012 World Series.

18. Peter Gammons, "Frank Robinson and the Boys of Winter," *Boston Globe*, February 3, 1974.

19. Curt Smith, *Voices of the Game* (South Bend, IN: Diamond Communications, 1987), 311.

20. Eisenberg, *From 33rd Street to Camden Yards*, 180.

21. Tom Adelman, *Black and Blue: The Golden Arm, the Robinson Boys and the 1966 World Series* (Boston: Little, Brown, 2006), 145.

Chapter 9

1. Doug Brown, "Robby Recovers from Knee Surgery Like It Was a Duster," *Sporting News*, December 10, 1966.

2. Eisenberg, *From 33rd Street to Camden Yards*, 184.

3. Jim Murray, "Injury Cost Frank Robinson 100 Homers," *Los Angeles Times*, May 11, 1974.

4. Bob Hunter, "MVP Robinson Shooting for Skipper Post," *Sporting News*, December 10, 1966.

5. Eisenberg, *From 33rd Street to Camden Yards*, 184.

6. Thomas VanHyning, *The Santurce Crabbers: 60 Years of Puerto Rican Winter Baseball* (Jefferson, N.C.: McFarland, 1999), 110.

7. *Sporting News*, September 14, 1966.

8. *Boston Record-American*, April 6, 1969.

9. Ibid.

Chapter 10

1. Robinson and Stainback, *Extra Innings*, 83.

2. Doug Brown, "F. Robby's Career as Manager Must Wait Until Bat Cools," *Sporting News*, May 3, 1969.

3. Ibid.

4. Baltimore relief pitchers such as Dave Leonhard, Moe Drabowsky, Eddie Watt and

Dick Hall often had great win-loss ratios because they benefited from Orioles come-from-behind victories in keeping with manager Earl Weaver's credo of "Good pitching, good defense, and three-run homers."

5. The Orioles didn't bunt much because Weaver did not believe in giving away outs. But he wasn't opposed to using every trick in his arsenal to win a ballgame. So while for him to win a ballgame with the use of a bunt was out of character, taking the opposition by surprise wasn't.

6. Doug Brown, "Frank Scoffs at Mets for Look of Losers," *Baltimore Sun*, October 12, 1969.

7. Eisenberg, *From 33rd Street to Camden Yards*, 218–219.

8. VanHyning, *The Santurce Crabbers*, 113.

9. Ibid.

10. Eisenberg, *From 33rd Street to Camden Yards*, 221.

11. Kevin Jackman, "Two Slams Put F. Robby in Records," *The Sporting News*, July 11, 1970.

12. Ibid.

13. The other two players to hit back-to-back slams in consecutive innings were Jim Gentile for Baltimore in 1961 and Jim Northrup for the Detroit Tigers in 1968. In Gentile's case, like Robinson's, the same three runners were on base for both slams. Gentile hit 46 homers for the Orioles in 1961 and, along with Roger Maris and Mickey Mantle of the Yankees, was in the chase for Babe Ruth's record of 60 for much of the season. His total of 46 was the Orioles team record until Robinson hit 49 in his Triple Crown year of 1966. Gentile was highly regarded by the Orioles but he was a first baseman, and, as he got older, was considered expendable when Boog Powell came up to the big leagues.

14. Robinson and Pappas, who did not know each other prior to the trade, had a strange professional relationship after the trade. In spring training of 1966, the Reds and Orioles played an exhibition game in Florida. A photographer approached Pappas before the game and said he'd like to get a photo of Pappas and Robby together, and Pappas agreed to it. A few minutes later, the photographer returned and told Pappas to forget it, that Robinson had declined. They never faced each other in a regular season game until 1972, when Pappas was with the Cubs and

Robinson was with the Dodgers. When high and inside and then struck him out. His second time up, he went down again. When the same thing occurred his third time up, Robinson was visibly angry and complained to the umpire but did not go after Pappas. After the game, Cubs catcher Randy Hundley asked Pappas what that was all about. Pappas said, "He refused to have his picture taken with me six years ago." Pappas tells of the incident in Eisenberg, *From 33rd Street to Camden Yards*, 150–151.

15. Skipper, *Umpires*, 90.

16. Dick Young, "Frank Robby in Pinstripes? Could Be," *New York Daily News*, December 3, 1970.

17. VanHyning, *The Santurce Crabbers*, 115. (Jackson may have cut down on his swing with Robby looking over his shoulder, but when he got back to the big leagues, he was swinging from the heels again. He struck out 161 times in 1971 and struck out 133 or more times in every full season he played, ending with 2,597 strikeouts for his career, the major league record.

18. Southworth was interviewed in 1969 by Neal Russo in a story published in *The Sporting News*, August 9, 1969. When the story was published, the Cardinals were vying for their third straight pennant. They didn't make it, losing out to the Mets. Southworth's 1944 Cardinals team did win a third straight pennant and won more than 100 games for the third year in a row.

19. Phil Jackman, "F. Robby Strictly Business, No Idle Chatter with Foes." *Sporting News*, April 10, 1971.

20. The last team to have four 20-game winners prior to the 1971 Orioles was the 1920 Chicago White Sox, who had Red Faber with 23 wins, Lefty Williams with 22, and Dicky Kerr and Ed Cicotte each with 21. Only five teams have won 100 or more games three years in a row: Connie Mack's Philadelphia A's, 1929–1931; Billy Southworth's St. Louis Cardinals, 1942–1944; Earl Weaver's Baltimore Orioles, 1969–1971; Bobby Cox's Atlanta Braves, 1997–1999; and Joe Torre's New York Yankees, 2002–2004.

21. Eisenberg, *From 33rd Street to Camden Yards*, 242.

22. Arthur Daley, "Newest Member of the 500 Club," *New York Times*, September 22, 1971.

23. Ibid.

24. Roger Angell, *The Summer Game* (Lincoln: University of Nebraska Press, 2004), 112.

25. Phil Jackman, "Once More, Orioles Ask: What's F. Robby Worth?" *Baltimore Sun*, December 11, 1971.

Chapter 11

1. Eisenberg, *From 33rd Street to Camden Yards*, 257.

2. "Dodgers Have Another Robinson; He's a Leader, Too," *New York Times*, May 28, 1972.

3. Ibid.

4. Robinson and Stainback, *Extra Innings*, 92–94.

5. "Trade Okay with Robby," *Los Angeles Times*, February 16, 1973.

6. Ibid.

7. Robinson and Stainback, *Extra Innings*, 96.

8. Dick Miller, "Peace in Our Time? Winks, F. Robby End Feud," *Los Angeles Times*, June 29, 1974.

9. Ibid.

10. Dick Young, "What's Going On Here?" *New York Daily News*, June 30, 1974.

11. Nolan Ryan and Ed Libby, *The Other Game* (New York: Word, 1977), 124.

12. Robinson and Stainback, *Extra Innings*, 100–101.

13. Ross Newhan, *The California Angels: A Conplete History* (New York: Simon & Schuster, 1982), 142.

14. Ibid.

15. Terry Pluto, *The Curse of Rocky Colavito* (New York: Simon & Schuster, 1994), 136–137.

16. Ibid.

17. "One Black Manager Enough? Too Many?" *New York Times*, September 8, 1974.

18. Ibid.

19. Werber is exaggerating. Robinson was arrested for not having a gun permit. The incident occurred in a diner, not a "beer dive."

20. "One Black Manager Enough? Too Many?" *New York Times*, September 8, 1974.

21. "The Commissioner's Reply, *New York Times*, September 8, 1974.

Chapter 12

1. *Cleveland Plain Dealer*, October 3, 1974.

2. The Associated Press story was published in newspapers throughout the country. The entry cited here was published in the *San Franciso Examiner*, October 3, 1974.

3. *Cleveland Plain Dealer*, October 3, 1974.

4. *Youngstown Vindicator,* January 23, 1975.

5. *Guideposts*, May 1975. *Guideposts* is the magazine of a faith-based organization by the same name founded by Dr. Norman Vincent Peale in 1945. The magazines emphasis is on stories on faith, hope and inspiration, and Robinson's essay was obviously written with that audience in mind.

6. United Press International story, February 27, 1975.

7. Robinson and Stainback, *Extra Innings*, 116–117.

8. Pluto, *The Curse of Rocky Colavito*, 140.

9. Robinson and Stainback, *Extra Innings*, 119.

10. *Cleveland Plain Dealer*, April 9, 1975.

11. Pluto, *The Curse of Rocky Colavito*, 144

12. Robinson and Stainback, *Extra Innings*, 122.

13. *Cleveland Plain Dealer*, July 11, 1975.

14. Pluto, *The Curse of Rocky Colavito*, 146.

15. Springfield (Massachusetts) Republican, April 18, 1976.

16. *Cleveland Plain Dealer*, July 2, 1976.

17. There are many published accounts of Joe Tait's radio comments and his reply to Robinson, including the used here, from Pluto, *The Curse of Rocky Colavito*, 150–151.

18. *Sporting News*, October 23, 1976.

19. Pluto, *The Curse of Rocky Colavito*, 155.

Chapter 13

1. Don Baylor and Claire Smith, *Don Baylor: Nothing But the Truth* (New York: St. Martin's Press, 1989), 110.

2. Jim Mandelaro and Scott Pitoniak, *Silver Seasons and a New Frontier: The Story of the Rochester Red Wings* (Syracuse: Syracuse University Press, 2010), 175.

3. *Orange County Register*, March 8, 1981.

4. *Christian Science Monitor,* March 18, 1981.

5. Ibid.

6. On September 6, 1975, Rennie Stennett got 7 hits in 7 at-bats in a game in which the Pittsburgh Pirates beat the Chicago Cubs, 22–0, at Wrigley Field. He is the only player in major league history to get seven hits in a nine-inning game.

7. *San Francisco Chronicle*, April 23, 1981.

8. Robinson and Stainback, *Extra Innings*, 187.

9. *San Francisco Examiner*, November 2, 1982.

10. The difference between the Giants signing Barry Bonds and not signing him was $5,000. After he played at Arizona State, the Pittsburgh Pirates drafted and signed him. Bonds went on to have a major league career in which he hit 762 home runs, more than any other player in history. The first 176 of those were with the Pirates. When he finally did sign with the Giants after several successful years with Pittsburgh, the first salary they paid him was $4.5 million plus bonuses.

11. *USA Today*, April 27, 1983.

12. *San Francisco Chronicle*, June 9, 1984.

Chapter 14

1. Robinson and Stainback, *Extra Innings*, 251.

2. Ibid., 270.

3. Eisenberg, *From 33rd Street to Camden Yards*, 391.

4. *Washington Post*, April 13, 1988.

5. Eisenberg, *From 33rd Street to Camden Yards*, 396.

6. *Los Angeles Times*, April 30, 1988.

7. *Washington Post*, June 21, 1988.

8. Ibid.

9. Ibid.

10. *New York Times*, July 12, 1989.

11. Eisenberg, *From 33rd Street to Camden Yards*, 410.

Chapter 15

1. Robinson cites many more examples of how he thinks blacks were passed over for baseball front office jobs in *Extra Innings*, a book published in 1988, about a year after Campanis' appearance on the *Nightline* television program in which Al Campanis said, "they lacked the necessities."

2. Eisenberg, *From 33rd Street to Camden Yards*, 453.

3. Robinson spent four years as an assistant general manager gaining the experience he needed and still didn't get the job. The reason may have been that his job was largely ceremonial—the Orioles rewarding him for his performance as their player and manager.

Gillick's experience was not ceremonial. He was an experienced, hands-on general manager. As Eisenberg points out, he made several deals, acquiring future Hall of Fame second baseman Roberto Alomar, outfielder B. J. Surhoff, reliever Roger McDowell and closer Randy Myers, moves that helped elevate the Orioles into pennant contention.

4. *New York Times*, April 20, 1997.

5. *New York Post*, February 14, 1997.

6. *Washngton Post*, May 6, 1997.

7. *Cincinnati Enquirer*, May 21, 1998

8. Ibid.

9. *Baltimore Sun*, February 28, 2000.

10. Ibid.

11. *Seattle Post-Intelligencer*, May 18, 2001.

12. *New York Times*, May 8, 2000.

Chapter 16

1. *USA Today*, February 13, 2002.

2. Blog.

3. The Expos' acquisition of Bartolo Colon and use of him for half a season offers an interesting perspective in how things sometimes work in baseball. In order to get Colon, the Expos gave up Grady Sizemore, Brandon Phillips and Cliff Lee. In addition to Colon, the Expos received pitcher Tim Drew. Sizemore, Phillips and Lee went on to have successful major league careers and were still active in 2014. Lee had seasons with the Indians in which he was 18–5 and 22–3. Sizemore was a clutch hitter and great defensive outfielder for the Indians for a decade until injuries started to limit his playing time. Phillips had a .272 lifetime batting average going into the 2013 season, most recently playing for the Cincinnati Reds. In exchange for those players, the Expos got Colon and Drew, who was 1–2 in two seasons with Montreal and was out of the big leagues after 2004. When the Expos traded Colon to the Chicago White Sox, they received pitchers Rocky Biddle, Orlando Hernandez and infielder Jeff Liefer. Biddle was 9–16 in two years with the Expos and he too was out of big league baseball after 2004. Hernandez did not play in 2003 and in fact never pitched for Montreal. Liefer appeared in 35 games, hit .193 and was picked up by the Angels on waivers in June. Colon, meanwhile, won the Cy Young Award for California in 2005 and was still pitching in 2014.

4. *Montreal Gazette*, November 20, 2002.

5. *Baltimore Sun,* April 3, 2005.

6. Ibid.

7. It was the only home run Bennett hit all year. In a 13-year major league career with several teams, mostly as a backup, he hit a total of 22 home runs.

8. *USA Today,* June 6, 2005.

9. *Washington Post,* June 16, 2005.

10. *Baltimore Sun,* June 16, 2005.

11. *Los Angeles Times*, June 16, 2005.

12. *New York Times*, June 21, 2005.

13. *Washington Post*, June 2, 2010.

14. *Washington Times*, May 26, 2006.

15. Ibid.

16. *Washington Times*, June 19, 2006.

17. *Washington Post*, October 1, 2006.

18. Ibid.

19. Ibid.

20. *New York Times*, October 1, 2006.

Chapter 17

1. Okrent and Lewine, *The Ultimate Baseball Book*, 294.

2. *Washington Post*, January 12, 2007.

3. *Washington Post*, January 12, 2011.

4. *Baltimore Sun*, February 24, 2011.

5. Ibid.

Bibliography

Books

Adelman, Tom. *Black and Blue: The Golden Arm, the Robinson Boys and the 1966 World Series.* Boston: Little, Brown, 2006.

Angell, Roger. *The Summer Game.* Lincoln: University of Nebraska Press, 2004.

Baylor, Don, and Smith Claire. *Don Baylor: Nothing But the Truth: A Baseball Life.* New York: St. Martin's Press, 1989.

Brosnan, Jim. *The Long Season.* New York: Harper & Row, 1960.

_____. *Pennant Race.* New York: Harper & Brothers, 1962.

Cook, William. *Big Klu: The Baseball Life of Ted Kluszewski.* Jefferson, N.C.: McFarland, 2010.

_____. *Pete Rose: Baseball All-Time Hit King.* Jefferson, N.C.: McFarland, 2004.

Eisenberg, John. *From 33rd Street to Camden Yards: An Oral History of the Baltimore Orioles.* New York: Contemporary Books, 2001.

Honig, Donald. *Baseball America.* New York: Macmillan, 1988.

James, Bill. *The Politics of Glory: How Baseball's Hall of Fame Really Works.* New York: Macmillan, 1994.

Jordan, David. *Pete Rose: A Biography.* Westport, CT: Greenwood Press, 2004.

Mandelaro, Jim, and Scott Pitoniak. *Silver Seasons and a New Frontier: The Story of the Rochester Red Wings.* Syracuse: Syracuse University Press, 2010.

Newhan, Ross. *The California Angels: The Complete History.* New York: Simon & Schuster, 1982.

Pluto, Terry. *The Curse of Rocky Colavito.* New York: Simon & Schuster, 1994.

Robinson, Frank, and Berry Stainback. *Extra Innings.* New York: McGraw-Hill, 1988.

Ryan, Nolan, and Ed Libby. *The Other Game.* New York: Word, 1977.

Skipper, John C. *Billy Southworth: A Biography of the Hall of Fame Manager and Ballplayer,* Jefferson, N.C.: McFarland, 2013.

_____. *Inside Pitch: A Closer Look at Classic Baseball Moments.* Jefferson, N.C.: McFarland, 1996.

_____. *Umpires: Classic Baseball Stories from the Men Who Made the Calls.* Jefferson, N.C.: McFarland, 1997.

Smith, Curt. *Voices of the Game.* South Bend, IN: Diamond Communications, 1987.

Sokolove, Michael. *Hustle: The Myth, Life and Lies of Pete Rose.* New York: Simon & Schuster, 2005.

VanHyning, Thomas. *The Santurce Crabbers: 60 Years of Puerto Rican Winter Baseball.* Jefferson, N.C.: McFarland, 1999.

Walton, Ed. *The Rookies*. New York: Stein and Day, 1982.

Ward, Geoffrey C., and Ken Burns. *Baseball: An Illustrated History*. New York: Alfred A. Knopf, 1994.

Wilson, Doug. *Fred Hutchinson and the 1964 Cincinnati Reds*. Jefferson, N.C.: McFarland, 2010.

Media

"Aaron and Robinson Coast into Hall of Fame." *Boston Globe*, January 14, 1982.

"A.L. Wouldn't Stand for Robby's Stance." *New York Times*, October 9, 1961.

Andriesen, David. "Major League's Lord of Discipline. *Seattle Post-Intelligencer*, May 18, 2001.

"Baseball: Robinson and Rodriguez Are Suspended." *New York Times*. April 11, 2006.

Beaton, Rod. "Robinson Returning as Manager." *USA Today*, November 20, 2002.

Bodley, Hal. "Robinson Hoping Giant Headache Will Go Away." *USA Today*, April 27, 1983.

_____. "Robinson in Unique Position." *USA Today*, February 13, 2002.

Boswell, Thomas. "A Bad Break." *Washington Post*, January 12, 2007.

Broeg, Bob. "Reds Could Get Hit by Boomerang Robinson." *St. Louis Post-Dispatch*, October 9, 1970.

Brown, Doug. "Catcalls Follow Robby Even When Birds Fly High." *Baltimore Sun*, August 3, 1968.

_____. "F. Robby's Career as Pilot Must Wait Until Bat Cools." *Sporting News*, May 3, 1969.

_____. "F. Robinson Powers First Drive Out of Orioles Park." *Sporting News*, May 21, 1966.

_____. "Frank Scoffs at Mets for Look of Losers." *Baltimore Sun*, October 12, 1969.

_____. "Robby Recovers From Knee Surgery Like it Was a Duster." *Sporting News*, December 10, 1966.

_____. "Woes Piling Up for F. Robby." *Baltimore Sun*, June 8, 1968.

Burick, Si. "Robby Becomes Reds All-Time Scorer." *Dayton Daily News*, September 4, 1964.

Cannon, Jimmy. "Frank Robinson Tells of Managerial Job." *New York Journal-American*, April 5, 1969.

Cannon, Jimmy. "The Spokesman." *New York Journal-American*, March 24, 1966.

Chass, Murray. "After Spending His Life Inside the Game, Robinson Finds Himself Out of It." *New York Times*, April 20, 1997.

_____. "Punishments Require Suspension of Disbelief." *New York Times*, June 21, 2005.

_____. "Robinson Does Turnabout After His Threat to Resign." *New York Times*, July 12, 1989.

Comak, Amanda. "The Day Davey Johnson Saved Frank Robinson from Drowning." *Washington Times*, May 18, 2012.

"The Commissioner's Reply." *New York Times*, September 8, 1974.

Connolly, Dan. "Dawn of a New Day for Ex-Expos in D.C." *Baltimore Sun*, April 3, 2005.

Curry, Bob. "New Pilot Robinson Refuses to Predict How Indians Will Finish." *Youngstown Vindicator*, January 23, 1975.

Daley, Arthur. "Newest Member of the Five Hundred Club." *New York Times*, September 22, 1971.

Dickey, Glenn. "The Giants Simply Stink." *San Francisco Chronicle*, June 9, 1984.

"Dodgers Have Another Robinson; He's a Leader Too." *New York Times*, May 28, 1972.

Drebinger, John. "Robinson of Reds Is

Most Valuable." *New York Times*, November 23, 1961.

Edes, Gordon. "Oriole Victory Is Good News to Forum Crowd." *Los Angeles Times*, April 30, 1988.

Elderkin, Phil. "Frank Robinson Stresses Basics for the Giants." *Christian Science Monitor*, March 18, 1981.

Eradi, John. "1956: Merging Forces." *Cincinnati Enquirer*, March 30, 1998.

"F. Robby Gets Chance to Manage in Puerto Rico." *Sporting News*, September 14, 1966.

"F. Robinson Is Valuable Unanimously." *Chicago Tribune*, November 9, 1966.

Feldman, Jim. "Apple Pie, Ice Cream Man." *Cincinnati Post*, August 8, 1956.

Ford, Bill. "MVP Robinson in Fold for Estimated $50,000." *Cincinnati Enquirer*, January 4, 1962.

_____. "Names Called Before Fight. *Cincinnati Enquirer*, August 16, 1960.

_____. "Reds' Frankie Robinson Admits to Having Batting Weakness." *Cincinnati Enquirer*, March 11, 1958.

"Frank Met Wife as Result of Mixup in Parking Lot." *Sporting News*, August 22, 1966.

"Frank Robinson, Aaron Elected to Hall of Fame." *New York Times*, January 14, 1982.

"Frank Robinson's Homer Puts Him on Hit Plateau." *New York Times*, July 10, 1971.

Gammons, Peter. "Frank Robinson and the Boys of Winter." *Boston Globe*, February 3, 1974.

Grady, Sandy. "Bad Winter Spurs Robinson's Fine Summer." *Philadelphia Bulletin*, August 10, 1961.

_____. "Who Stuck a Pin in Robinson's Psyche?" *Philadelphia Bulletin*, June 9, 1963.

Graham, Frank, Jr. "Cincinnati's Million-Dollar Baby." *Sport*, October 1957.

Gross, Milton. "Robinson Had to Grow Up." *New York Post*, October 4, 1961.

Hecht, Henry. "Robinson Never Ducked a Fight." *New York Post*, July 30, 1982.

Hertzel, Bob. "Another Look." *Baseball Prospectus*, April 20, 2010.

Hobson, Geoff. "Reds Finally Say Thanks to Robinson." *Cincinnati Enquirer*, May 21, 1998.

Hunter, Bob. "MVP Robby Shooting for Skipper Post." *Sporting News*, December 10, 1966.

Jackman, Phil. "F. Robby Strictly Business, No Idle Chatter with Foes," *Sporting News*, April 10, 1971.

_____. "Once More, Orioles Ask: What's F. Robby Worth?" *Baltimore Sun*, December 11, 1971.

_____. "Season Has Hardly Begun for F. Robby, Orioles' Bat Baron." *Baltimore Sun*, August 7, 1971.

Jares, Joe. "The Birds Fall Down on Broken Wings." *Sports Illustrated*, July 17, 1967.

Kaegel, Dick. "Echoes of Jackie at Cooperstown." *The Sporting News*, August 9, 1982.

Keegan, Tom. "Robby Would Be Great Commish." *New York Post*, February 14, 1997.

Kelly, Ray. "Reds' Robinson Became a Hitter By Talking it Over—with Himself." *Philadelphia Bulletin*, March 21, 1962.

King, Joe. "Tebbetts Backs Down After Prod by Giles." *Cincinnati Times-Star*, July 18, 1957

_____. "Tebbetts Charges Bias in Robinson Beaning." *Cincinnati Times-Star*, July 17, 1957.

Kram, Mark. "Discord Defied and Deified." *Sport*, October 5, 1970.

Lang, Jack. "Hank Settles for 97.8 Percent." *The Sporting News*, January 30, 1982.

Lawson, Earl. "Birdie Charges Rival Hurlers Pick on Robby." *Cincinnati Times-Star*, July 17, 1957.

_____. "Gabe Tells How Ace Might

Have Been Lost." *Cincinnati Post & Times-Star,* August 11, 1961.

_____. "Looks Like Robbie's Back." *Cincinnati Times-Star,* March 30, 1959.

_____. "Robby's Beaning Poses Questions." *Cincinnati Times-Star,* April 10, 1958.

_____. "Robinson Always Stars in Debut." *Cincinnati Times-Star,* April 19, 1956.

_____. "Robinson Plans to Quit Baseball." *Cincinnati Post & Times-Star,* September 29, 1962.

_____. "Robinson's Grin Hides Sadness Over Trade." *Sporting News,* December 28, 1965.

_____. "Slugging Robby Wraps Up Reds Records by the Dozen." *Cincinnati Post & Times-Star,* September 29, 1962.

_____. "Tears and Cheers as Robby Bids Reds Fans a Fond Adieu." *Cincinnati Post & Times-Star,* February 12, 1966.

Leavy, Jane. "Frank Robinson? Yes, Really!" *Washington Post,* June 21, 1988.

Lebovitz, Hal. "Robbie: His Time Has Come." *Cleveland Plain Dealer,* October 3, 1974.

Madden, Bill. "F. Robinson, Aaron, Chandler Join Hall." *New York Daily News,* August 2, 1982.

Maisel, Bob. "Baltimore Loves You, Frank." *Baltimore Sun,* August 2, 1982.

Maske, Mark. "Excited F. Robinson Is Returning to Baseball." *Washington Post,* May 6, 1997.

Mazer, Rosalyn A. "Frank Robinson Inspires Oriole Magic." *The National Pastime.* Cleveland: Society for American Baseball Research, 1992.

McGrath, Don. "Robinson in the Hall." *San Francisco Chronicle,* August 2, 1982.

Merchant, Larry. "Two Strikes, Then Pow." *Philadelphia Daily News,* August 10, 1961.

"Mental Errors Put Giants on Rocks, Robby on Fire." *San Francisco Examiner,* May 23, 1981.

Miller, Dick. "Peace in Our Time? Winks, F. Robby End Feud." *Los Angeles Times,* June 29, 1974.

"More on Frank Robinson's Speech." *Baltimore Sun,* February 24, 2011.

Moses, Ralph C. "Vada Pinson." *The Baseball Research Journal.* Cleveland: Society for American Baseball Research, 1996.

Murray, Jim. "Injury Cost Robinson 100 Homers." *Los Angeles Times,* May 11, 1974.

Myles, Stephanie. "Robinson Stays Put." *Montreal Gazette,* November 20, 2002.

"N.L. Hurlers' Credo—Don't Rile Robby." *Sporting News,* May 22, 1965.

"One Black Manager Enough? Too Many?" *New York Times,* September 8, 1974.

"Only Fair I Use Needle on DeWitt—Robinson." *Sporting News,* November 12, 1966.

"Oriole Flag Fades from Focus as Frank Fights Fuzzy Vision." *Sporting News,* July 29, 1967.

"Orioles Fire Cal Ripkin, Sr." *Washington Post,* April 13, 1988.

"Orioles: Let's Make a Deal." *Baltimore Sun,* November 30, 1970.

Pepe, Phil. "Hope for the Orioles." *Sporting News,* March 7, 1966.

Reel, Ursula, "Torre Wishes Robby a Speedy Recovery." *New York Post,* August 14, 1999.

"Rescue Revealed: When Robby Nearly Died." *New York World Journal Tribune,* October 11, 1966.

"Robby Hears Swap Rumors, Just Grins." *Cincinnati Post & Times-Star,* December 6, 1965.

"Robby Leaves 'Em Laughing With Quip Over Salary Slash." *Sporting News,* February 27, 1964.

"Robby Rates AL Umpires." *Cleveland Plain Dealer*, July 11, 1975.

Robinson, Frank. "What Everybody Should Know About Managing." *Guideposts*, May 1975.

Robinson, Frank, with Dave Anderson. "How a Pennant Race Tests Your Guts." *Sport*, September 1965

"Robinson Arrested on Weapons Charge." *Cincinnati Post & Times-Star*, February 9, 1961.

"Robinson Blasts Reds." *Philadelphia Bulletin*, April 4, 1966.

"Robinson Fined on Gun Charge." *Cincinnati Post & Times-Star*, March 20, 1961.

"Robinson Hits Three Homers." *Los Angeles Times*, August 23, 1959.

"Robinson Is Manager of the Year." *San Francisco Chronicle*, November 2, 1982.

"Robinson Named Tribe Manager." *Cleveland Plain Dealer*, October 3, 1974.

"Robinson Out as Manager." *Washington Post*, October 1, 2006.

"Robinson's First Order: No Curfew for Indians." *Sporting News*, March 1, 1975.

Rosenbaum, Art. "Ex-Bad Boy of Oakland." *San Francisco Chronicle*, August 30, 1982.

Ross, George. "All-Time Legion Team? Oakland Draws Support." *Sporting News*, August 22, 1964.

Russo, Neal. "Don't Count Cardinals Out, Says Ex-Pilot Southworth." *Sporting News*, August 9, 1969.

Schmuck, Peter. "F. Robby Batting Third in Baseball's Hierarchy." *Baltimore Sun*, February 28, 2000.

_____. "Robinson Still Knows How to Bring Heat When Needed." *Baltimore Sun*, June 16, 2005.

Schneider, Russell. "Hendrick Walks Out Before Tribe's Finale." *Cleveland Plain Dealer*, October 3, 1974.

_____. "MacPhail Upholds Umpires, Fines, Suspends Robinson." *Cleveland Plain Dealer*, June 7, 1975.

_____. "Reynolds Threatened to Get Robby." *Cleveland Plain Dealer*, July 2, 1976.

_____. "Seghi and Rehired Robby Clear Air in Wigwam." *Sporting News*, October 23, 1976

Sharnik, Morton. "The Moody Tiger of the Reds." *Sports Illustrated*. June 17, 1963.

Simers, T.J. "Robinson Refuses to Budge When it Comes to a Grudge." *Los Angeles Times*, June 16, 2005.

Smith, Red. "The Shrine by the Lake." *New York Times*, December 18, 1981.

Strege, John. "The New Zookeeper: Franks Robinson Brought in to Tame a Team with Giant-Size Problems." *Orange County Register*, March 8, 1981.

"Surgery Successful for Frank Robinson." *New York Times*, August 12, 1999.

Svrluga, Barry. "Five Years Ago, the Washington Nationals Were on Top of the World." *Washington Post*, June 2, 2010.

Swope, Tom. "Reds Will Go Down Line with Robinson." *Cincinnati Post*, April 18, 1956.

"Trade Okay with Robby." *Los Angeles Times*, February 16, 1973.

Vecsey, George. "The Dean of Discipline Is on the Case." *New York Times*, May 8, 2000.

Watson, Emmett. "In Sunshine and in Shadow." *Sports Illustrated*, August 26, 1957.

"Whatever Robby Got, It's Got Him Down." *Sporting News*, July 31, 1965.

White, Joseph. "Nationals Fine Ohka for 'Contempt' Against Robinson." *USA Today*, June 6, 2005.

Young, Dick. "Frank Robby in Yankee

Pinstripes? Could Be." *New York Daily News*, December 3, 1970.

_____. "What's Going on Here?" *New York Daily News*, June 30, 1974.

_____. "Young Ideas." *New York Daily News*, September 9, 1963.

Zuckerman, Mark. "Mounting Friction." *Washington Times*, June 19, 2006.

_____. "Robinson Tearful After Win." *Washington Times*, May 26, 2006.

Index